CMOK to YOu To

A Correspondence

Nina Živančević and
Marc James Léger

punctum books ℗ earth, milky way

First published in 2016 by
Dead Letter Office,
a division of punctum books (Earth)
operated by the BABEL Working Group
punctumbooks.com | babelworkinggroup.org

The BABEL Working Group is a collective and desiring-assemblage of scholar-gypsies with no leaders or followers, no top and no bottom, and only a middle. BABEL roams and stalks the ruins of the posthistorical university as a multiplicity, a pack, looking for other roaming packs with which to cohabit and build temporary shelters for intellectual vagabonds. We also take in strays.

It is a fine consolation among the absent that if one who is loved is not present, a letter may be embraced instead.
—Isidore of Seville

ISBN-13: 978–0615988047
ISBN-10: 0615988040

Cover design: Dragana Nikolić.
Book design: Chris Piuma.

Before you start
to read this book,

take this moment to think about making a donation
to punctum books, an independent non-profit press,

@ http://punctumbooks.com/about/

If you're reading the e-book, click on that link
to go directly to our donations site.
Any amount, no matter the size, is appreciated
and will help us to keep our ship of fools afloat.
Contributions from dedicated readers will also help us
to keep our commons open and to cultivate new work
that can't find a welcoming port elsewhere.

Our adventure is not possible without your support.
Vive la open-access!

Preface

CMOK to YOu To presents in slightly modified form the email correspondence of the Serbian-born poet Nina Živančević and Canadian cultural theorist Marc James Léger from the period February to May 2015. In December of 2014 Léger invited Živančević to contribute a text to the second volume of the book he was editing, *The Idea of the Avant Garde – And What It Means Today*. Taken with each other's idiosyncrasies, their correspondence gradually shifted from amiable professional exchanges and the eventual failure to organize a scholarly event to that of collaborating on some kind of writing project, which eventually became *CMOK*. Several titles were attempted for this book – *Marshmallow Muse: The Exact and Irreverent Letters of MJL and NZ*, *The Orange Jelly Bean, or, I Already Am Eating from the Trash Can All the Time: The Name of This Trash Can Is Ideology*, *The Secreted Correspondence of Mme Chatelet and Voltaire*, and *I'm Taken: The E-Pistolary Poetry of Kit le Minx and Cad* – but none of these proved to be more telling that *CMOK*, the Serbian word for kiss, which sums up the authors' quest for "harmony" in an altogether imperfect world and literary medium.

With regard to the following presentation, some names have been changed in order to protect people who might otherwise be offended by unguarded or absurdist commentary. For the sake of clarity, the emails are presented in their respective email threads. As the daily correspondence becomes more frequent, however, there are at times near-simultaneous responses to different threads. On the whole, the dialogue is more coherent when the individual emails are presented in their respective threads even if on occasion this confuses the real-time chronological sequence. The clock readings refer to Marc James Léger's Montreal Inbox, North American Eastern Daylight Time, which comes six hours later than the Central European Time Zone in Paris and Belgrade.

Rép: Re:
From Nina Zivancevic

Marc Léger <leger.mj@gmail.com>
To: zivancevicn65 <zivancevicn65@gmail.com>
13 February 2015 at 13:41

hi Nina,
i received your books a few weeks ago and managed to read two of
them and am just now sitting down to *Death of NYC* and should say that
so far i liked Cure especially and look forward to these other poems

speaking of avant garde this poetry project seems interesting, no?
http://www.lanaturnerjournal.com/contents/print-issue-7-contents-2

since you are a person of many places it makes no sense for me to talk
about Yugoslavia in particular but i will say that i recently did an interview
with Janez Emil Janša, a really nice person and doing great work

and also look for my contribution in *Grey Zones of Creativity and
Capital*, edited by Gordana Nikolic and Sefik Tatlic for the Museum of
Contemporary Art Vojvodina, Novi Sad

otherwise I'm looking forward to your contribution to Idea of the Avant
Garde, vol.2; the contributors so far include: Oliver Ressler, Pauline
Oliveros, John Tilbury, Lucien Kroll, Richard Barbrook, Condé &
Beveridge, Alfredo Jaar, FREEE, David Tomas, David Thomas, Kelly
Copper, Gavin Grindon, Gabriel Rockhill, Machete Group, Georgina
Born, Massimo Ricci, Marcelo Exposito, Mitch McEwen with Dawn
Lundy Martin, Matthew Shipp, Robert Wilson, Eda Cufer, Bonnie
Marranca, Sylvere Lotringer/Semiotext(e), Bruno Bosteels, Thomas
Burkhalter, Chika Okeke-Agulu, Mark McElhatten, McKenzie Wark,
Marijeta Bozovic, Go Hirasawa, Jessica Zychowicz, Reverend Billy,
Benjamin Noys, Christian Bok, Patricia Yberra, Nina Zivancevic, Zoe
Beloff, Map Office, Carrie Noland, Carla Harryman, Ultra Red, Edith
Brunette, Raymond Gervais and Jean-Marie Straub

and i also sent you one of my books via slow boat across the atlantic

best regards
Marc

Zivancevic Nina <zivancevicn65@gmail.com>
To: Marc Léger <leger.mj@gmail.com>
13 February 2015 at 17:18

Hi Marc! Although your name reads Léger, I see you are not taking
things "à la légère" and your excellent work attests to it --
here we are suffering from
many things which I'm afraid not very "avant-garde" and which concern
public civility,
so, I've been getting ready to sit down and write something for your no.2-
but these awful political climate takes much away of my time,
anyways, I"ll get to it soon, and I would like to know -- how long my
contribution should be, in printed pages I mean..
I've checked first Juliana Sphar's article as she edited my booklet a long
time ago, and she's someone I've known a bit, but I have a different idea
of the project.
I look forward to reading your work and your compilations- thank you so
much for yr attention to my work,
keep the flame burning
much love
à bientôt
Nina

Marc Léger <leger.mj@gmail.com>
To: Zivancevic Nina <zivancevicn65@gmail.com>
13 February 2015 at 18:45

Bonjour Nina,

Actually, my professor of medieval history told me that my name comes
from the middle ages and means (meant) "lecher" but even here I'm
afraid I have been somewhat taking things easy - à la Légère - and
not like your famous countryman Sade - encore un effort, citoyens! Of
course you will forgive me if my favourite is Žižek and I am only starting
to know about Zupancic.
The contributors are free to send in what they like and I have no word
limit except maybe your own sense of what you would like to contribute
to a book with 50 other people. Pauline Oliveros and John Tilbury sent in
about 500 words each. Lucien Kroll sent in 14,000 words, which is quite
a lot and a very good text in fact. My prediction is that your contribution
will come somewhere in between ...
Yes, Juliana Spahr in this anthology is very good and I liked also her
collaborator Joshua Clover's piece. There is also this book that came

out, with 100 contributors in creative writing on related matters: http://
entropymag.org/the-force-of-whats-possible-ed-lily-hoang-and-joshua-
marie-wilkinson/

all my best
Marc

Zivancevic Nina <zivancevicn65@gmail.com>
To: Marc Léger <leger.mj@gmail.com>
14 February 2015 at 19:17

My dear Marc- thank you for the link and yr smart response- indeed, the
entropy is the state of my spirit and my mind..
hmmm.. Žižek - I tried to understand and like, sort of before I read a
brilliant book "Žižek Manifest" by Darko Jelicic.. I wish I cld translate
THAT one into English... The author, despite his collateral damages
(former minister of culture who ended up in a Stalinist type of jail cell
etc) dismantled Žižek along the seams of his high-fashion thinking,
deconstructing his thought – that reached us in a form of the high
commercial philosophic commodity- but, he (Jelicic) did it in such a
brilliant way and manner that's it's worth reading it
and.. yes of course, many "Eastern European" or "central European"
philosophers are jealous of Žižek – as he had got to West European
market earlier than they did, however-- some of them, like this Jelicic,
are also brilliant in their analysis of the Žižek phenomenon etc etc

Zupancic, may be a good thinker, may not, I haven't read this one from
my primary school days...-- you should check into Crnjanski, by far one
of the best Central European Moderninsts.. he's our Kafka..
So, good night dear Marc, please take a look at our editorial activities
, the mag "Les Intempestives" and the anarchist site edited by Žižek 's
(and my close) friend Giancarlo Pizzi, Orpheerouge.org. We've been
working very hard on several topics at the same time!

best,
Nina Zee

Fwd: tande noam chomsky (22 janvier)

Zivancevic Nina <zivancevicn65@gmail.com>
To: Marc Léger <leger.mj@gmail.com>
17 February 2015 at 16:30

Marc—here's a piece of "my reality" included here as seen by Noam...so to speak
I just wanted to tell you that I came back home tonite and I opened my mailbox and found your "collector's item" in it!
I was very happy- my classes are over for 2 weeks, we ahve a winter break plus I'll have a pleasure of reading your good book!
thank you! a VERY timely arrival of this package.. more later--
à bientot
nina

Attachment: **NOAM CHOMSKY : "BEAUCOUP DE JOURNALISTES ONT AUSSI ETE ASSASSINES A GAZA"**
> Noam Chomsky: « Beaucoup de journalistes ont aussi été assassinés à Gaza » Par Noam Chomsky le 22 janvier 2015 Crises/guerres France Médias Propagande Après l'attentat terroriste contre Charlie... (http://www.jacques-toutaux.pro/article-noam-chomsky-beaucoup-de-journalistes-ont-aussi-ete-assassines-a-gaza-125422022.html)

Marc Léger <leger.mj@gmail.com>
To: Zivancevic Nina <zivancevicn65@gmail.com>
17 February 2015 at 16:49

just a warning Nina, the first essay in the book would seem to be the most controversial with readers and so maybe it's better to start backwards and move your way to the first essay - but in any case if you are familiar with Žižek's arguments about "postmodernism or class struggle" in Hegemony, Contingency, Universality, then what I say is redundant

i have invited a Palestinian architect to write for volume 2 but no word from her yet - and also Emily Jacir has made some good projects http://electronicintifada.net/content/material-film-retracing-wael-zuaiter-part-1/7054

best M(a)rc

Marc Léger <leger.mj@gmail.com>
To: Zivancevic Nina <zivancevicn65@gmail.com>
17 February 2015 at 18:44

about Charlie, thanks for the Chomsky

yes, the reaction to the CH massacre was entirely foreseeable, and even after 9/11, I was living in the US, I knew there would be reaction - i dread that now France wants to pass a patriot act -- two days after CH, I wrote this piece, obviously less detailed than Chomsky:
http://legermj.typepad.com/blog/2015/01/against-victim-politics.html

and then for some good news
http://www.democracynow.org/2015/2/17/the_next_syriza_as_greece_rejects

all the best
Marc

Zivancevic Nina <zivancevicn65@gmail.com>
To: Marc Léger <leger.mj@gmail.com>
18 February 2015 at 04:35

Dear Marc, thank you so much for sharing these links with me- I was not aware of your blog-- too much work around here--but your text is excellent and of course much more coherent and substantial (technically speaking etc) than my would be 'controversial' blog I wrote the day following the Charlie event, My friend Wael, assistant to Badiou and Rancièr won't talk to me now.. eh.. too bad in regards to losing friends.. Anyways, the PODEMOS case and Syritza case I've been following and as the matter.. this afternoon our editorial group led by my good friend, aka Toscanini, has a meeting. Our editorial now is Tancelin (taught aesthetics at Paris 8), Pizzi, friend of Toni Negri, who also did time because of the Red Brigades, Bruno Dequinot (teaches art, media at Paris 3) Pablo, a Podemos activist, Gerard da Silva, a wild Portugese writer, Mariola O., a Grotowski specialist, and mini-me...
You can check us out on www Orphéerouge.com.. or org..?I'll bring yr blog to the meating, i really love it! anyways, The Neoliberal Undead is next to my pillow and waiting to be read.. am likely to go back to "Art" my favorite lollypop of all times..

btw, have i sent you my book "Onze femmes artistes.." ?where trodding along E Said's steps i try to deciphre the question

What does (and how much) an artist gains by leaving his homeland and what does s/he lose? i
Have a very very nice day on the top of the "Real Mountin" or wherever you are!
nz

Attachment: Text by NZ, "Rally Against the Terrorism of...Our Minds"

Marc Léger <leger.mj@gmail.com>
To: Zivancevic Nina <zivancevicn65@gmail.com>
18 February 2015 at 10:17

Nina,

i see that you came out of it right away - it took me a little while to see that people were going to start to get emotional about it but without any consideration. it's too bad that Wael is so PC - I tried that once and after that was finished I wrote a few things

the Art lollipop I have a lot to say about, as do you, and this article here is just the tip of it: http://www.metamute.org/community/your-posts/revolution-going-to-be-communist

yes, I have Onze Femmes Artistes here with me - thank you - the notion of exile did not stand out for me as strongly as the resemblance to a book I used to have (now at Rosika's) called Onze Artistes from the 50s, with Picasso, Cocteau, Brancusi and others - portraits of artists in their studio - i like this Ken Russell territory on the lives of artists, which my colleague Bruce Barber loves also with his "born under Saturn" way of seeing things and also representations of artists as deviants in the movies - but these women artists, isn't it Victoria Vesna and not Vesna Victoria ? Abramovic was discussed in Volume 1 of Idea of the Avant Garde by Moe Angelos - that's a good question, about the costs and benefits of leaving one's homeland, I can talk about it too

yes, we have a "the mountain" in Montreal - i will go back when the snow melts

all the best
Marc

Zivancevic Nina <zivancevicn65@gmail.com>
To: Marc Léger <leger.mj@gmail.com>
18 February 2015 at 18:17

Yes, you're right this book 'Onze femmes' I conceived in the 1990s but is pertinent as it examines the involuntary (political post-Marxist) exiles of Koshara Bokshan and Ljubina Jovanovic (oldest members here) who failed to get arrested by OZNA in 1950 because they said they had liked Chagal!!!
Then I tried to show that they were two women-artists in our Fluxus and that there was Marina but also Eugenija Demnievska (they started our 'body art' and performance minimalism), and onto Kirila Faeh, Oli de Mejcen etc etc..The task was big and now i hear that i did not handle it well..Certainly it may be, but i am always writing from a position of a writer, and that's how I'd take my task of writing for you about the "Avant-garde". There's no historical one.
We are already history. I hope you agree to that. Let us see what we can think up in a new and entropic manner. How are you doing on Mannerism? I have to see every barberic manner in the political surroundings here in France, and yet! It was Averroes who called the Westerners Vandals thus Vandalusia, Andalusia, as what we approach often borders on vandalisms in thinking and action.

Thanks for sharing your Web garden with me! You are a very kind and open person! best,
nina zee

Marc Léger <leger.mj@gmail.com>
To: Zivancevic Nina <zivancevicn65@gmail.com>
18 February 2015 at 19:46

Nina Zee - what you have to say about avant garde is what you have to say and i look forward to it – it's for everyone involved as they like it - even though the other day I tried to coax someone into giving me more than 50 dismissive words and then he started accusing me of being Hitler so it got a little crazy real fast - but I try to be a good comrade

now what are they doing ?
http://pitchfork.com/news/58520-pussy-riot-enlist-richard-hell-yeah-yeah-yeahs-nick-zinner-miike-snows-andrew- wyatt-for-eric-garner-inspired-video-i-cant-breathe/

best
Marc

Zivancevic Nina <zivancevicn65@gmail.com>
To: Marc Léger <leger.mj@gmail.com>
19 February 2015 at 02:18

accusation? you, being HITLER..? who could THAT be?(i hope not
richard hell)
i am not like that, i am much more subtle in my approach in my writing,
most of the time--although some people don't know how to read it....
but sophisticated people like you- pethaps, why not. I am delighted that
you've invited mini-me to participate in yr project and i hope to be at 'la
hauteure" of such a task..
one more thing: ONE should not come too close to the artists or
movements s/he analyses, the artists in question start hating you, f
they flash the accussations etc etc- won't go into the psychoanalysis
of the phenomenon, and you just kill yourself to bring into light our
respective existence..
OK, please-- have a nice day!
best,
nina

Fwd: Invitation a la Sorbonne

Zivancevic Nina <zivancevicn65@gmail.com>
To: Marc Léger <leger.mj@gmail.com>
19 February 2015 at 10:22

Dear MJL I even ordered yr book on the Brave New Avant Garde
through Amazone...to get acqainted w yr style/mode of thinking. And to
format my essay..
I was joking about the gift phenomenon which is real..but not for this
purpose of your project
You must be tired or real busy... as you sort of misread some of my
mails.but
to reassure you: i have to swallow an important conference on the AG
in April, was invited by Georges Banu himself, so I will shape up my
contribution to you as well (out of it). And out of Kantor's body and the
East European cum post AG theater vs performance practice(evreything
I did and was and am and will be) So,
out of the body of that text I'll assemble a baby new born text fr you.
Sounds good to you?
Yrs Truly
Nz
Nz ps: all yr texts are REALLY excellent!

Marc Léger <leger.mj@gmail.com>
To: Zivancevic Nina <zivancevicn65@gmail.com>
19 February 2015 at 10:56

Nina ZEE, I'm not sure if how or why i misread your emails, but I assure
you i did not intend (I try not to have my nose up against the glass), but
anyhow it all seems interesting to me, especially as my writing somehow
automatically seeks to mimic yours - so you will recognize that my form
responds to yours - as so in this regard I look forward to sharing my new
book *Drive in Cinema*, which will come out in September - but I will send
you also the *Millet Matrix*, which I think you would like

thanks for ordering BNAG; you could say that BNAG goes with NU,
but that whereas NU is more activist, BNAG makes some theoretical
departures, especially Welcome to the Cultural Goodwill Revolution
and The Subject Supposed to Over-Identify, which is the starting point
for most of what I've done since then - deepening: 1) the class analysis
of the real subsumption of labour in biocapitalism/post-fordism, 2) the
limitations of activism-massism within biocapitalism, 3) the relevance of
artistic avant-gardes and political vanguards in this context

for the volume 1 i wrote a very short introduction, This Is Not an Introduction, because with 50 contributors, and now 100, I do not ask contributors to be concerned with the editorializing - this is a discussion amongst ourselves and others, which I parametered as three generations: 60s-70s neo avant-gardes, 80s-90s (anti)post-modernists, 2000s activists - in the context of today's international crises, and inter-disciplinary, because different fields respond to AG with different references that the others can benefit from knowing more about – and so not so much a textbook, but to be used by users

still working on:
idiots: nomadic practices: discourse of the hysteric
morons: critically affirmative: discourse of the university
imbeciles: avant garde: discourse of the analyst

but now Žižek is coming out with his Discourse of the Master, which to me is simply Art, which causes a lot of problems (maybe not for Badiou), but my essay in BNAG you will see is about the Analyst

so yes, please send me your baby and i will do my best to be your meta-mom and this is good company, 100 people or more and now also Kantor theatre n perf ... thank you!!!

best
Marc

Zivancevic Nina <zivancevicn65@gmail.com>
To: Marc Léger <leger.mj@gmail.com>
19 February 2015 at 17:40

Dear M(a)rc, or should I say M(e)rc,
which is our (:ar) in French. Come to think of it, it sounds like Merk or Merkel, but then this already sounds like Hitler to you, I bet.
You see how we get into linguisctic taxonomies- and I am glad that you reminded me that I should be more serious in terms of my style of writing, or at least more sounding English than French.. Ay, you see what the French have done to me?
A couple of years ago I spoke and wrote perfect English but now I really sound like thinking in French and writing in English..
However, having said all this, I should warn you (ach, what should I warn You?) not to enter my form in writing simply because
you are my editor and you should correct my errors and insufficencies rather than "responding to my form".Imagine what a disaster it would be

if the contents resemble one another as well as our respective forms? However, I find this correspondence highly amusing, as much as you do, and I notice that it has started invading my 'real'(ity), I was opening my mail tonight hoping that I'd find your response, or as Badiou has nicely remarked in his "A la recherche du réel perdu".. he says something like " Faut-il alors dire que le réel ne se laisse appréhender que du coté de l'expérience, de la perception sensible, du sentiment immédiat, voir de l'émotion, ou même de l'angoisse? C'est une longue tradition en philosophie." And then, "C'est dans ces termes, finalement, que Pascal entreprend de ruiner la rationalisme cartésien, que les empiristes s'en prennent à Leibniz, que Kierkegaard critique Hegel,, ou que l'existentialisme remplace la vérité par la liberté".

And I was happy to find your message that you were planning to share your new book, Drive in Cinema with me- you probably know that it would make me very happy to read it and perhaps, if I like my own reading of it, publish a review somewhere etc.

You could even come to Paris to make a presentation/promotion of it, I surely know a couple of places which would be happy to host your conference. Until that happy day when your book arrives, I will probably sit here anxiously (biting my nails over Kantor) but as Badiou has also said

"Disons que la question philosophique du réel est aussi, et peut-être surtout, la question de savoir si, étant donné un discours selon lequel le réel est contraignant, on peut, ou on ne peut pas, modifier le monde de telle sorte que se présente une ouverture, antérieurement invisible, par laquelle on peut échapper à CETTE contrainte sans pour autant nier qu'il y a du réel et de la contrainte..."

Has this passage explained my fear that you might have misunderstood my emails? I always misunderstand some- many people have already started numerous arguments because of the misunderstanding of emails. It is much better and nicer to talk to the Other (as Levinas wld say), directly, as the electronic communication becomes obtrusive . It is a new form of psychological warfare brought by the empires such as Google or Smoogle and Doodle..if you know what I mean. And of course you do!

And I am deeply moved that you want to be a meta-mom for my text, as you see that I need someone to mother my texts in English- here every editor is going to have plenty of work, hands full of work . If you can edit my writing I'd say it wld be great, and if you cannot really- I'll give my article to one of my American friends to correct the basics. And you will always remain the "meta-pop" for this piece of writing, as you sollicited it..

Btw, how did you find my address? Who gave it to you? Meaning-- is there any friend in common who suggested you to contact me?

I hear you saying "the world and the web is very big.."

Anyways, please think about a possible presentation of your work here in Paris. One could invite to your evening all these bigwigs whom you've been reading and quoting... but for such an event, I wld have to contact all the idiots, morons and the imbeciles who you had mentioned in your letter. Voila! I wish you a very
good evening,
nina zee

Marc Léger <leger.mj@gmail.com>
To: Zivancevic Nina <zivancevicn65@gmail.com>
19 February 2015 at 20:20

Dear Nina Zee, I see no choice here but to respond in between the lines, not unlike the white and black stripes that we love so much in underground Parisian fashion of the 50s (maybe even Germany in the 20s)

On 19 February 2015 at 17:40, Zivancevic Nina <zivancevicn65@gmail. com> wrote: Dear M(a)rc, or should I say M(e)rc, which is our (:ar) in French. Come to think of it, it sounds like Merk or Merkel, but then this already sounds like Hitler to you, I bet.

I like (e) but maybe in like Kurt Schwitters' M(e)rz and a home full of Marzbau friends - which was my point sending you Rosika's Mary Linwood Napoleon - her friend made one of George III after Benjamin West - but more to evading your typographic whatnots

You see how we get into linguisctic taxonomies- and I am glad that you reminded me that I should be more serious in terms of my style of writing, or at least more sounding English than French.. Ay, you see what the French have done to me?

I see nothing but I can take your word for it and maybe also the imagined sound of your speeches to the French parliament.

A couple of years ago I spoke and wrote perfect English but now I really sound like thinking in French and writing in English..

that's what they said about Gabrielle Roy, which led to Anne Hébert and Marie Claire Blais - I asked her for a signed copy of *La belle bête* and she said, "oui, c'est de ton age"

However, having said all this, I should warn you (ach, what should I warn You?) not to enter my form in writing simply because you are my editor and you should correct my errors and insufficencies rather than "responding to my form".Imagine what a disaster it would be if the contents resembles as well as our respective forms?

yes, that's very true, though you should not underestimate my knowledge of the Black Arts - I am happy to do some editing work on your text and this reminds me are you doing this to be like the Others? - in any case it is my pleasure

However, I find this correspondence highly amusing, as much as you do, and Inotice that it has started invading my 'real'(ity), I was opening my mail tonight hoping that I'd find your response, or as Badiou has nicely remarked in his "A la recherche du réel perdu".. he says something like

you should email my pen pal - though he has been sick lately - poor little Bill ... his photographs remind me of your poems ...

Faut-il alors dire que le réel ne se laisse appréhender que du coté de l'expérience, de la perception sensible, du sentiment immédiat, voir de l'émotion, ou même de l'angoisse?

what is he saying ?

C'est une longue tradition en philosophie.

this is also -In- *Praise of Love*, which I endorse

And then, "C'est dans ces termes, finalement, que Pascal entreprend de ruiner la rationalisme cartésien, que les empiristes s'en prennent à Leibniz, que Kierkegaard critique Hegel,, ou que l'existentialisme remplace la vérité par la liberté".

when in doubt ... truth procedure!

And I was happy to find your message that you were planning to share your new book, Drive in Cinema with me- you probably know that it would make me very happy to read it and perhaps, if I like my own reading of it, publish a review somewhere etc. I'd be happy to attempt at clarifying some issues of your good book with the general readership, so to speak..

I have to warm you there are some difficult essays in there

You could even come to Paris to make a presentation/promotion of it, I surely know a couple of places which would be happy to host your conference. Well, yes, such things have to be planned in advance, we all know that. Until that happy day when your book arrives, I will probably sit here anxiously

at least I will, and this is August or September I think - but you can also promulgate The Idea of the Avant Garde, volume 1, which came out last September and still needs readers and reviewers - so maybe that's something you would like to suggest - as for Paris! oh yes! and perhaps I could present something on the films of Vera Chytilova's (RIP) Daisies, which I do with a comparison to Vaclav Vorlicek, Who Wants to Kill Jessie? in relation to psychoanalysis - I have not yet presented this material anywhere - I heard that in France they love their art rupestre and so it should go over well - I should maybe write something about Fruit of Paradise, which is maybe an even better film

(biting my nails over Kantor) but as Badiou has also said

the relation of the negation of the relation

"Disons que la question philosophique du réel est aussi, et peut-être surtout, la question de savoir si, étant donné un discours selon lequel le réel est contraignant, on peut, ou on ne peut pas, modifier le monde de telle sorte que se présente une ouverture, antérieurement invisible, par laquelle on peut échapper à CETTE contrainte sans pour autant nier qu'il y a du réel et de la contrainte..."

in relation to an invitation by me to Badiou through his friend in NY said "he doesn't care about your Québec" - well, these punk girls, that say what? "And if you need to use institutions to make sure the world doesn't cop out, we're going to use them." cop?

Has this passage explained my fear that you might have misunderstood my emails. I always do- many people have already started numerous arguments because of the misunderstanding of emails. It is much better and nicer to talk to the Other (as Levinas wld say),

yes, but the Other is always up to his phenomenology - les malheurs de M. Merleau-Ponty as Lefebvre put it - my hero - but you know if someone wants to give me some face, what am I to say - no thanks, I'm good - but I am not one for moral panics, only Freudo-Marxism and maybe a little bit of Kristeva

directly, as the electronic communication becomes obtrusive .

obtrusive? what's your solution to obtrusive? kill, kill, kill !!!

It is a new form of psychological warfare brought by the empires such as Google or Smoogle and Doodle..if you know what I mean. And of course you do!

yes, thank you for the compliment ?

And I am deeply moved that you want to be a meta-mom for my text, as you see that I need someone to mother my texts in English- here every editor is going to have plenty of work, hands full of work . If you can edit my writing I'd say it wld be great, and if you cannot really- I'll give my article to one of my American friends to correct the basics. And you will always remain the "meta-pop" for this piece of writing, as you sollicited it..

I have to say I would you prefer to do it myself, unless it's incomprehensible to the uninitiated – I'm a greedy little editor

Btw, how did you find my address? Who gave it to you? Meaning-- is there any friend in common who suggested you to contact me?

aliens

I hear you saying "the world and the web is very big.."

you can quote me on that in your review and it occurs to me that the notion of post-enlightenment schizo-something has something to say to this web which is not One - that's from Yurchak too - do you know him? - an article he wrote on late socialism was terrific and repeats a lot of those jokes about the socialist in hell who is up to his neck in it

Anyways, please think about a possible presentation of your work here in Paris. One could invite to your evening all these bigwigs whom you've been reading and quoting...

it should go the oher way around

but for such an event, I wld have to contact all the idiots, morons and the imbeciles who you had mentioned in your letter. Voila! I wish you a very good evening, nina zee

splendid, as Kant used to say
ours is like Amiri Baraka's dispute with Barrett Watten, but the opposite

Zivancevic Nina <zivancevicn65@gmail.com>
To: Marc Léger <leger.mj@gmail.com>
19 February 2015 at 20:48

what was Amiri Baraka's dispute with Watten?
Amiri as a post-colonial continentalist and Watten of an analytic
philosopher?
Look, you don't have to give me an answer-- as you're in quandry
whether I'd get what you mean or not...perhaps i just mean what i say
and probably you do too, but always swimming in the river of terms for
which i need a special Latin dictionary. I don't think that even the network
of the networks could help me here..
Have no regrets though- if I manage to make anyone laugh,a serious
artist like you... that's already a punk accomplishment..
ach, and I have to go back to Schleiermacher now, some new problems
on the horizon here, 3am in Paris..
best,

Marc Léger <leger.mj@gmail.com>
To: Zivancevic Nina <zivancevicn65@gmail.com>
20 February 2015 at 09:31

Zena, Here is another link for you, though I fear I may be maxing out
your clicker:
[Essay on Barrett Watten and Amiri Baraka.]
I imagine that Schleiermacher's at 3am in Paris is a script for a play ?
Marc

Zivancevic Nina <zivancevicn65@gmail.com>
To: Marc Léger <leger.mj@gmail.com>
20 February 2015 at 09:55

Hi,
I am glad that Nancy J. can write such a coherent and comprehensible
review:
like I said last night- Stanley Cavell could possibly.. help yr or my own
case
but
in
no
way

our dialogue cld be reduced (are you a reductionist?)
to
"   These two modes of debate — one rooted in formal discourse
and the other in quick rhetorical insults — made this a tough match to
watch. The contrast of these two extremes made it apparent that these
were two men who could not speak to each other because of their very
different approaches to speech and language. Each represented their
time and the radically different ways that they experienced the historical
realities of the past 40 years — and neither seemed willing to listen, or
learn from the other.
    Through the course of the match they became caricatures of
themselves: The Opaque Gunslinger vs. the Verbal Terminator."
I imagine that I wld be a Gunslinger and Theee- the Verbal T...? selon
l'age et l'experience..
I am sure that our dialogue is a bit more meaningful (ah, Cavell!!) than
that.. although
I am a more radical poet than Baraka, and you are a more radical thinker
than Watten (oh, boy! oh girl)
I think I trashed inadvertently yr mail with your Rosika's Napoleon link,
you can send these links along, thank you, you're not "maxing out my
clicker although I might be busier than u at this time of the year) and
probably need more time- to get all things done
like to put Hermeneutics into a capsule of MLA scholarship,East
European style at 3am in paris etc.. a scrip for a horror movie?.
Indeed. Typing all my silly thoughts into 4-5 languages all the time (for
the last 30 years)..Boy, do i get tired! I wish you a good day and a less
condescending stance vis-a-vis yr less talented (verbally) collegues
in fact
I play scores, violin scores all the time.. the words fatigue me and i am
EVER more at home in the realm of pure..
V.Yankelevitch.
Yours Truly,

Marc Léger <leger.mj@gmail.com>
To: Zivancevic Nina <zivancevicn65@gmail.com>
20 February 2015 at 10:48

Zena, , , I can see that the global conspiracy has also caught up with
you and that now we are forever expanding the range of possibilities in
this capsule. I think that you would make an excellent gunslinger and I
have to say I know something in this area. This can be worked up into
a horror cross-genre if you like but you know who really surprised me it
was Claude Lelouche with his nice adoption of our Guenevere and your

Lancealot in Another Man, Another Chance. One of the best opening sequences for a Western, which starts in the context of the Paris Commune.

I think though that you should be a Mexican bandita and you can be played by Julie Delpy. What do you say?

Zivancevic Nina <zivancevicn65@gmail.com>
To: Marc Léger <leger.mj@gmail.com>
20 February 2015 at 11:21

Hahahaha!
Of course that I disagree!
Jus' tell me smth ..before I join bela bartok forever..& you..bela lugoshi.
Is claude lelouche a cousin of marc lelecher?
Tsss..a film crotic..a Member of the French Fed of Cinema Crots I never got to know..i like his girl, Huppert..but I prefer
True Faux.
And you?
Ok. U r still in kowboi lands I see..
Come to paree and i'll take u to the movies.
"see ya at the movies"

Zivancevic Nina <zivancevicn65@gmail.com>
To: Marc Léger <leger.mj@gmail.com>
20 February 2015 at 11:36

Aussi:
Thanks for the links! u shd not joke w that "bandita" stuff though...some people shared the same opinion platform and started contemplating my acting avatars..and hop! Forever forbidden to enter the paradiso of the US.! The amer.gvmt says that I am a female version of ginsberg and chomsky cum stalin cum malcoma x cum...the policemen always come when I try to cross the us borders so I think I won't even try again
Yr Paloma Rodriguez

Marc Léger <leger.mj@gmail.com>
To: Zivancevic Nina <zivancevicn65@gmail.com>
20 February 2015 at 11:40

my preference is for the unforgiven JLG (see attached),
but I did visit Day for Night at Père Lachaise
and i love this rebekah del rio with buttons for you to click since you're
very fast from this other side of paradise - quick, give her something to
read and i would like to request your unconditional surrender and your
signature here:
https://www.youtube.com/watch?v=xrC3Bf-CvHU
[Rebekah del Rio performance of Roy Orbison's "Crying" (Llorando) in
David Lynch's *Mulholland Drive*]

Attachment: MJL essay on Godard's *Film Socialisme*

Zivancevic Nina <zivancevicn65@gmail.com>
To: Marc Léger <leger.mj@gmail.com>
20 February 2015 at 12:27

Thank YOU! I have already eaten from this trashcan called
The Unconditional Surrender
But hmmmm.. If really necessary- I.ll sign the damned thing again...
Here: I'm signing the contratct!

Zivancevic Nina <zivancevicn65@gmail.com>
To: Marc Léger <leger.mj@gmail.com>
21 February 2015 at 09:18

Dear Marconi Legerissimo, have'nt had time to open my comp at home
since yesterday..the ugly gargoyles of capitalism
Money and time, have swallowed all my activities..tonite I hope I will look
at all clips and give you my humble op..my small Samsung cannot open
heavy files
And this Nina-Marc email or 'emaille' file becomes hefty and quite big..it
reminds me of...
No, in fact. It does not remind me of anything I've already seen...
A ce soir...

Marc Léger <leger.mj@gmail.com>
To: Zivancevic Nina <zivancevicn65@gmail.com>
21 February 2015 at 10:19

keep me posted - i am now reading "the age of the poets" for real

Zivancevic Nina <zivancevicn65@gmail.com>
To: Marc Léger <leger.mj@gmail.com>
21 February 2015 at 11:03

I'll certainly keep YOU posted even if I have to trash 50 other emails
waiting for my response...
How do u like that big book(age du poetes)??
Let me know..
The Goldslinger

Marc Léger <leger.mj@gmail.com>
To: Zivancevic Nina <zivancevicn65@gmail.com>
21 February 2015 at 12:27

seems like with his notion he's trying something like the time-image ...

Goldslinger theme

Marc Léger <leger.mj@gmail.com>
To: Zivancevic Nina <zivancevicn65@gmail.com>
21 February 2015 at 14:59

portable zen(a)
let meow no wha?
and my foray into avant-theatre-performance with bruce barber

http://legermj.typepad.com/blog/2012/04/six-authors-in-search-of-a-character-a-reading-and-writing-of-bruce-barbers- e.html

http://legermj.typepad.com/blog/2012/04/saying-something-about-e-an-interview-with-bruce-barber.html

---

Marc Léger <leger.mj@gmail.com>
To: Zivancevic Nina <zivancevicn65@gmail.com>
21 February 2015 at 16:54

Poem for Nina Zee

julie delpy, click here:
https://www.youtube.com/watch?v=OmLOt9mRD18
[Elvis Presley, live performance of "Unchained Melody" 1977]

Zivancevic Nina <zivancevicn65@gmail.com>
To: Marc Léger <leger.mj@gmail.com>
21 February 2015 at 17:14

Marconi!
thank you for the song via Prelvis Esley,
lemmie jus' watch these x2 videos and- ..
see ya at the movies...

Zivancevic Nina <zivancevicn65@gmail.com>
To: Marc Léger <leger.mj@gmail.com>
21 February 2015 at 17:53

Ah, has anyone told you that – you're too much, Marco legerus
(sounds like a Roman xcenturion, no re to Barbars) now onto Barber E

performance- it was a strange day today
as I've just got Perec's EEE book (Espèces d'espaces) and bunch of
other videos..
but barber's got it wrong when he said "about Brecht (is) that you could
see the apparatus, so there's no illusionistic distancing"
just the contrary (see Innis, etc etc)- brecht was for the intellectual
distance, so the whole theater of Images (via Foreman) comes from him,
he didn't want to bother the spectator in any way--
and it was Piscator who was for "no illusionistic distancing".. PLEASE!! i
f you want me to write a text for you- a painfully correct la Sorbonne type
of info has to go into yr book.
And i don't think that Julie Delpy's lovely image goes with me.. Yeah, I
am really sweet and naive
but more like that image downhere (sort of VEEERY determined)
and always agreeing with you! yes!
Thank you so much, Marc- you really ma

Image: [next page]

Marc Léger <leger.mj@gmail.com>
To: Zivancevic Nina <zivancevicn65@gmail.com>
21 February 2015 at 19:20

well, this E was not written for the book on [performance] so that is
just as well then given that bruce got it backwards - judith malina sent
me something on Piscator for volume 1 and i should get to know my
dramaturgs better that's for sure - in the semiotexte book on Müller he
says just days before the wall came down that he thinks it will never
come down, so that must have taken everyone by surprise, especially
the wall - which is, you know, gone

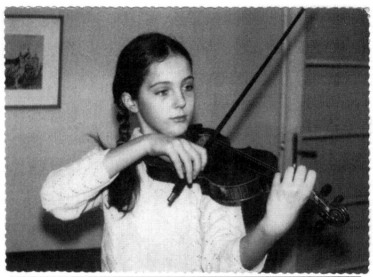
Nina Zee playing the violin.

brilliant!

Zivancevic Nina <zivancevicn65@gmail.com>
To: Marc Léger <leger.mj@gmail.com>
21 February 2015 at 18:14

can we have some more of this salad for lunch, please? (Regarding MJL essay "Drive in Cinema: The Dialectic of the Subject in *Daisies* and *Who Wants to Kill Jessie?*")

I LOVED it!
thank you

Zivancevic Nina <zivancevicn65@gmail.com>
To: Marc Léger <leger.mj@gmail.com>
21 February 2015 at 19:15

Wait a minute..now it gets really interesting..i.m finishing the godard text..will send u a response in a sec..am really impressed
"are u real, my ideal?" James? (but joyce)

Marc Léger <leger.mj@gmail.com>
To: Zivancevic Nina <zivancevicn65@gmail.com>
21 February 2015 at 19:35

there is a true sandwich story there that actually happened where Here Comes Everybody was dropped at the start of *Marxism and Urban Culture* (to which Cayley and me contributed an essay on psychogeography and protest marches) that i found a little bit planted and then the former editor of Parachute invited me to Dora Garcia's Finnegan's Wake reading group at which I was sentenced to pharmakon as usual - but this should be extended into a monologue or a memoir which is one thing i don't have in me - my guess is it's mostly all on tape, or in this email, which is somehow involution of the convolution

---

Zivancevic Nina <zivancevicn65@gmail.com>
To: Marc Léger <leger.mj@gmail.com>
21 February 2015 at 19:45

I don't want to sound repetative, but I really really liked yr Godard -God vs Dog review,

I wrote of review of it in serbian and i guess you cannot read it
nor the video done a

Zivancevic Nina <zivancevicn65@gmail.com>
To: Marc Léger <leger.mj@gmail.com>
21 February 2015 at 19:50

oops, a year later in Dec 2013 where the images were supplied (that is
a film in the background by Godard's right hand, Lou Kokowski, simply
called the Film.
But Lou went to see him last year and found him in a very poor state ,
impoverished in a village in Switzerland i love that man (Godard) and
often see myself as a silly version of Ana Karina where I stroll through
the Alphaville of New York and Paris and London and Belgrade
looking for people "who did not forget how to cry", but is that Uncle big
Art? is it.. AG? I don't know,
but I totally agree with you when you say that a "provisional definition
of an AG artist can be his acceptance of NO aesthetic criteria", as
exemplified and "taught " by Duchamp

Zivancevic Nina <zivancevicn65@gmail.com>
To: Marc Léger <leger.mj@gmail.com>
21 February 2015 at 19:57

that there are no guarantees for the social importance of artworks
therefore it goes without saying
and perhaps the artist should not really worry about the importance
(once he understood that he's got only his walk along the narrow
"passage from creativuty to consequences"..
Well, he shd be balanced out.. sort of so as not to confuse this absence
of social importance for his deep Desire (yes Lacan)for air and airy
abstraction
which some of us imbeciles call "l'art pour l'artism" etc etc..
here's my video..
no, wait, i have to use the We trasfer i guess it's really heavy;o

---

Image: [next page]

Les deux Ninas. Le FUMOIRE bar, Paris, 2014.
Photo by Margo Berdishewsky.

Zivancevic Nina <zivancevicn65@gmail.com>
To: Marc Léger <leger.mj@gmail.com>
21 February 2015 at 20:18

now i see.. it's almost.. 3 am in Paris and I've been reading Marc J Léger
all night long-- which is a much nicer task indeed that going back
to Schleiermacher,
althogh some people might say "it's the same thing but upside down"
however, as a former member of the Living theater—I'm always for "the
Living" and the dead authors.. well, we admire some of them, don't we?
but hard to keep up with that dialogue!
I may be going back to my violin, luckily, have veeery good neighbors
(they never complain when i play)
hasta la vista
y muchos besos

Zivancevic Nina <zivancevicn65@gmail.com>
To: Marc Léger <leger.mj@gmail.com>
21 February 2015 at 20:27

aaaa, now i'm really going to cry-- as I had sold my coffret with all his
films (Jonas Mekas)- i was THAT hungry
and that was before i signed my bancrupcy act and sold my apartment..
but his retro at the Serpentine was really great, this i remember and i am
glad that everything stays in my head, sort of stuff you cannot sold or
buy, certain types of memories..

Marc Léger <leger.mj@gmail.com>
To: Zivancevic Nina <zivancevicn65@gmail.com>
21 February 2015 at 20:37

i have an answer to this artist poor artist idea (ars gratia artis, just in time
for the Oscars) but i,m not saying it straight out - but you have more in
my writings in terms of the basic structure - and am still developing this
aspect --- yes, we love Ana Karina as perhaps JLG/JLG could not or only
as he would have liked us to

Zivancevic Nina <zivancevicn65@gmail.com>
To: Marc Léger <leger.mj@gmail.com>
21 February 2015 at 21:01

Mr Leger,
thank you for these two .. silly me I sent you the second part of the
performance which you cannot understand anyways..
here's a reading of the Cure - for good night..
thank you fr yr overall care and thinking of me
i wish you a very nice evening indeed..
NZ

Attachment: Two audio works by NZ: "4 philosophers death" and "5
doctors come and go"

Zivancevic Nina <zivancevicn65@gmail.com>
To: Marc Léger <leger.mj@gmail.com>
21 February 2015 at 21:21

then i don't know what to do with you, a rat that i am.. I wish I were
a gentle creature, something like a mouse..

Marc Léger <leger.mj@gmail.com>
To: Zivancevic Nina <zivancevicn65@gmail.com>
21 February 2015 at 21:23

Poem for Nina Zizancevic

twas the night before Christmas
and all through the house
Nina was stirring
not even a mouse

Zivancevic Nina <zivancevicn65@gmail.com>
To: Marc Léger <leger.mj@gmail.com>
21 February 2015 at 21:28

not at all, the sad truth Marc is-- that i am a mutant, a replicant escaped
from that old movie by Scott(?)

see, my head is full of movies, extended paintings in movement as i call them,

my father was a director of the national museum, a really cultured guy, but a bloody perfectionist..

he wanted me to describe, write down every image i see in galleries etc since age 5..

i adored him and hated, both, as he was my "missing father", a point addressed in a long analysis i undertook a couple of years ago

---

Marc Léger <leger.mj@gmail.com>
To: Zivancevic Nina <zivancevicn65@gmail.com>
21 February 2015 at 21:35

yes, we were all the children of Marx and Scott but because of him we were not allowed to forget it –i used to work in two national museums so i understand completely

but I have to go for now xena, the warrior photocopy machine

Zivancevic Nina <zivancevicn65@gmail.com>
To: Marc Léger <leger.mj@gmail.com>
21 February 2015 at 21:40

good night, brave knight,
see you at the movies..(and other virtual realms)

about schleiermacher

Marc Léger <leger.mj@gmail.com>
To: Zivancevic Nina <zivancevicn65@gmail.com>
21 February 2015 at 21:03

i did a piece that he might have liked
it was a bottle of painters' medium - with the title:
*eucharis: unfinished thanks to the trait in the other and the
imponderables contained in the phrase 'alter ego'*
but that was context specific

Zivancevic Nina <zivancevicn65@gmail.com>
To: Marc Léger <leger.mj@gmail.com>
21 February 2015 at 21:10

wait.. was that a theater piece? or what else..?
and do you have any trace or trait of it left for the eternity? let me know..
xxx

Marc Léger <leger.mj@gmail.com>
To: Zivancevic Nina <zivancevicn65@gmail.com>
21 February 2015 at 21:17

yes, it was theatre and everyone pretended i was not happening, which
was false -
these are the indirectest traces ...

Attachment: Images of MJL artwork, *Thieves Like Us*, Karel Appel and
CoBrA t-shirt designs, "Proud to Support Karel Appel" and "Proud to
Support CoBrA"

Zivancevic Nina <zivancevicn65@gmail.com>
To: Marc Léger <leger.mj@gmail.com>
21 February 2015 at 21:23

this is a lovely poster, Marc,
do you know that I met him once (Appel).. with Allen, his great friend at
Naropa that is, in 1981.....

Marc Léger <leger.mj@gmail.com>
To: Zivancevic Nina <zivancevicn65@gmail.com>
21 February 2015 at 21:24

he made everything okay and is one of my favourites in the way that his ars gratia artis also carried into its broader frames of creation, so I'm not convinced the imbeciles are at all Kantian, more hegelo-lacanian, given the context-specificity of the unconscious

---

Zivancevic Nina <zivancevicn65@gmail.com>
To: Marc Léger <leger.mj@gmail.com>
21 February 2015 at 21:38

I don't want to bore you with my memories and my silly stories any more..
my failing health tells me that i should rest.. and still, it is so pleasant having this virtual conversation with you..
somewhat like in a film Bettie Blue, where someone starts reading, yeah, a guy starts reading his wife's manuscript and he cannot stop.. so he goes on and on and on.; and discovers a lot of things about a woman he had just married.. but i wld like to see these two films you spoke of.. Daisies and Jessie..
i am so ignorant, i am like a dummy sitting here in paris, reading theory all the time..

De ta lectrice dévouée

Zivancevic Nina <zivancevicn65@gmail.com
To: Marc Léger <leger.mj@gmail.com>
23 February 2015 at 12:14

Dear MJL
Im terribly sorry for evertaking yr special presence for granted in my lousy boxes.
Are you too "BB" or too BBT"?*
*too Busy to Breathe or too Busy to Be True?
At any rate ..now that u groomed me (a bit like a pet or those abused kids) to click every message of yours, you disappeared. Now that the hour of the virtual conditioning is over just tell me smth: was that a dream, a hacker's joke or yr own flight into nz's imagination?

A little girl lost
(Blake, part 2)

Marc Léger <leger.mj@gmail.com>
To: Zivancevic Nina <zivancevicn65@gmail.com>
23 February 2015 at 13:03

warning: free nonsense verse - do i sound like a flarf barf mark lark ?
i was hoping you would read this for fear that filling out boxes marked x for Xena has become a leisure past time for me, and was cry-y-y-y-in over you - now that we have wedding plans in Paree, and one more thing about Kant's imerative i can't won't didn't do - you cannot socially construct one to know one - WE,RE INCORRUPT MAXIMALISTS

Zivancevic Nina <zivancevicn65@gmail.com>
To: Marc Léger <leger.mj@gmail.com>
23 February 2015 at 13:25

Ohhhh
U know Brad..i just want to tell you
That even drowning
I won't ask u for help
Zena Lichtenstein

Marc Léger <leger.mj@gmail.com>
To: Zivancevic Nina <zivancevicn65@gmail.com>
23 February 2015 at 13:37

Comrade Anais Nina
please tell me the one about the *enragés*

Zivancevic Nina <zivancevicn65@gmail.com>
To: Marc Léger <leger.mj@gmail.com>
23 February 2015 at 17:01

Dear dr John Schmoo
I think im goin off my clicker
I read this guy's article cum study about Godard and...
I decided to marry him right away although I have no idea if he.s
married, buried, gay or sad...
I don't care
Im in love w his scriblin
Can you help dear doc?this had never happened before..i mean
Not recently..not since 2001

I rhink im in a big trouble
I have to get back home
To open ALL of yr attachments
This is my attachment to yr letters
Whoever YOU
May be
Sending you the Stranglers link in my spirit "tango in paris"..
Am amazed at all this..let me dwell or droole in my
Amazement..
Please help!!
Yr Zina Dostoyevich, phd.

Marc Léger <leger.mj@gmail.com>
To: Zivancevic Nina <zivancevicn65@gmail.com>
23 February 2015 at 18:04

hold on, i have to go take my shower, back shortly

Marc Léger <leger.mj@gmail.com>
To: Zivancevic Nina <zivancevicn65@gmail.com>
23 February 2015 at 18:38

ok, that's better, hygiene is very important
now, dr Zhivago, let me see about your unchained malady

Dear dr John Schmoo
I think im goin off my clicker

that is not a problem, here you go:
http://www.lacan.com/journal9/?p=520

I read this guy's article cum study about Godard and...
I decided to marry him right away although I have no idea if he.s
married, buried, gay or sad...

nous n'acceptons plus
des cours de soir
les rois de l'impérialisme
le progrès technologique
appartiennent au gai savoir
pratique et théorie
– e.e. cummings

I don't care

me n'either - you can make a credit card payment at the desk

Im in love w his scriblin

flattery will get you

Can you help dear doc?this had never happened before..i mean
Not recently..not since 2001

where does it hurt ?

I rhink im in a big trouble
Please help!!
Yr Zina Dostoyevich, phd.

Stalinists! Your Nina is with us!

Zivancevic Nina <zivancevicn65@gmail.com>
To: Marc Léger <leger.mj@gmail.com>
23 February 2015 at 18:44

now i don't know about the socially undermined and really homeless
but can relate somewhat to all the movements type "occupy wall street"
don't forget i was that Tama Yanovic's "slave of NY" working dead shifts
on Wall street, sucking dicks (metaphorically) to all Wall street lawyers
and what do i think about les enragés?
what do you?
have you taken your shower and got all ready for the Midnight town
special show where you can quote, yet again, the symbols of a certain
human rebellion - be it Badiou, or Deleuze or my late friends Baudrillard
and Bourdieu

what can i tell you while you're taking this divine shower thinking
who's that crazy woman from paree sending me all this messages..
i don't know.. I was in mourning (le deuil) for many years and i stopped
dialoguing in any meaningful way
i was so glad to have found you in this virtual forest of (w)(b)irds
birds!
zina nee

Marc Léger <leger.mj@gmail.com>
To: Zivancevic Nina <zivancevicn65@gmail.com>
23 February 2015 at 19:02

how could I forget that!? I mean, those were the days my friend
but really, it's Candy Darling that got the best of me
but my feeling is that Niko was the true artist, no ?

Fwd: Tr : Fwd: merej/ projo

Zivancevic Nina <zivancevicn65@gmail.com>
To: Marc Léger <leger.mj@gmail.com>
23 February 2015 at 18:53

Your take on me being a verbal version of yr Billy Dane is a

JEUDI 5 MARS 20H30 PENICHE CINEMA 59 BD MAC DONALD 75019
PARIS METRO PORTE DE LA VILETTE PROJECTION DU FILM TU
CROIS QU'ELLE VA VENIR?

Texte : Pierre Merejkowsky **Réalisation** : Jean Philippe Reymond
Production Hibou/Télébocal, CNC COSIP **Interprètes** le metteur en
scène : Christophe Correia l'actrice célèbre et célébrée : Claure Nebout
Pierre Merejkowsky: Pierre Merejkowsky
A cette occasion sera proposé à la vente par Patience le texte Tu crois
qu'elle va venir? de Pierre Merejkowsky (Les Editions du Crime et du
Châtiment)
Prix : 3 euros TTC (2 euros tarif réduit sans justificatif)
(aucun carton d'invitation ne sera demandée à l'entrée)
intention

Le spectateur
Les dialogues de Claire, de Christophe sont entièrement écrits
PM n'étant pas répertorié dans la catégorie INSEE des travailleurs
exerçant une profession de comédien professionnel, la thématique,
ainsi que la fin et du début des verbales et gestuelles de PM moi seront
écrits. Claire et Christophe auront ainsi la possibilité d'intercaler leurs
dialogues et gestuels écrits dans l'autisme revendiqué de PM moi
Un autisme, qu'il ne paraît pas opportun de qualifier de psychiatrique
mais au contraire de politique.
En effet PM moi réfute dans ses interventions et sa gestuelle la notion
d'auteur définie par les sociétés d'auteurs qui considèrent que l'Auteur
est le CREATEUR de droit divin et du siècle des lumières avec son
cortège de droit patrimonial et de défilés du Ministre de la Culture.
Pour PM moi la ligne politique, affective, sexuelle, morale est clairement
et définitivement définie
L'auteur n'existe pas. le Droit d'auteur existe.
L'auteur n'est pas Dieu, ni Staline, ni Maître
Il est réceptacle
Perroquet
du monde extérieur, de son passé, passé des ancêtres, de sa mère,
de sa grand mère, du présent, du futur, de la conscience collective, de
l'espoir, du renouveau, de la naissance. Et de la Résurrection.
Nous sommes tous le présent
je suis une archive

je suis moi PM
Le vécu devra OBLIGATOIREMENT respecter la mise en scène définie
sans aucune dérogation possible ainsi que le stipule les contrats de
travail enregistrés et tamponnés par le service compétent
La Scène du théâtre, le café, le banc public, le passé, le présent, le café,
le critique, le Ministre de la Culture, la rencontre sont Pensées
donc créations.
Vive le théâtre
vive le désir
vive la vie

Zivancevic Nina <zivancevicn65@gmail.com>
To: Marc Léger <leger.mj@gmail.com>
23 February 2015 at 18:59

strange representation of some desolate images
in my poetry, i don't know
what to tell you..?
if i ignore interspaces and interpunction that is because Crnjanski said
that "the punctuation is a violation of the side of an author .. of his public"
so i don't want to impose my thinking on anyone , especially not on you,
my dear and very very very dear colleague (as they say here "mon cher
collegue"), so, hmm whatever, I'll be here to welcome you if you come to
paree
you just have to tell me the dates
and also if you have no place to stay- don't go
to a hotel, you can stay with me- in my small studio (26m sq) i can even
leave and leave you the keys
and you can keep my paintings on the walls-- if you like to
jerk off while viewing Carravagio..
zee

Zivancevic Nina <zivancevicn65@gmail.com>
To: Marc Léger <leger.mj@gmail.com>
23 February 2015 at 19:09

but the best summery of your friend
going towards youz
and description in this film of Pierre
which says
TU CROIS QU'ELLE VA VENIR?
now yr turn to answer..

Marc Léger <leger.mj@gmail.com>
To: Zivancevic Nina <zivancevicn65@gmail.com>
23 February 2015 at 19:19

i'm not as fast a bronzeslinger maybe
but i have to have an all expenses paid trip otherwise not possible
so maybe our wedding will be cancelled after all but it was nice knowing
you and carravagio
but if your sorbonne wants some funny art rupestre I propose we team
up
but maybe that was just me falling for your stratégies
Mayakovsky's mother calls again

Zivancevic Nina <zivancevicn65@gmail.com>
To: Marc Léger <leger.mj@gmail.com>
23 February 2015 at 21:14

Hmm I dont know what yet
New theories or strategies to think
Up in this academic dessert full of
simulacra to bring you to my enchanted forest
Some people really think that I might be some dangerous witch and I
dont deny it but thee who had seen a little girl..and also yr
Very good writing took that magic power away
Baudrillard loved fish for dinner and I
Wld like to cook the same thing for u
And dont worry abt the wedding
We will always..as FOH said
Once we were we always will be
The reason to cancell my fifth wedding? Wld be with you now? I will
send her the bill as ive already bought the dress for the ocassion snd it
will be hard for me to find a guy to match this gown
You were perfect!!

Marc Léger <leger.mj@gmail.com>
To: Zivancevic Nina <zivancevicn65@gmail.com>
23 February 2015 at 22:02

et in arcadia i go
you can be certain that when I say "oh yes!" I mean
it's just that my situation has been depleted since 2009 and also 1999,
and also 1978

and so pre-paid air plan and hotel-or-no-hotel and i will covet my own
baguette
anything that does not require a credit card with money on it
and yes, let me talk to y'all about the Avant Garde without a dash that
would interest me
i am plenty interested in your witchy web-o-grams

i would like to do the show more in a cavern like
i don't know if you can swing that kind of gig
i have a two hour sho in mind, we can sell tickets for money
i don't know how it would go off, honestly
kind of like a performance piece called Girls Gone Godard
and you have a special part to play if you are consenting
not sure how this will fly with the blasé blasers
might seem a little bit risqué
but you give me courage
it would be like Barrett and LeRoi rides again
or, maybe you could also suggest something and i'll work it in
i'm all about experimental music and avant rock

This Heat
Red Crayola
Carla Bozulich
Nena Zee and the Maniacs

Zivancevic Nina <zivancevicn65@gmail.com>
To: Marc Léger <leger.mj@gmail.com>
24 February 2015 at 06:19

this is what I call- a total success: we moved from a total
misunderstanding to: the prenuptial agreement here it is, a perf which i
will do as a part of our larger project

Marc Léger <leger.mj@gmail.com>
To: Zivancevic Nina <zivancevicn65@gmail.com>
24 February 2015 at 13:57

well now this fiction thing is hetting hot! - so i am not only cold and bitter
for this massage thing but you already have an X inscribed in you
i read your fine print and let me know - i,m happy to steal your show and

pre-nups and do Girls Gone Godard, especially if you want to share the limelight
we could get some dry ice to go with the cat food

Zivancevic Nina <zivancevicn65@gmail.com>
To: Marc Léger <leger.mj@gmail.com>
24 February 2015 at 14:19

I'm totally open to your persona and all yr suggestions and gimmicks as I hate doing things all alone
And hate even more doing them with stupid people
You can count on me in every respect
You lucked out this time with me as I'm zen(a) and totally open to you
(happens every 100 years here, but shit happens)
But we can do a mock performance on it...back to work.
Tjink about that plane offer
Yrs Truly...

Zivancevic Nina <zivancevicn65@gmail.com>
To: Marc Léger <leger.mj@gmail.com>
24 February 2015 at 15:16

Ok Marc jL
So are you going to sign the pre-nups or are u willy-nilly and
All tis just a "poet's joke"?
An dont u steal my show please cause I am an innocent girl and a collooque..collegue of yrs..
Tout d.abord.the show has to start with very loud mendhelson's wedding march bringing us on stage..
Then..more onto the ornaments and info when my friend Dan leaves..
hasta tonite..

Marc Léger <leger.mj@gmail.com>
To: Zivancevic Nina <zivancevicn65@gmail.com>
24 February 2015 at 16:31

i have to confess i have a little bit of an aversion to mendelsohn ever since i worked for revenue canada - how about elgar's pompadour and circustance - it would seem he regretted having written that composition and so our wedding should be in the finest of petty bourgeois traditions - no compromise on the i dos and do nots - and it should go well - i would like you to dress up as Godard himself if that's okay and i will do my thing ... by any means necessary

---

Zivancevic Nina <zivancevicn65@gmail.com>
To: Marc Léger <leger.mj@gmail.com>
24 February 2015 at 16:56

ok, i've just played elgar on my violin
yes, pompe and circonstance.. sounds good
you can dress up if you like you can be Miranda Pampelos and I could be a noble torrero Midealdo de Rojas
.....a bit like marlene ditrich upstaging von strocheim..
as you wish.. but the perf must go on!

Zivancevic Nina <zivancevicn65@gmail.com>
To: Marc Léger <leger.mj@gmail.com>
24 February 2015 at 17:29

Oh, also what I'm sending you is a DVD of les peripheriques vous parlent, and a film on Eduard Glissant
- this could be a good place for us to perform
- then there is this association of IVRY- they wld like us to do the performance there that is, our wedding where I what..?
I become mme Léger!!!! wof!!!
i don't even know how you look like- aside from that kitty photo
who are you, my husband, my door of perception, the love of my life?
who's going to be yr maid of honnor? who's my man?
who is going to serve champagne?
i,m not a boozer but some folks around here like that bottle..
etc etc
we'll invite Badiou and Jean-Pierre Faye to grace the event.
they can write a book together about the event.
yes.
let's do that.

Zivancevic Nina <zivancevicn65@gmail.com>
To: Marc Léger <leger.mj@gmail.com>
24 February 2015 at 17:30

yet another place for us to perform is a theater space of my friend Tania
(angels' theater)
she was Guattari's last girlfriend, he died in her arms so to speak..
So will i get to die in yr arms? ha, Marc? you answer that one..

Marc Léger <leger.mj@gmail.com>
To: Zivancevic Nina <zivancevicn65@gmail.com>
24 February 2015 at 18:53

i'm a little confused
is it a lecture, performance, trapeze act, or a crucifiction, or a caveman
wedding
in any case i think we should call off the wedding and just consider
ourselves Xs, unfortunately, RT has already started reporting on our
shenanigans

assuming you still like me and want me to go on
the title of our piece de résistance is:
"Girls Gone Godard"
i would ask you to read aloud the Godard theses
what is to be done – que faire
i cue you and i do the rest
plus entrance music and exit
French or English, as you like it
can I do my part in English, or should I translate everything ?
my French is not as good as my English
and i have to renew my passport
i was doing that this week
best to make no plans until May Day
let me know if you get funding - it'll be fun

Zivancevic Nina <zivancevicn65@gmail.com>
To: Marc Léger <leger.mj@gmail.com>
24 February 2015 at 19:03

Ah my dear
All of the above is ok and feasible
Except for funding
Which is always smth to be planned well in advance.
What about the Cultural center/mission of Canada.do they have any
funds? If I ask from the french side, and I can, this all goes well in
advance, translation perheps cld be funded, i'll ask CNL for advice..
Otherwise all other things cld be done in no time..
I am sorry you're cancelling the nups, just as I was planning to go for a
sax or sex change just to please you..but now I have to find some other
ideas for a burlesque .
I. Havent tried that genre..this time it seemed purrrrfect
Love those cats!
Yr devoto howardella

Marc Léger <leger.mj@gmail.com>
To: Zivancevic Nina <zivancevicn65@gmail.com>
25 February 2015 at 08:49

of an obscure disaster
ode to a cis-poet
Je vous salue Nina
vous êtes bien attachée
le seigneur est avec vous
priez pour les tickets
vraiment maintenant

Zivancevic Nina <zivancevicn65@gmail.com>
To: Marc Léger <leger.mj@gmail.com>
25 February 2015 at 09:10

Marc, it seems you are more "léger" than myself- as the name says..
I've been on the real rails of reality when i said "in advance" -- look here,
we have a friendly invite hello from Gua (like the Indian "being", "nicara-
gua", etc)

Marc Léger <leger.mj@gmail.com>
To: Zivancevic Nina <zivancevicn65@gmail.com>
25 February 2015 at 09:19

Guat ?

Zivancevic Nina <zivancevicn65@gmail.com>
To: Marc Léger <leger.mj@gmail.com>
25 February 2015 at 09:19

hmm Guattari and his last chance/fiance Tania
she said she'd host us even if we'd all have to rob the bank for this show
(how guattaresque of her)
so we have the place, Theater of Angels- as long as we want (like a
week or so) and then all other smalltime venues..
now .. the ticks.. OK, when wld u/cld you like to come to paree? i'll be
reading my poem w/ yr pics (those kitties) plus
that sublime Richard cum Nick songs- i like them a lot, what else (given
my perso background)
all on March 22 when Tania hosts me & JP Faye for an evening, book
promo- my book Airplane Sonnets and Faye's lofty "éclats dans la philo"
will be presented. with fanfare.
so, ticks, yeah, ok, but what about food etc- perhaps you could earn
yr budget here by selling the entrance- yeah, i think i can attract large
audiences w: my preaching nonsense that i do once in a while
and the prenups... -- that cld stay for the "right place right time" like La
Cantada bar where ML Questin runs the continuum of what used to be
Briands "Cabare du Neant" (lovely title)
Cabaret which was started at le CHAT NOIR (everth turns around chats
chez nous) in the 19 century
as France had stopped all her activities in the beginn of the 20th cent.,
sort of..

Zivancevic Nina <zivancevicn65@gmail.com>
To: Marc Léger <leger.mj@gmail.com>
25 February 2015 at 09:24

ok, good- YOUR best QUALITY, MJL
is your humor (shd be engraved on yr grave)

but i've jus realized that my acute loneliness had been aggravated to the
point of inviting you incessantly here and there
my dear camrade-- whenever U (Thou) decide to come over and
DO the show
2. Sell yr books
3. Find the translators here and certain funds
-- i am open and even more open than you think i am
Yours Truly and
Perpetually,
Nina Zee

Marc Léger <leger.mj@gmail.com>
To: Zivancevic Nina <zivancevicn65@gmail.com>
25 February 2015 at 09:36

  great, let's do it at the Panthéon
  in the shadow of Alechinsky and la petite bière belge
  now I have a really big feeling
  if you were to give me lessons in creative writing
  i would be at the back of the class
  reading Nina Zivanchevic and the time that she said fooey, that man
  they are all the same as Gonzo Schleiermacher
  i have a feeling this will write itself out

Zivancevic Nina <zivancevicn65@gmail.com>
To: Marc Léger <leger.mj@gmail.com>
25 February 2015 at 09:38

  plus: thanx for Kinski's output brrrrr (to close to my commie home and
  the police cum customs officers tortures i've been through..)
  YOU are quite an artist, pal! That shark thing and a kitty inside is
  REALLY MY life, quintessentials!!
  I'll print it and frame it, put in the bathroom or better: in the kitchen so
  that i can lose weigth- any t i want to eat, i look at it and
  FREEZE!!
  ok, i freeze scene now

Re: nina la rouge minimaliste

Zivancevic Nina <zivancevicn65@gmail.com>
To: Marc Léger <leger.mj@gmail.com>
25 February 2015 at 15:20

but if u like red... i'll take u to the Maison Rouge here,
the temple of Pop und Minima art

Marc Léger <leger.mj@gmail.com>
To: Zivancevic Nina <zivancevicn65@gmail.com>
25 February 2015 at 16:17

my passport will be available as early as April
just in time to walk and talk with you about the moulin
with a petite bière belge after to chase the blues away

Zivancevic Nina <zivancevicn65@gmail.com>
To: Marc Léger <leger.mj@gmail.com>
25 February 2015 at 16:52

Oh...in that case.. if you feel like coming in April-- wld you like to be on a
panel with me?
(meaning all sorts of panels) as my book "Airplane Sonnets" is just about
to come out!
I have gigs scheduled: March 13,14.. 22, 28, 29
and the big gig on April 25.. and a conference on Kantor April 14 and 15
but if you know.. how to present me (that surely u can do blindfold) and
if you knew really and truly how to play an instrument(for an intermezzo)i
cld even get you some money , a honorarium-
please
don't worry
about
money..
it is necessary but we can pay in sea shells, like the Maori..
I have this important gig at the Serbian Cultural Center, my violin teacher
will play smth too (i hope), and the whole diplomatic core will be there,
Toscanini and Roger Fry and Genevieve Laurin will do their bla bla as
Fry wrote a preface and Toscanini a postface
but you could intervene as well and i cld announce our performance to
happen afterwards

Marc Léger <leger.mj@gmail.com>
To: Zivancevic Nina <zivancevicn65@gmail.com>
25 February 2015 at 17:03

anytime on April 1 would be excellent
perhaps at the cinematheque française, if they do lectures
i could introduce you and you could read my paper
okay, but money is always an issue, even in sea shells

Zivancevic Nina <zivancevicn65@gmail.com>
To: Marc Léger <leger.mj@gmail.com>
25 February 2015 at 17:06

But cinematheque IS an institution, you see..they take 1-2 years to
decide on things, if u see what i mean could it be a private gallery? or
April 1 is the Fool's day.. u want this one? I'll start looking for the ticks...

Marc Léger <leger.mj@gmail.com>
To: Zivancevic Nina <zivancevicn65@gmail.com>
25 February 2015 at 17:09

yes, I want ... the fool's day
Plato's cavern and bar

Zivancevic Nina <zivancevicn65@gmail.com>
To: Marc Léger <leger.mj@gmail.com>
25 February 2015 at 17:19

wait a minute.. what cld be done in such a short time (they're all slow
around here)..
I mean what wld exactly you like to do?
Screening of the film?
Performance before, within, after? Lecture? All of the above?
but what if you don't.. and you have the ticks..?
.. we have one month..
do u think i can do it.. find that place, yes, tomorrow night at the Cabaret
of Neant.. I'll ask them right away for the screening and the rest..

Marc Léger <leger.mj@gmail.com>
To: Zivancevic Nina <zivancevicn65@gmail.com>
25 February 2015 at 18:17

thanks for your kind generosity
i don't have a passport number just yet - they said it will take around
2 weeks before I receive it we could organize for late April, if you think
there would be students-people still around

either way i don't think you should pay for the tickets, as Cayley and me
think this is too extravagant - we should get a sponsor
la sorbonne or i could ask the canadian embassy in france
i'm not institutionally affiliated here
i would stay 3-4 days max since right now i'm not supposed to be out of
the country
we could present GGG or i could present the Daisies/Jessie piece
i am also happy to talk about the avant garde material ...

Zivancevic Nina <zivancevicn65@gmail.com>
To: Marc Léger <leger.mj@gmail.com>
25 February 2015 at 20:07

1.
-- yes, me too, but these places never pay for the tickets here and
almost anywhere (the National Education is like that), I had to pay for
my tickets to go to highly official invitations to Columbia U in NY, to Peru
last year, I couldn't go to Melbourne or Seoul for the same reason and
that's why I said "check with the Cultural sector with the embassy or the
ministry of culture". Anyways I know how these institutions (don't) work.
That's why we- the radical workers around here, prefer to do things (as
any avant-garde) in bars, associations, independent spaces.. which you
are going to hear in my contribution about the contemp AG around here-
I started interviewing some artists..

yes, it is absolutely wiser for you to present your new books, and the
screening and/or performance can be a special bonus. The best thing
is really September, if you can do it at that time. I'd be happy to connect
you with the organizers of the said departments, but really, you should
decide which project or screening you'd like to do and I will fill in the slots
with the addresses of the right institutions

you should tell yr friend not to worry-- I was planning of staying with
my friend during yr stay, and as for the tickets- like I said it seems

extravagant but you should see it on a larger scope and scale as my wish to help a friend/collegue and a scholar who also thought so highly of my work by inviting me to participate and be a part of his family- so you should not see it as a movement of temporary folly or any ulterior motive on my side

I am here in this world to support art and critical thinking in so many different ways.
So perhaps you should look into different possibilities on yr side of venues and decide, but really decide what you'd like to do most
yr friend, Nina Z.

Marc Léger <leger.mj@gmail.com>
To: Zivancevic Nina <zivancevicn65@gmail.com>
25 February 2015 at 20:40

given all this i feel like finally the avant garde cannot arrive, not for the moment anyway - i was worried there but now i'm reassured that nothing will get in the way of this underground email connection we have cultivated - life is sweet

---

Zivancevic Nina <zivancevicn65@gmail.com>
To: Marc Léger <leger.mj@gmail.com>
26 February 2015 at 04:15

OK, dr Leger, I feel better too, as the light of reason is piercing through- whatever happens next- I am addamant- you should take care of yr wellbeing and NOT come over here in a hurry for 3 days (I wld feel like the murderer in Hasenclaver's MURDERER , of the AG and it's most brilliant exponent- MJL!
This action, that is trip, has to be planned a bit - way too much in advance
thanks for Filliou review, yeah, what to say more? And Palais de Tokyo is hosting now a disco-club, which is not the worst aspect of an AG activity... let us see next---
in any case they'll be tired and slow
that's why I like talking to you- you're not slow..
your friend, Nina

Marc Léger <leger.mj@gmail.com>
To: Zivancevic Nina <zivancevicn65@gmail.com>
26 February 2015 at 10:41

dear Dr Zhivago,
now that we've flatlined, what comes next ?
since it has been found that you can flatline with a well-tempered
Hasencleever, i would like to change this nopertunity into another shall
we - almost anything goes in the nachtraglicheit of our writing, yours
which has quite some style and mine that doesn't really - i don't know
what all the antique references could be but i imagine that you will have
something profound to say - i could apply my synapses to this new
literary medium. you could do it with your eyes closed as you count to
three and that would give me a chance to escape -- i won't say more
except to say now i'm really scarred

Zivancevic Nina <zivancevicn65@gmail.com>
To: Marc Léger <leger.mj@gmail.com>
26 February 2015 at 12:19

Hmmmmmmmm..

Marc Léger <leger.mj@gmail.com>
To: Zivancevic Nina <zivancevicn65@gmail.com>
26 February 2015 at 19:05

what i propose for us is that we commit to print - i would really love to
duet with you now that we're not going face to face with Levinas big
Other - unless you don't consider me your freedom fighting equal, in
which case, i don't know, Beaubourg, i understand you -- always the
themes, the cheerleading – but with your minimalism and black paint i
think we could do something worthy of your delphyne timelessness

Zivancevic Nina <zivancevicn65@gmail.com>
To: Marc Léger <leger.mj@gmail.com>
27 February 2015 at 06:35

OK my camrade Marc (my X and the father of my kid is also Marc, but Sorrodjé),
we can do all of the above and much more (to come),
F-Beaubourg- I performed there only once, Pierre (the Filliou guy) had invited me, but
I want to say that there are many OTHER places, which belong to Big Other, this afternoon I am going to La Chaine, the biggest art squat here to talk to their director Fabian (a smart bauhaus German, they had lovely people aside from Hitler), so that I intervene on March 1é,13 and on we go...
we could (as we write fast and well) set up a working hour and write a book of dialogues or something which cld be turned into a script/ performance or a book on its own
it cld be better than Heiner Muller sorry i missed the umlauts ü..
so think about it.. even if you show up
for 2 days and do your "preaching" gig on AD or Arriere garde (a bit into history) wld be great..
yours truly,

Zivancevic Nina <zivancevicn65@gmail.com>
To: Marc Léger <leger.mj@gmail.com>
27 February 2015 at 06:50

yeah, also I realized that with our jokes and pre-nups etc we have gone a bit too far,
now my friend Toscanini took yr email address from me- he wld like to write to you and discuss some interesting things like Agamben, yr opinion on Negri etc-
but what he really wants to do is "what do you intend to do with my girl Nina.." I imagine..
So if you get an email from him - just be delighted
as he's someone
 really
interesting
like all of us..
xxx, Zena Parkins

Marc Léger <leger.mj@gmail.com>
To: Zivancevic Nina <zivancevicn65@gmail.com>
27 February 2015 at 08:24

okay, i'll think about it and xena, the umlat machine
an entire paragraph is more than i could have hoped for and i imagined
it in a high key which somehow implies double entendre - but also
aspiration and climbing the mountain to see the other side - whatever
you decide is okay with me - i had a Chaplin Book in mind, obviously, but
maybe you think it should be performed on a rainy stage with Toscanini,
Sorrodjé and Macbeth - in any case i never thought (a) could be so
much more than a - thank you for this bebopportunity to sing along – it's
as you wish and as I could only imagine – and if we're lucky we'll get one
of those Acker awards

Zivancevic Nina <zivancevicn65@gmail.com>
To: Marc Léger <leger.mj@gmail.com>
27 February 2015 at 09:35

Hey..hey hey!!
(more later)

Zivancevic Nina <zivancevicn65@gmail.com>
To: Marc Léger <leger.mj@gmail.com>
27 February 2015 at 09:56

As long as we are open and straigthforward ..but less like those trickters
three card montys from g.de la tour's painting
We can get many great things done
together..or w one another.. (never figured that idiomatic expression..)
More later

Marc Léger <leger.mj@gmail.com>
To: Zivancevic Nina <zivancevicn65@gmail.com>
27 February 2015 at 10:21

you'll have to set up some parameters – but me i'm nothing if not Manet
(is that okay, i can change it to Rimbaud if you prefer)

Zivancevic Nina <zivancevicn65@gmail.com>
To: Marc Léger <leger.mj@gmail.com>
27 February 2015 at 10:26

I started asking around about the possible venues for you- I think even
beau bourg will be contacted
Then the Czeck institute as well I also started interviewing artists around
to get their feeling what they consider to be the actual AG..i stopped
doing that 15 years ago, but yes thank u camrade Ilich
I will check on them again..interesting(as always) what they have to say..
like it is there but more yhan ever Invisible because they hate going to
beaubourg palais Tokyo to hang out w people like koons and his chica.
we understand them.
As to my friends S.,T. , or whoever there may be, dont worry, they wont
spoil our wedd performance or honeymoon..but yr girlfriend seems more
seriosly upset about yr trip..

Marc Léger <leger.mj@gmail.com>
To: Zivancevic Nina <zivancevicn65@gmail.com>
27 February 2015 at 10:50

thanks to all your friends at the petit Palais the big Palais and please
tell them the avant garde is back and forth and back and forth - i
have nothing against Chico Marx and Harpo but some people, whew,
they take what they can get - my girlfriend likes to go to the Nieme
arrondissement to see the commune – she's nothing if not a comrade

Zivancevic Nina <zivancevicn65@gmail.com>
To: Marc Léger <leger.mj@gmail.com>
27 February 2015 at 11:13

You have to set yr parameters for me dear Marc, u as well
And yes, me too, thank u, as my mom was constantly telling the same
thing..
I shd not dissipate and shd infiltrate my thought and action to the nicer
forms of survival .than this one..
I am so happy to get to know you! It.s like…discovering a twin brother
lost since toddlership (here.s this neologism just for you)
Are we like these tigers in Arnaud's movie "Two brohers"..?
you should know this by now...

Zivancevic Nina <zivancevicn65@gmail.com>
To: Marc Léger <leger.mj@gmail.com>
27 February 2015 at 12:52

As just one hour ago I visited that friendly squat cum great performance space and the director said to his friends an collabs: "please bring a chair fpr THE madam.
wld u like some tea or coffee? U see, mafame had worked with the living, la mama, the dalai lama etc etc etc.."
I felt very old. All of a sudden.
They almost made me cry.
One of them worked w Marcel m.
And I told them that it was albert vender and bareau who kept me in France- they offered me some cake.

Fwd: My Room

Zivancevic Nina <zivancevicn65@gmail.com>
To: Marc Léger <leger.mj@gmail.com>
1 March 2015 at 09:45

i hope your whiter night was whiter than the shade of pale
and that it was productive, fruitful etc
yr friend, lectrice devouée

Attachment: Image of NZ's room with violin

Marc Léger <leger.mj@gmail.com>
To: Zivancevic Nina <zivancevicn65@gmail.com>
1 March 2015 at 11:21

my dear miu miu,

i wonder what we have done to deserve this transatlantic resistance to
things on this side of the ponderosa - but I also think this can't be true,
you seem so comfortable in new york, unless i missed something, so
please don't explain and i know what i know

your viola has a photographer but no player, making me wonder
what Jacques Rancière would say in this regard about the movie that
Rosselini would make of your life and times – how you worked the room

---

Zivancevic Nina <zivancevicn65@gmail.com>
To: Marc Léger <leger.mj@gmail.com>
1 March 2015 at 14:10

Who said that Beauty is in the eye of the beholder
And who said or asked us how to tell el dancer from the dance?
Yeats daddyo is this your chance?
I had to spend a day with my british editor, the smartest armenian on the
planet,working on and at the same time obfuscating my web site
a tout a l'heure
N

Zivancevic Nina <zivancevicn65@gmail.com>
To: Marc Léger <leger.mj@gmail.com>
1 March 2015 at 14:12

And there.s also Woolf.s room of one.s own
And when you enter it there.s no one to bother you
How do you enter a room of one.s own and u r not that person?

Marc Léger <leger.mj@gmail.com>
To: Zivancevic Nina <zivancevicn65@gmail.com>
1 March 2015 at 14:18

"Uplift everybody, and uplift yourself." – Yogi Tea

Zivancevic Nina <zivancevicn65@gmail.com>
To: Marc Léger <leger.mj@gmail.com>
1 March 2015 at 17:14

Also, Dr Leger,
here you find two things..
the sound recordings of my "French" avangarde artists (ready to be
uploaded into yr flea zoo)
and a brief moment of "illumination" of yr russian doll aka camrade "Zee"
it was shot in India, a month ago.

Attachment: 10 images of NZ with bindi chakra

Marc Léger <leger.mj@gmail.com>
To: Zivancevic Nina <zivancevicn65@gmail.com>
1 March 2015 at 18:17

here, you're welcome

Image: Flea Circus, Tivoli – Copenhagen: "A performance with human
fleas pulling carriages, Juggling, walking the tightrope, playing football
etc."

i have many loves among the avant garde but i would say that for the golden era of you tube it has to be the Egyptian correspondent; my Skype address: http://www.lacan.com/zizlacan4.htm

Image: Gene Tierney in an Egyptian costume reading a script on the set of *Sundown* (1941)

Zivancevic Nina <zivancevicn65@gmail.com>
To: Marc Léger <leger.mj@gmail.com>
2 March 2015 at 13:17

Marc, Thank you so much..for yr overall attention to me and to my special cage in yr circus... And for sending these entire movies..really lovely..
I wish I had more time to watch them.
Today..the whole day at the UN ..giving exams. I like yr "Skype" address [Lacanian Ink], sounds ok to me but it wld be better if we cld see more of.. Marc J Leger in it..and less Lacan or Zizek..whom we admire..but the admiration shd also be
handled..with moderation.
Don.t take it personally, you r our hero and a star over here and u shine the brightest!
This fr the time being_

—

Yr Sylvia Bataille

Zivancevic Nina <zivancevicn65@gmail.com>
To: Marc Léger <leger.mj@gmail.com>
2 March 2015 at 13:34

And most of the time in yr NL zombie you come back 'to yr own mind' so to speak, when you brillig analyze the idea of socalled cult. Produ,tion vs. neolib.culture..i want to hear..and here I do, more of Marc JL and.. less all the rest..
Hey, but who am I to ask for anything? (paul ricoeur enters here)
Live ya, zee

a poem

Marc Léger <leger.mj@gmail.com>
To: Zivancevic Nina <zivancevicn65@gmail.com>
3 March 2015 at 19:46

Where Is My Pal?

Where did Nina go?
Was it to New York?
Was it to Paris?
Am I bothering her?
I wonder if she is doing something important
and here i am
with my links
I like to think
that our chaplinbook
is coming along nicely
Who knows what Marjorie Perloff would say
or Gerald Raunig
can I be rehabilitated?
after all this?

Zivancevic Nina <zivancevicn65@gmail.com>
To: Marc Léger <leger.mj@gmail.com>
4 March 2015 at 05:16

Ahhh Wunderbar!! Danke shoen
Ich liebe dich and above all yr lovely attention ,a proof that there is some
consistency and stability in this world
And, we are at Madelaine metro stop now..
No, I cannot say anything that was not said before in this world..

Concorde stop now,...
But at least we always try desperately to put it in a new form..at least
there are some other people who can tell us smth new..like last night..

Asseble Generale stop..f..i wont get sny time here to read today.s
newspaper..
Last night I conducted a GREAT interview with Marc Louis Questin, a
pillar of the cont. French AG who is also a guy who organized , renewed
Briand.s Cabare du Neant, author of Magie du Chaos.

,Sevre Babylone stop....
And.a friend of Hakim Bay aka Peter Lamborn Wilson.great, Marc,

we will have something valuable, a testimony on the activities here...
Rennes!!! Off I go into the day,
Love ya,
Nin

Zivancevic Nina <zivancevicn65@gmail.com>
To: Marc Léger <leger.mj@gmail.com>
4 March 2015 at 05:16

U can read my previous email as a poem..depends on yr reading of it..

Zivancevic Nina <zivancevicn65@gmail.com>
To: Marc Léger <leger.mj@gmail.com>
4 March 2015 at 09:20

Please do send yr pertinent links and musings..very few people in this
world
Pay attention
To someone else.s interior
Enterrier
Why this ocean between us..?
So far away...

Marc Léger <leger.mj@gmail.com>
To: Zivancevic Nina <zivancevicn65@gmail.com>
4 March 2015 at 13:56

beware: impertinent link and musings on someone elses underground
https://www.youtube.com/watch?v=INauGnZv3BQ
[Shozin Fukui's *Gerorisuto* (1987)]

Zivancevic Nina <zivancevicn65@gmail.com>
To: Marc Léger <leger.mj@gmail.com>
5 March 2015 at 05:23

thanks for yr visual poem,
but mind you, my dear,

the parisian metro- much more toughter than the japanese
less money in France, less comfort
my vision: people on top of each other like the chemical layers of cake
on top of each other, no air to breathe..
it takes 1 day for a human being to recover from this metro..
hmm but i'm not human- i'm a replicant no NYC 3000000044444777
i go there every day, to work and back ay ay ay ayyyyyyyyyyyyyyyyyyyyyy
yyyyyyyyyyyyyyyyyy

Marc Léger <leger.mj@gmail.com>
To: Zivancevic Nina <zivancevicn65@gmail.com>
5 March 2015 at 11:00

The Replicant in the Gray Flannel Suit

The year's at the spring,
And day's at the morn;
Morning's at seven;
The hills-side dew-pearled;
The lark's on the wing;
The snail's on the thorn;
God's in His Heaven -
All's right with the world!

Zivancevic Nina <zivancevicn65@gmail.com>
To: Marc Léger <leger.mj@gmail.com>
5 March 2015 at 17:29

Veery true..
More on my plate
Tonite..a great screening of pierre merejkowski..more on the soul of an
artist under- socialism..

Fwd: Micika

Zivancevic Nina <zivancevicn65@gmail.com>
To: Marc Léger <leger.mj@gmail.com>
9 March 2015 at 18:55

my pen friend! on my return from Zurick i found yr good book in my
mailbox! but i haven't finished the Neolib zombie!
i'll do it tonight, and then into the new adventures of the latest Marginal
garde of the guards!
i do have some comments to make!
i may not share them with you (as you're the illustous author, right?)
will write soon,
love,
Nin

Image: Micika (cat)

Marc Léger <leger.mj@gmail.com>
To: Zivancevic Nina <zivancevicn65@gmail.com>
9 March 2015 at 19:18

dear professor, please do make comments on anything that comes to
your stream
the cover of BNAG is from the film Partisan Songspiel by Chto Delat,
who you probably know - they were also featured recently in 032c
fashion magazine and much to my narcissism mentioned me and John
Roberts
a new contributor to vol 2, Marieta Bozovic, will be writing about the
comrade of Chto Delat, Kirill Medvedev - she says she really loves the
Nina, as do I, as does Mabuse

Image: Mabuse (cat)

Zivancevic Nina <zivancevicn65@gmail.com>
To: Marc Léger <leger.mj@gmail.com>
10 March 2015 at 05:07

hey, I did not mean it that way – "the professor" part, and Lo', Dog knows
that you have to format that "stream of c." for any more serious approach
and analysis.. I'll write, so I'm doing,

I will check on these clicks- fashion mag, why not, fab-ulous!!
off I go into the day, yeah, graceful cats keep stream of our soulful
content...
love, Nin

Marc Léger <leger.mj@gmail.com>
To: Zivancevic Nina <zivancevicn65@gmail.com>
10 March 2015 at 09:31

please send stream o' graceful cats and soulful content
i have now with me the "phenomenology of spirit"
so that should be interesting, as it so happens

Zivancevic Nina <zivancevicn65@gmail.com>
To: Marc Léger <leger.mj@gmail.com>
10 March 2015 at 15:39

And tonite, the poet, russian translator John High said.."my words are
against the propaganda of meaning"
I liked that one

Wow

Zivancevic Nina <zivancevicn65@gmail.com>
To: Marc Léger <leger.mj@gmail.com>
10 March 2015 at 14:34

Phenomenology of spirit! Wow! Stay with that Hegel, dont ever leave him..we need that guy!
xxxxxxxx

Marc Léger <leger.mj@gmail.com>
To: Zivancevic Nina <zivancevicn65@gmail.com>
12 March 2015 at 20:38

i click therefor i am but who are you
https://www.youtube.com/watch?v=9zkwj2JwB7w
[Nick Cave talks about Nina Simone]

Zivancevic Nina <zivancevicn65@gmail.com>
To: Marc Léger <leger.mj@gmail.com>
16 March 2015 at 10:52

Hi Marc- should I interview my friends David Graeber and Niall Mc Devitt? for our Territory unit purpose (AG)- they are congenial Brits and you've been quoting the former one, right? I see them every so often in London..How are u??? kissssssssssssssssssssssssssssssss
ssssssssssssssssssssssssssssssssssssssssssssssssssssssssssssssssss
sssssssssssssssssssssss

Marc Léger <leger.mj@gmail.com>
To: Zivancevic Nina <zivancevicn65@gmail.com>
16 March 2015 at 13:48

dr. Nina X - punk goddess, interviews BiLL Blake

Marvin: You William Blake?
William Blake: Yes, I am. Do you know my poetry?
Nobody: Things which are alike, in nature, grow to look alike.
William Blake: Do you still have my eyeglasses?
Nobody: No, I traded them. Do you have any tobacco?
William Blake: No, I traded it.

Nobody: For what?
William Blake: I'm not telling.
Nobody: Liar.
William Blake: Thief.
Nodoby: It is strange that you do not remember any of your poetry,
William Blake.

Image: Andre Csillag photo of Deborah Harry (aka Blondie) with Doctor
X T-shirt at Hammersmith Odeon, London, January 1980

Zivancevic Nina <zivancevicn65@gmail.com>
To: Marc Léger <leger.mj@gmail.com>
16 March 2015 at 16:23

where are the interviews.. am I missing something? (obviously, many
things..)
please send them along!
thank you so much!
Of course that I love punk, in fact, every form of Baroque (and its
extensions, expressionism, punk, neo-ex etc)
xxxxxx

Marc Léger <leger.mj@gmail.com>
To: Zivancevic Nina <zivancevicn65@gmail.com>
17 March 2015 at 11:55

EIN POEM FUR DR NINA XXXXXX

Was the coalition government necessary?
How should we understand Varoufakis?
Have the Marxists gone Keynesian?
What happened in the negotiations?
What do the next few months hold?
How would a "negotiated" exit look?
What kind of capital controls are needed?
Isn't eurozone exit risky?
And the impact of devaluation?
What of the social movements?
Does Syriza need uncritical support?

Zivancevic Nina <zivancevicn65@gmail.com>
To: Marc Léger <leger.mj@gmail.com>
18 March 2015 at 03:29

Hello- usually poems need no answers or answering,
but as this one does, you'll have to wait a bit for the response- have
these two books coming out now- one of them
Living on Air is already an ebook (you can get it on Amazon if u have
many and time
time and money, gargoyles of capitalism
as to David- you want me to intervene? ask why he's not responding?
have a good email address?
xxxx

Marc Léger <leger.mj@gmail.com>
To: Zivancevic Nina <zivancevicn65@gmail.com>
18 March 2015 at 10:32

Hello - that,s okay, the *Comrades* book is definitely on the back burner;
so i don't know yet about your book but the horses make it look like a
country album cover and also i thought i was waiting for you to send
something else, but in any case i will splurge when the time comes and it
will come soon enough

Стихотворение для Нины

Image: Far Side cartoon. A cow reads a poem to a room of cows:
"Distant Hills. The distant hills call to me. Their rolling waves seduce my
heart. Oh, how I want to graze in their lush valleys. Oh, how I want to run
down their green slopes. Alas, I cannot. Damn the electric fences. Damn
the electric fences. Thank you."

Zivancevic Nina <zivancevicn65@gmail.com>
To: Marc Léger <leger.mj@gmail.com>
18 March 2015 at 17:44

I don't know what exactly you've been waiting to get from me
as to my article for you: it has to be written!
I have so much work to do around here—it's not even funny or fun any
longer...

thank for the entertainment, the famous music by the gang of 4.
are we the gang of 5?
pleasant evening, Marc James!

Marc Léger <leger.mj@gmail.com>
To: Zivancevic Nina <zivancevicn65@gmail.com>
19 March 2015 at 09:25

i thought you had said you sent something but no matter - i will look into getting a copy of the book you read in front of the Beat Hotel - yes, as the Gang says: it's a factory, so for us, the Gang of 5, we don't know what it is but please enjoy, as our friend Bifo recommends to all of us

---

Zivancevic Nina <zivancevicn65@gmail.com>
To: Marc Léger <leger.mj@gmail.com>
20 March 2015 at 09:28

Oh yes. I sent you a DVD of les Peripheriques Vous Parlent with Eduard Glissant and a book . Hasn't it arrived yet? I will interview the guy next week, that is the person in charge of that group/movement "Peripheriques".. They've done many good things here in Paris , actions of social value like "against toxic pollution of the environment" etc
But the most important interviews I've done for yr AG anthology..are gone! I've lost them with my mobile, stolen from me a week ago. I'll be transferring it from now on right away
I am in a hospital now, was operated on my ankle again..it was broken a year ago but never properly recovered...ay...
Talk to u a bit later, camarade Legerevitch!

Marc Léger <leger.mj@gmail.com>
To: Zivancevic Nina <zivancevicn65@gmail.com>
20 March 2015 at 09:45

Get Well Soon: this, to help you with your Kantor conference and ankle ankh, uncle Hank perhaps some day semiotexte will publish our chapbook - dizzy derata

Image: Cover of Kathy Acker and McKenzie Wark, *I'm Very Into You: Correspondence 1995-1996*

Zivancevic Nina <zivancevicn65@gmail.com>
To: Marc Léger <leger.mj@gmail.com>
22 March 2015 at 04:43

Oh, thanks, but I do not see exactly what Acker's correspondence has
to do with Kantor? Surely if i looked at and into the book the answer wld
arrive to me
Don't you know that I am Acker's translator into Serbocroatian?
At any rate, I loved the woman, she housed my ex-hub Mike Levin (aka
Black Eagle Press) for a year, after I kicked him out of our Suffok St
apartment in NY
but the highlight of my relationship w/Acker came -after she died. I wrote
a short necrologue (for you to read the second part in English, though u
cld try serbian too if u were to learn it-- for the ocassion of the pre-nups
etc etc (see file: Leger-Zivancevic))
enjoy ! Sunday morning, I mean
I have to go back to camarade Kantor..
xxx

Attachment: NZ obituary for Kathy Acker

Zivancevic Nina <zivancevicn65@gmail.com>
To: Marc Léger <leger.mj@gmail.com>
22 March 2015 at 05:21

In fact, Dizzy,
i am not so dizzy after my coffee and
I am sending you the correct version of my necrologue,
for our book, I don't know, our correspondence acquired "leger" tone and
i don't know if all this stuff is publishable-- i mean, if u read no matter
whose correspondence, you wld see people discussing worthwhile
issues at LENGTH, we do it but in a short version so that wld be a very
very short book
I mean,
one cld get going with the project of keeping the correspondence (i just
hope that my terrible depressions don't get hold of me- which prevents
my writing so to speak),
okay dear Marc,
have a great Sunday morn, again
xxx

Marc Léger <leger.mj@gmail.com>
To: Zivancevic Nina <zivancevicn65@gmail.com>
22 March 2015 at 10:35

Image: Snoopy pacing in front of a typewriter

yes, i could see that would be depressing to you as i don't normally write about anything at such length, at least not without sending things for you to click and jokes that semiotexte doesn't want to publish - i suppose you must be a connection to la Chanson de Gest that somehow has an underground, i mean, ... what i'm saying is i could write a whole book on that but i'm not sure i follow you on the not that interesting verdict - feel free to nevermind this Balony Facebook process over here and concentrate on more important things

my poem to you for our book that doesn't fit our list:
зашто постоји песма а не ништа

Zivancevic Nina <zivancevicn65@gmail.com>
To: Marc Léger <leger.mj@gmail.com>
22 March 2015 at 16:37

baloney! what's for you LOve Supreme?
and who do you think you are?
And who do you think I am?
please answer all this
NOW
(with or without clicks!!)

Marc Léger <leger.mj@gmail.com>
To: Zivancevic Nina <zivancevicn65@gmail.com>
22 March 2015 at 17:59

oh dear me, i believe i have stirred you up - who are we, what the bleep are we doing here as cis-poet and clicko-maniac when all is not right up there in the world, but still, no excuses, it doesn't have to be Ferlinghetti - i mean, our corr. that's what i call sunday morning cartoons and monday morning and tuesday and wednesday... but for this facebook i am certainly going to sit in your class, so you can be Suzanne Stone Maretto and I'll be Lydia Merz and we'll call the whole thing stories from the principal's office

---

Zivancevic Nina <zivancevicn65@gmail.com>
To: Marc Léger <leger.mj@gmail.com>
22 March 2015 at 18:01

and don't get angry if
I'm not into all that career climbing and montineering
I am just a simple creature from Mitteleurope
I am a Vieniesse (Vienna) girl who likes fun
but the editors of Holy Church of publishing
always want to read something more than the clicks
see where Charlie Hebdo ended up?
And when i really invited you over here to give conferences (or to
arrange for some of them)
you took my offer to be a joke and gave me some really lame excuses,
and OK, we're all - the way we are..
but you should not think that I can dance to any trance music coming to
my ear through the air..

Zivancevic Nina <zivancevicn65@gmail.com>
To: Marc Léger <leger.mj@gmail.com>
22 March 2015 at 18:03

yeah
sorry (I guess I got really angry)

Marc Léger <leger.mj@gmail.com>
To: Zivancevic Nina <zivancevicn65@gmail.com>
22 March 2015 at 18:47

so ... what are you trying to say ? ...

Zivancevic Nina <zivancevicn65@gmail.com>
To: Marc Léger <leger.mj@gmail.com>
23 March 2015 at 06:58

mmmmmmmmmmmmmmmmmm; I was operated on my leg on Friday,
still on crutches, plus the doc forgot a metal piece in it- so, most likely i'll
have yet another surgery, really not in a great mood, have to teach this
afternoon from one to 8pm- sorry to bring up my existential problems,

but, yeah, this is exactly what i was trying to say: i'm taking each and every slice of reality as it comes along (and not a sandwich that Ken Jordan is editing "the reality sandwiches", you can check that out www. reality..) trying at the same time to maintain my sanity and read yr book, read David's "Utopia of Rules", Porter's "Fall of the Sassanian empire" and Fiatti's Mitteeurope. With that stupuid Scarpetta's intro on Kantor.. and the kids are yelling: Teacher teacher why did you give me 10 out of 20 and my friend
Jo Smuck got 15 out of 20?
do i deserve all this?
do you?
i hope i did not wear you out with my problems xxxxxxxxxxxxxxxxxxxxxx
xxxxxxxxxxxxxxxxxxxxxxxxxxxxxxxxxxxxxxxxxxxxxxxxxxxxxxxxxxxx

Marc Léger <leger.mj@gmail.com>
To: Zivancevic Nina <zivancevicn65@gmail.com>
24 March 2015 at 10:49

Prof. Z, i'm listening to your dvd right now and sliding into Sartre in the 60s with some kind of Deleuzian under-taste; tell your undergraduate devotees all they need to know: please keep me in your list of tgings to do and your reality sandwich and let me know on a scale of 1-2-10 my favourite "bas-fonds" in Paris right now is not that rogue painter but the wonderful cis-poet, held captive in the Carnavalet

---

Image: François Boucher, Étude de pied (1751), Musée Carnavalet, Paris

nina z

Zivancevic Nina <zivancevicn65@gmail.com>
To: Marc Léger <leger.mj@gmail.com>
25 March 2015 at 14:03

Hi Marc! wow! i knew that it was YOU! When i dreamt of yr lovely
personna 10 years ago
and before going back to my monastery i felt that we wld connect. but i
did not know of yr name exactly
however, i had a dream and you were in it
please stay in there
never go away
life is so short and cruel with or without Caravaggio
you are sorely missed on this side of the ocean
am going to watch Pynchon film now. hope it's not as awful as Tim
Burton's that i glanced at 3 hours ago.
my problem is that i hve patience to watch the movies only for 20
minutes, than i know what they're all about
then i walk out.. see, you wldn't like to have me for a close friend- i wld
drive u crazy
or you're crazy already?
my love to you, camarade Legerovitch

Marc Léger <leger.mj@gmail.com>
To: Zivancevic Nina <zivancevicn65@gmail.com>
25 March 2015 at 19:20

yes i thought this Pynchon movie was not the worst thing i've sat
through, especially the first 20 minutes - and this anne wiazemsky book -
the first 20 minutes
http://www.gallimard.fr/Media/Gallimard/Entretien-ecrit/Entretien-Anne-
Wiazemsky.-Un-an-apres

Zivancevic Nina <zivancevicn65@gmail.com>
To: Marc Léger <leger.mj@gmail.com>
25 March 2015 at 19:37

Ha! Thank you camarade Legerovich! Blondie- the first time
i met her with Rich Hell she seemed VERY old to me, and somewhat
provincially arrogant- now it's arrogant to say so, but
hey, I'd rather take Blondie than Pynchon film (book is.. always a book
and I try not to watch the "books") Heroin is the main hero in the movie,

and
that role I liked a lot- although it was a bit longer than i cld take..
thank you for yr enthusiasm as well, you're quite a poet, Marc James,
if you keep sending me these clips, i am likely to think that "i've got a
pen friend" in Montreal and will visit you one day- if you don't make it to
Paree..
have a nice day, as they say

Marc Léger <leger.mj@gmail.com>
To: Zivancevic Nina <zivancevicn65@gmail.com>
25 March 2015 at 20:03

maybe but your friend Gérard Courant should know that Godard did
this ff for the trailer for FilmS a few years ago - am going to watch all
of this video one more time and so it might take a while before i bother
you again with my chätouillement but rest assured that i'm not going
anywhere in particular with all this; all this against the backdrop of (your
answer here)

GC ici
https://www.youtube.com/watch?v=v-ZDg1jmy8M
[Compression *La Dérive* de Paula Delsol (2014) by Gérard Courant]

Zivancevic Nina <zivancevicn65@gmail.com>
To: Marc Léger <leger.mj@gmail.com>
26 March 2015 at 05:12

oooooh, you got it wrong again!
I was not snotty nor condescending not self assured not self important
not--
but as I'm coming to terms now as to where i come from and where i'm
going to.. (all within big nothingness) I wanted to tell you-- as I'm a tiny
girl coming from the 'Byzantine empire' such a condensed tough term..
very complex.. like.. Baroque..
I have no special love at this moment for the prefabricated stuff that
Neoliberalism has offered to us ..
(be it Blondie, be it benita Morena..be it the Waters' Redheads..)
I cried for hours though when Freddie Mercury died
I did not say Marcury
Marc, please never die and never go away from my heart!
you are so precious! I'll never say it again

Marc Léger <leger.mj@gmail.com>
To: Zivancevic Nina <zivancevicn65@gmail.com>
26 March 2015 at 09:31

okay, so i will be placid, staying here, never going away or anywhere
like justinian and theodora but without all the killing
and please don't cry
i have this thing for your heart thing
dangerous, edgy, wordy
with a sweet pitch and a soft landing
okay, so i promise i will take this lesson from Badiou

1. the description is artificiality, technology, the background is a screen
2. the description is its own seeming, without external explanation
3. it is not the double of our lives (Badiou's rule); it is a constructive
deconstruction
4. it is more intense than actual life, fragile

i'm digging deeper
and then the prefabs come again
more of them
Blondies, Zivancevics, Cleopatras, Delsols
you had a big Baroque nothingness complex
a special love
your heart come and goes
a photocopy machine
an impression
something to send our publisher
something for all of middleeurope
you'll see, a cis-poet and a click-o-maniac can also be

Zivancevic Nina <zivancevicn65@gmail.com>
To: Marc Léger <leger.mj@gmail.com>
26 March 2015 at 10:19

Cmon Marc
You're quite a poet!
But i'm NO Mussolini nor Anthony nor Cleopatra
I'm a black lesbian marxist

Zivancevic Nina <zivancevicn65@gmail.com>
To: Marc Léger <leger.mj@gmail.com>
26 March 2015 at 10:40

My poet friend
U r deconstructing this fragile construction successfully
Nô, i Will never set you free.
We Will always live happily
But much after
Everafter
Like i the movie "only lovers stay alive"

Thanx for comparing me to Theo or Justin(justinian)
They were good people, smart
S(he) ruled the country
And h(s)e played music, paying off brothels and slaves
Yes. Badiou was her favorite pet.

Marc Léger <leger.mj@gmail.com>
To: Zivancevic Nina <zivancevicn65@gmail.com>
26 March 2015 at 10:41

i'm thinking a smutty bestseller true crime sci-fi psychedelic political tract
with a goldslinger western theme + your 80s fashion sense - heavens

---

Zivancevic Nina <zivancevicn65@gmail.com>
To: Marc Léger <leger.mj@gmail.com>
26 March 2015 at 12:29

Justin--
Try
To sell our correspondence
We can doll it up a bit
Social issue here and
A bit of polit bureau agit prop there
The irreverant aesthetica
And a bit of a rigmarole advertizing
We cańt go wrong
A bit of
Something for éveryone

Lets do it
(That´s the way i run my whorehouses)
Theo, the funny girl from Pigalle

Fwd: Tr: La Couverture

Zivancevic Nina <zivancevicn65@gmail.com>
To: Marc Léger <leger.mj@gmail.com>
26 March 2015 at 07:53

Marc-- Perhaps my next one perhaps that one will
it will certainly contain some memories of you...

Marc Léger <leger.mj@gmail.com>
To: Zivancevic Nina <zivancevicn65@gmail.com>
26 March 2015 at 10:18

who is this Alain-Robbe Zivancevic - who does he think he is ?!

Marc Léger <leger.mj@gmail.com>
To: Zivancevic Nina <zivancevicn65@gmail.com>
26 March 2015 at 10:51

black lesbian marxist
trans-arab proudhonista
terrorist chic cis-poet
napoleonic french cabaret salon singer
ottoeroticnarcotic

Zivancevic Nina <zivancevicn65@gmail.com>
To: Marc Léger <leger.mj@gmail.com>
26 March 2015 at 12:50

Justin--
It´s just my french editor (auditor) Jérôme Carassou, he aint no b-friend
of Théo

Marc Léger <leger.mj@gmail.com>
To: Zivancevic Nina <zivancevicn65@gmail.com>
26 March 2015 at 13:05

of course, i forgot my NZ keywords and glossary: tempestuous, cajoling,
enticing, desiring, adorable, 80s, living, mischievous, recondite, fussy,
musical, beatnik, sneaky, on the line

Zivancevic Nina <zivancevicn65@gmail.com>
To: Marc Léger <leger.mj@gmail.com>
26 March 2015 at 13:11

Oh...
This had happened sooooo
Long ago.. I was reading
Justin's poem
Sort of drooling over it
When i missed my train and took
A totaly wrong direction to St. Denis
Either Justin is a veeery good poet
Or i Like him beyond possible
Or both.
At any rate my undergraduate court will miss my class now
Shit
Eer..but what a lovely feeling!!
Theodora phd.

Marc Léger <leger.mj@gmail.com>
To: Zivancevic Nina <zivancevicn65@gmail.com>
26 March 2015 at 13:29

kissing, getting me to write
Nina, Queen of the Night

Zivancevic Nina <zivancevicn65@gmail.com>
To: Marc Léger <leger.mj@gmail.com>
26 March 2015 at 14:45

But i have never been a beatnik really
More punk than beat!
And was born on the same day and date as Johnny rotten
Love that guy!

Zivancevic Nina <zivancevicn65@gmail.com>
To: Marc Léger <leger.mj@gmail.com>
26 March 2015 at 14:57

Oh...ho.
You got me speechless
Sir Justinian Legerovich- ha, u must be a shrink of some sort
Anyways i hope you dont charge me much when i come to you
One of these days and seek help
This day may arrive pretty soon
I may burn all my marbles and get off my rocker
Right now i'm still functioning but my soul is in danger and
I am not Spinoza to love everything and éveryone in nature I
'm more like Leibnitz
Yeah i'll stick to Hegel
I'll always love you

Marc Léger <leger.mj@gmail.com>
To: Zivancevic Nina <zivancevicn65@gmail.com>
26 March 2015 at 18:45

how long a visit would you like
1 month, 10 years ...

if you had to play a prefabricated character in my forthcoming novel
would it be
Audry in Unbelievable Truth
Maria in Trust
Elina in Simple Men
Katie in Surviving Desire
Isabelle in Amateur
Fay in Henry Fool
Magdalena in The Book of Life
Beatrice in No Such Thing
or The Girl from Monday in The Girl from Monday
I hope you choose Isabelle

Marc Léger <leger.mj@gmail.com>
To: Zivancevic Nina <zivancevicn65@gmail.com>
26 March 2015 at 18:62

this is the lecture i will be giving in Paris after my morning latte across
from la madeleine:
https://www.youtube.com/watch?v=Cm7XLRoD02k
[Die Tödliche Doris, "Die Über-Doris"]

Fwd: [SAES] [COLL] [Erratum] Programme du colloque international « Ici et ailleurs dans la littérature traduite », Université d'Artois, 21-22 mai 2015

Zivancevic Nina <zivancevicn65@gmail.com>
To: Marc Léger <leger.mj@gmail.com>
28 March 2015 at 07:27

So Marc
Do u think i like to hear u first thing in the morbing
Or some Florent Monocle who sends his stuff stiffen geshift on translation?
Listen to Kathleen Ferrier
Xx

Marc Léger <leger.mj@gmail.com>
To: Zivancevic Nina <zivancevicn65@gmail.com>
28 March 2015 at 09:34

sorry, i try to geshift stiffen to you in the morning
so i can check my mail and see what the comité scientifique has recommended
i think you probably wore headbands in the 80s and i would imagine one of those aerobics outfits
now you seem so sad in the Bay Area and K is sure to be stranded at the gates of Nina - it seems to me like the poets have got something here about writing it all down and i have to say everything i know about you i learned from you and this here prefabricated (   ) Living on Air

**oh well this amorphous
thing**

Zivancevic Nina <zivancevicn65@gmail.com>
To: Marc Léger <leger.mj@gmail.com>
26 March 2015 at 19:30

Attachment: *Living on Air* Manuscript and Book Cover

Marc Léger <leger.mj@gmail.com>
To: Zivancevic Nina <zivancevicn65@gmail.com>
27 March 2015 at 09:15

Dr X - this is on my list for today but i have a few tasks to take care of
first and then i will light incense to get in the mood and get back to you
on this polyamorphous thing ...

Zivancevic Nina <zivancevicn65@gmail.com>
To: Marc Léger <leger.mj@gmail.com>
27 March 2015 at 11:15

Well, perhaps you don't need that incense unless there's sense to it, if
your bathroom is clogged etc-
i hope my mnsc does not STINK, but hey, anything is possible
It's more like Education Sentimentale, young girl in big town(s) etc
By the way, did you know that my grandma was a Richard Strauss fan?
Plus I've written this text so long ago that now, while proofreading it, i try
to undestand it myself and not hate it..
Gooood-luck with it!!

Marc Léger <leger.mj@gmail.com>
To: Zivancevic Nina <zivancevicn65@gmail.com>
27 March 2015 at 11:31

I knew that about your grandmother, but i thought you said you were a
big Johann Strauss fan, born in Vienna and all that - see what you've
done to me with your poetess and young girl playing violin - i will read
you and be the judge but it's going to be difficult after everything that has
passed between us, so basically, we'll see - i will put on my black outfit
(like I've joined the Frenchie King gang or something), or is it a hippie
theme? and get ready to be swept away

Zivancevic Nina <zivancevicn65@gmail.com>
To: Marc Léger <leger.mj@gmail.com>
27 March 2015 at 13:37

I am no Johann Strauss fan-- you really think so lowly of me, I see, and, on top of, with that incense insense stuff- who wld like to read me? And don't, please do not read that book as it happens to be very self-revealing, it will definitively destroy our already destroyed prenups and you will never write or click to me again..
xxxxxxxxxxxxxx

Marc Léger <leger.mj@gmail.com>
To: Zivancevic Nina <zivancevicn65@gmail.com>
27 March 2015 at 13:52

that was a lot of fun. since then I have become somewhat more familiar with the poésie d'auteur or politique de poésie or whatever they call it, avant-Byzantine -- what, no Strauss? i guess that means i won't be introducing you to my father

Zivancevic Nina <zivancevicn65@gmail.com>
To: Marc Léger <leger.mj@gmail.com>
27 March 2015 at 14:11

ha ha ha! I am sure you "were serious" about it!
hey, it was nice meeting you! see you at the movies! i cannot leave Europe anyways, really and truly i'm forever stuck in one of these castles -- and i gather you have a different future. Say hello to your father though! he must be a nice guy!
NZ

Marc Léger <leger.mj@gmail.com>
To: Zivancevic Nina <zivancevicn65@gmail.com>
27 March 2015 at 15:36

oh sure, now that i made arrangements for us to meet in little tokyo
you were not in little Tokyo
like it's nothing between us, just words,
like ha ha and faster pussycat

like hi, I'm Nina Zivancevic
i did not say anything about the future
what i said was honest and true
like the movies
well, okay, so what's up with with Paris 8?
what's taking them so long?

Zivancevic Nina <zivancevicn65@gmail.com>
To: Marc Léger <leger.mj@gmail.com>
27 March 2015 at 16:08

what about Paris 8?
what's your plan exactly?
Xcuse me, but it's hard to make any plans with you -- cause YOU've
been changing yr mind!

If you'd like me to act on your behalf-- and I said I liked yr writing enough
and MORE than enough—I'd be happy to arrange smth

but 1. You have to tell exactly what sort of event (book promo,
conference..?
2. and when wld you like to do it
However, I must tell you (unless you're Bill Gates or someone like that,
accustomed to frequent flights) it wld be wise for you to stay more than
a day or two in Europe, as it's really hard on yr body and nervewracking
plus, you're not rushing to a funeral, so a 4 or 5 day stay wld just be
more sane and healthier on you
xxxxxxxxxxxxxxxxxxxx

Marc Léger <leger.mj@gmail.com>
To: Zivancevic Nina <zivancevicn65@gmail.com>
27 March 2015 at 16:31

well, it could be a lecture-performance on "what is to be done with Spring
Breakers" and it could be conjoined or not with a lounch of The Idea of
the Avant Garde, for which i could give my lecture but in Languedoc. so
that's two possibilities that would be easy enough to prepare - the SB is
more cavern-style

yes, i could stay 4 to 5 days, but not 10 days - a short while also
because i am not supposed to be outside the country - but i do now have

my passport - but damn, haven,t read a word of yr book yet - wild horses could,t drive me away - of course you are aware of Sir Charles's Living on Thin Air

---

Zivancevic Nina <zivancevicn65@gmail.com>
To: Marc Léger <leger.mj@gmail.com>
27 March 2015 at 16:49

you DONT have to read it
by teeth skin you escaped
OK i authorize you-you dont have to read it

Marc Léger <leger.mj@gmail.com>
To: Zivancevic Nina <zivancevicn65@gmail.com>
27 March 2015 at 18:42

i'm reserving my comments for after reading the book but before that i want to say how i really enjoyed it and i think that you need to see a doctor or maybe even a veterinarian - your prose is terrific, stylish, and coyishly disarming - there seems to even be a détournement of balkan mysticism, a listlessly toying with the clichés; this prose work should not fool the inattentive reader - it is essentially film segments of acatalectic verse - we haven,t seen prose like this since michel deguy

---

Zivancevic Nina <zivancevicn65@gmail.com>
To: Marc Léger <leger.mj@gmail.com>
27 March 2015 at 20:32

????
To see a veterinarian? My dear pal, what is the name of the planet you grew up on?
It wasnt a planet for polite animals, was it??
Please give me its name... Now:

Marc Léger <leger.mj@gmail.com>
To: Zivancevic Nina <zivancevicn65@gmail.com>
27 March 2015 at 20:43

i see in the book you've characterized Jesus as an airline stewardess - nice! ...

Zivancevic Nina <zivancevicn65@gmail.com>
To: Marc Léger <leger.mj@gmail.com>
28 March 2015 at 05:14

Thanx . Better than the advice to see the vet,,
You must also be quite busy with your work, Justin.
Thanks for devoting time to my own
Xxxxx

Marc Léger <leger.mj@gmail.com>
To: Zivancevic Nina <zivancevicn65@gmail.com>
28 March 2015 at 09:43

i'm a slow reader but i can see you were trying to do something for all human animals there

---

Zivancevic Nina <zivancevicn65@gmail.com>
To: Marc Léger <leger.mj@gmail.com>
28 March 2015 at 10:12

Here is the latest:
Slow Justinian, you've got to help me now- my publisher Barncott press needs a new blurb for the jacket.
Slow or not, or what? Can you kinfly supply one of your famous dittos (you've said smth already to the effect that the book is not undear to you)
I'll try Gerard Malanga as well
so two of you could be on the back cover.
Sounds good to you?
really many xxxxxxxxxxxxxxxxxxxx and yyyyyyyyyyyyyyyyyyyyyyyy
and you can have the whole alphabet from mexxxxxxxxxxxxxxx
nnnnnnnnnnnnnn mmmmmmmmmmmmmmmmmmmeeeeee

Marc Léger <leger.mj@gmail.com>
To: Zivancevic Nina <zivancevicn65@gmail.com>
28 March 2015 at 10:36

muzik to my ears
i will do my best for your B side
galant
promotional
literarily ravaged
and paired with one of the real warhol people !

Marc Léger <leger.mj@gmail.com>
To: Zivancevic Nina <zivancevicn65@gmail.com>
28 March 2015 at 11:54

okay but this is not something i normally do – i mean i'm not qualified -
the NYC review of books does not often invite the likes of me though i
was asked once to review something of a sci-fi novel by someone out of
the blue

anyway, this is option A:

*Nina Z. pursues the memory of (mostly) K. through places and times that
read like fictional worlds. She brings the underground in from the cold,
only to engage it in a conversation that is as coyishly sidelong as it is
enticingly sincere. Avant-byzantine mysticism with a smile.*
*– Marc James Léger, author of Brave New Avant Garde and Drive in
Cinema*

i'm working on options B to Zee as i go. let me know your honest opinion

---

Marc Léger <leger.mj@gmail.com>
To: Zivancevic Nina <zivancevicn65@gmail.com>
28 March 2015 at 13:47

dear
version B: i might take out the first line and switch Nina Z. to simply Z.
version C:

If you don't like typo's, read this book. – Marc James Léger,

---

Zivancevic Nina <zivancevicn65@gmail.com>
To: Marc Léger <leger.mj@gmail.com>
28 March 2015 at 14:04

Thank you. That´s called giving a helping hand.
Thank you my friend.

Zivancevic Nina <zivancevicn65@gmail.com>
To: Marc Léger <leger.mj@gmail.com>
28 March 2015 at 14:25

Your kind action really inspires me to continue my organizing
conferences on BNAG and DiC
But as you figured out
the academia out there is cold and cruel and it´s not enough
it does not suffice to snap one's finger for things to get done...
Wof wof
Kank u camarade MJL. The reason i put my early pics on is that i want to
be reminded what innocense was all about

Marc Léger <leger.mj@gmail.com>
To: Zivancevic Nina <zivancevicn65@gmail.com>
28 March 2015 at 15:35

speaking of innocence: version D, and still reading on

*Living on Air is nothing if not Nina Zivancevic – an avant-byzantine girl
on the lower east side of fiction. The question is: who does she work for?
– Marc James Léger, author of BNAG and DiC*

Marc Léger <leger.mj@gmail.com>
To: Zivancevic Nina <zivancevicn65@gmail.com>
28 March 2015 at 17:04

here are some A to Zs but i did not make it all the way there
i hope to make it up to you but right now i need to take a short break
back to you shortly

Nina Zivancevic pursues the memory of K. through fictional worlds, urban scenes and warm interiors. She brings the underground in from the cold, engaging it in a conversation that is as coyishly sidelong as it is enticingly sincere. Avant-byzantine mysticism with a smile.

Nina Z. brings the underground in from the cold, engaging it in a conversation that is as coyishly sidelong as it is enticingly sincere. Avant-byzantine mysticism with a smile.

Nina Z. brings the underground in from the cold, engaging in a narrative that is as coyishly sidelong as it is enticingly sincere. Avant-byzantine mysticism with a smile.

Living on Air is nothing if not Nina Zivancevic – an avant-byzantine girl on the lower east side of fiction. The question is: who does she work for?

Bringing it all back home, Living on Air is nothing if not Nina Zivancevic. An avant-byzantine mystic on the lower east side of fiction.

If the purpose of poetry is to divert people from acting foolishly, then the purpose of Living on Air is to remind us that love is poetry.

The bourgeois novel is dead and the global era of protest turns poets into politicians. Living on Air channels the underground to render a lover's tale woven of intimacy and art world striving.

It's not boring.

Go East and West, young man. That's what Nina Zivancevic did and she lived to tell the tale.

Zivancevic Nina <zivancevicn65@gmail.com>
To: Marc Léger <leger.mj@gmail.com>
28 March 2015 at 16:00

Btw I wish I were that East German spy lovely Nixon's girl in Washington .. She was well paid for a while but alas! Was quickly discovered as the double spying Irma..

Zivancevic Nina <zivancevicn65@gmail.com>
To: Marc Léger <leger.mj@gmail.com>
28 March 2015 at 15:58

I'd replace lower with "lowest East side of fiction (than we get the double innuendo emphasized)
She works for (and only for) Midnight Cowboy aka Marc James Léger
Author of Nagg and Dick
(They are working out.. Their perforating perfect performance conference)

Envoyé de mon iPhone

Marc Léger <leger.mj@gmail.com>
To: Zivancevic Nina <zivancevicn65@gmail.com>
28 March 2015 at 18:47

now i,m certain that you are that East German spy
hiding in plain sight
a real gone gal
yeah, it's going to be like the Ziegfried Kracauer Follies
or the Follies Burgers (as in Peter with the omelettes and coffee on u)
i'm okay with lowest East side in whichever combination you prefer

Envoyé de mon iPhoneZereforeiHam ...

Marc Léger <leger.mj@gmail.com>
To: Zivancevic Nina <zivancevicn65@gmail.com>
28 March 2015 at 19:04

i think i,m around L or M

Nina Zizancevic needs my endorsement like a fish needs a bicycle.
– Marc James Léger, author of Nagg and Dick

Zivancevic Nina <zivancevicn65@gmail.com>
To: Marc Léger <leger.mj@gmail.com>
29 March 2015 at 05:44

ha ha ha
stop it click-o maniac,
ah, i'm more like a maniac of letters than that famous spy
now let me ask you: who are you?
why can't you get out of country?
do you have a prison bracelet like those guys who have to check in
every three days to a precinct (scuse my spelling) ?
Now as to the spelling IT IS damn tireing to think in 4 languages all the
time and check the spelling- no mashine or program wld help me that
way
have a nice Sunday my dear camrade and fellow-sufferer
yr queen of no place/no idea, really lost but more like in words than
actions..

Marc Léger <leger.mj@gmail.com>
To: Zivancevic Nina <zivancevicn65@gmail.com>
29 March 2015 at 10:07

yes i,m wanted in several countries for a crime i will not commit
prison bracelet - you could say that, yes, but the diagnosis described it
some other way
there are stories there,
and lots of no thanks, i gave at the dead letter office
but yes, i can make it out of the country, that is, if you would be so kind
as to dig a tunnel for me - there are no restrictions – except vegetarian
meals in the tunnels only

i have to think more about the endorsement, dear me, another day of
slave work

*Look out Slavoj Žižek, here comes Darko Jelicic. If you want to know
what kind of person would say such a thing, read Living on Air. Rollover
Badiou, it's the avant garde!*

Marc Léger <leger.mj@gmail.com>
To: Zivancevic Nina <zivancevicn65@gmail.com>
29 March 2015 at 10:21

voici les glissements progressifs de l'alphabet
what will the people at Paris 1, 2, 3, 4, 5 ,6 , 7 and 9 say ???

There are no seduction scenes in here and nothing to turn your crank.
Nina Zivancevic doesn't write that way – she's not that kind of writer, and
we're all better off for it. She's selective and she knows what she's doing.
Still, Living on Air is sexy, cool, fantastic – an intimate voyage into the
underground lives of a literary maven and avant-byzantine emperess.

Zivancevic Nina <zivancevicn65@gmail.com>
To: Marc Léger <leger.mj@gmail.com>
29 March 2015 at 10:31

Oh now we're jumping into conclusions!
If I were u, I wouldn't trust much either Zizek or Jelicic, much less Badiou
(have u read his strange essay on Deleuze?)
In fact I don't even know who you are
U might be one of these shopping spree consumers of critical , French ,
Slovenian cum Yale theories
But I guess u are young and handsome
And soon enough
U will understand how relative all these things are as to the starving in
the streets of... Plus u wanted to hear my words
Plus you do not want to open yr mind to anything different than yr
conditioned Academic.. Ok
Thank u for the blurb and yr reading of ot
I will see if I should use yr negative outlook on the cover of my
manuscript

Marc Léger <leger.mj@gmail.com>
To: Zivancevic Nina <zivancevicn65@gmail.com>
29 March 2015 at 10:57

hey – don't be mad!! don't write me a tirade …
you know i have to be on the lookout for banditas
especially the one they call Ze Serbian

yes i read Badiou's "theoretical essays" on Zezeuze and i agree, there is too much "bad infinity" - as for the French elections, you can make your Faustian bargain and i will see you at the little bar on the rue Maurice Thorez

i know that you're a leading figure in the New York school and the avant-jazz drolling club - and so, i hope you have an open dust jacket

I first met Nina Zivancevic when she was a waitress at a restaurant with an Art Deco theme called Twenties. Since then she's built quite a reputation for herself as an artiste, writing poetry, performing on stage, sending me emails. Her latest accomplishment is Living on Air. I wish I had the words to describe it but I've never read Frank O'Hara and people like that and so what do I know. References to Lawrence Durrell don't quite do it either. Living on Air is what it feels like to be in love and to visit Paris, New York, San Francisco and every other place in the literary imaginary. It's tender, worldly, and it's sure to make you smile.

a photo of photo of a film in a film museum in an electronic letter in the mind of a cat

Image: Photograph of Musidora in a film still from Louis Feuillade's *Les Vampires* (1915) in the Cinema Museum in Frankfurt

---

Marc Léger <leger.mj@gmail.com>
To: Zivancevic Nina <zivancevicn65@gmail.com>
29 March 2015 at 11:09

let me know if this works better for you
my aim is true and i wouldn't mind it if you wore me on your sleeve
what am i your sycophant elephant in the chat room or something

Living on Air is avant-byzantine prose at its finest and Zivancevic's personal take on the life of a literary maven resembles Deleuze and Guattari's rhizome more than it does the traditional network or anything having to do with "truth procedure." Eileen Myles eat your heart out.

Marc Léger <leger.mj@gmail.com>
To: Zivancevic Nina <zivancevicn65@gmail.com>
29 March 2015 at 11:18

hey, I hope that you are well and this message finds you at an opportune moment. I've had the chance to read your terrific book and I'm very happy to write an endorsement for you. It's my privilege. Please find below a suggested endorsement. Let me know if you would like me to lengthen or shorten it or add sparkles or em-dashes or anything else. Your wish is my command. I expect I will never hear from you ever again, but that's the risk you take.

Living on Air is what I imagine Isabelle Huppert's character Isabelle in Hal Hartley's Amateur would write. Now all we need is a two-piece leather outfit and an electric drill at a lecture-performance and we're in business. Chris Kraus get a life.

Image: [next page]

Zivancevic Nina <zivancevicn65@gmail.com>
To: Marc Léger <leger.mj@gmail.com>
29 March 2015 at 11:29

And what's yr diagnosis?
I am a paranoid obsessive and perversely narcissistic kleptomaniac..
so what about you? Tomorrow at Paris 3 (otherwise called la Sorbonne Nouvelle) I will ask Bruno Pequinot to arrange a conference for you. Or to indicate how I cld go about it.
The vet gave me a lot of pills but my fur still keeps shedding..I think I am going to die soon , camarade Léger ,and our letters are going to be the only testimony to my sanity

---

Marc Léger <leger.mj@gmail.com>
To: Zivancevic Nina <zivancevicn65@gmail.com>
29 March 2015 at 11:34

whatever you do, don't take 100 horse pills and not call me in the morning
the world needs you
who is this Bruno? one of your dungeon pals?
and now, something completely different:

An endorsement by the likes of me could ruin a writer's reputation for life. That tells you something about Living on Air – a risky venture if ever there was one. Still, you have to hand it to Nina Zivancevic, or to her publisher, or to the bookstore, depending on how you look at it.

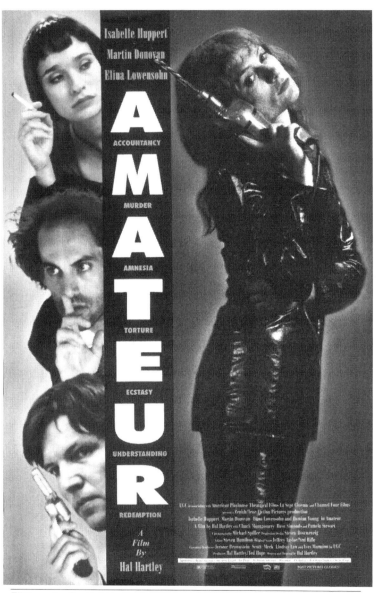

Film poster for Hal Hartley's *Amateur* (1994).
Courtesy of Possible Films.

Zivancevic Nina <zivancevicn65@gmail.com>
To: Marc Léger <leger.mj@gmail.com>
29 March 2015 at 11:42

The last take is beautiful
As u can tell I'm a sucker for Beauty
Oh! My sublime friend!
If you only knew.. How much I miss you! More than Plotinus and st
Augustine together
If I only worked on our extraterrestrial communicational commuting
You'd be able to brush up on the conventions and
Forget the Ghettoisation of my writing and persona altogether !
Why avant Byzantine ? Why do we need that ghetto like categorising
Black lesbian Marxist
White gay Foucault
Happy Canadian Marc
Fucked up Russian judo champion
C'mon Marc, u and I can do better than that...

Marc Léger <leger.mj@gmail.com>
To: Zivancevic Nina <zivancevicn65@gmail.com>
29 March 2015 at 11:49

i like you all ghetto :)

Among the fleas in Marc's flea circus, Nina Zivancevic is the one that
causes me to rethink, or man the torpedos, not sure which one. Living
on Air merely confirmed what I already knew: life's rich pageant is no fun
without the challenge of the underground. A literary diary full of surprises
and avant-byzantine verse.

Marc Léger <leger.mj@gmail.com>
To: Zivancevic Nina <zivancevicn65@gmail.com>
29 March 2015 at 11:53

maybe like this, for good measure ?

Among the fleas in Marc's flea circus, Nina Zivancevic is the one that
causes me to rethink, or make a sandwich, not sure which one. Living
on Air merely confirmed what I already knew: life is no fun without the

challenge of the ghetto underground. A literary diary full of surprises and avant-byzantine verse.
– Happy Canadian Marc

Marc Léger <leger.mj@gmail.com>
To: Zivancevic Nina <zivancevicn65@gmail.com>
29 March 2015 at 12:00

Nina, let me know what you think of the below possibility
if that doesn't work then i'll re-apply

Living on Air is avant-byzantine prose at its ghetto finest, and Nina Zivancevic is a Germany spy, I'm sure of it. Someone should do something about this fucked up Russian. Eileen Myles, where are you when we need you?

Zivancevic Nina <zivancevicn65@gmail.com>
To: Marc Léger <leger.mj@gmail.com>
29 March 2015 at 11:54

Oh .. Think u r confusing me with
Yet another gstring gfriend of yours..
Who dares take these pills in yr company
Who dares calling u at night?
Silverslinger will beat them up all..
Now onto more cultural matters
Please Google out Bruno Pequinot
He's running the Film and Art Media dept at Sorbonne nouvelle
I'll give him something to remember- a Byzantine blow job (wash shampoo and creamy head) so that he arranges that conference 4 u

---

Marc Léger <leger.mj@gmail.com>
To: Zivancevic Nina <zivancevicn65@gmail.com>
29 March 2015 at 12:09

now you've got me all serious
you have this kind of white gay Foucault word power
still, if you want to do me a favour

i would like to be on France culture
there is somebody i have to get back at

Living on Air is the finest work of prose-fiction this side of Nathalie
Cardot, and Nina Zivancevic is the most delightful literary maven to have
blessed the halls of the Sorbonne.
– Bruno Pequinot

Marc Léger <leger.mj@gmail.com>
To: Zivancevic Nina <zivancevicn65@gmail.com>
29 March 2015 at 12:14

more about whose confusing who and wha

Reading Living on Air is like counting down from A to Zee. It's like,
she has this kind of white gay Foucault word power. You find yourself
thinking like her, as if her world is your world, and then you're doing
weird things you didn't know you wanted to do. It's like, she says she's
not feminist, but can she be trusted?

Marc Léger <leger.mj@gmail.com>
To: Zivancevic Nina <zivancevicn65@gmail.com>
29 March 2015 at 12:24

this one is blurb x, XXX
i figure i earned my day's wages
with the devil behind me and death at my side

I gave up fiction for cultural theory around 1991. I figured the bourgeois
novel was finished anyway and so what more could it do. Living on
Air I can see has come to the same conclusion but keeps on writing,
animated as it is by personal and literary worlds and the compulsion to
get up in the middle of the night. It's irrepressible, like a black lesbian
marxist.

Marc Léger <leger.mj@gmail.com>
To: Zivancevic Nina <zivancevicn65@gmail.com>
29 March 2015 at 12:42

i suppose that my bateau ivre has either reached its destination or is lost at sea - i hope that there is something in my attachments that can be rescued or recombined - thank you for this nice visit

Why did Nina Zivancevic write Living on Air? That is the question. My guess is she needed something to do, someone or something to love. Disarming at the utmost and fanciful at its avant-finest. Z is for Nina Zivancevic. Living on Air is for those friends, lovers and comrades who will read it. A personal travelogue by a literary maven and underground emperess.

Zivancevic Nina <zivancevicn65@gmail.com>
To: Marc Léger <leger.mj@gmail.com>
29 March 2015 at 13:17

Marc! If I were a Visigoth I would've married you on the spot and had kitties with you of every shape and colour, but the absurdity of life is-- You tell me:

At any rate you are the eternal K I've been looking for, that is, according to the Egyptian cosmology, the eternal moving principle which moves from one body to another?
And...lovely you supported this early amorphous text, now I'm writing another one,
It's more structured, describes my PhD days in France...I'm a slow writer here and
I hate novel as genre but everyone wants u to sell yr product anyway.
Xxxxxxxxx

Zivancevic Nina <zivancevicn65@gmail.com>
To: Marc Léger <leger.mj@gmail.com>
29 March 2015 at 13:52

Auyy now you talk passion..
Did u know that Myles lusted over me but really Lily Marlene
But so rude and waspish and uncooth..

Marc Léger <leger.mj@gmail.com>
To: Zivancevic Nina <zivancevicn65@gmail.com>
29 March 2015 at 15:18

and that jeans and t-shirt look
like it's the empire of Clovis and the Saxons have not even left germany

Poem for Lily Marlene

I lurped up Living on Air like a bukkake princess.
– Gerard Malanga

Zivancevic Nina <zivancevicn65@gmail.com>
To: Marc Léger <leger.mj@gmail.com>
29 March 2015 at 16:34

Hahaha Marc! Where are you??!!
My life was so sad without your miaow miaow miu...

Zivancevic Nina <zivancevicn65@gmail.com>
To: Marc Léger <leger.mj@gmail.com>
29 March 2015 at 16:45

Ha ha ha
Thank you Momo Schmomo for giving my private address to MJL
He is my virtual cloud and there are 9 of us in it
His cat is better than Satrapi's psycho killer's pussy cat

from Nina Z.

Zivancevic Nina <zivancevicn65@gmail.com>
To: Marc Léger <leger.mj@gmail.com>
30 March 2015 at 18:23

Camarade Legerovich,
mission completed. Or almost so—we've had an interesting association
meeting this evening..mainly focused on the advancement of the right in
this country. And I spoke to Bruno about your (our?) project in general
and yr presentation and authorship in particular.
He asked me if you spoke French (hmmmm?) and if you could send him
your CV and a letter, telling what you'd like to present. Like an official
envoie, so that he could work on our behalf. Very pompous on the side
of the French who always refuse to understand anything in English.. But,
ok, I guess that's sort of feasible-- if you write such an official "hello" and
etc.- I could translate it for you and send it back, that you to him- this has
to be coordinated , sort of, and please
-- forgive all these stupid big wigs (Baudrillard and Michel F. could
not do anything with them) and try to do it, if you will. I am just a fly in
the wind here, and i try to do things the other way round.. I am a truly
subversive force in this university, one could tell hmmm..
OK,
à tres bientot
your friend
Nina

Marc Léger <leger.mj@gmail.com>
To: Zivancevic Nina <zivancevicn65@gmail.com>
30 March 2015 at 19:30

dear insider subversive - i will write something in french to get this
mission accomplished but it might sound a little Brittany - not britney
spears but my ancestors les Bretons, but they are used to it i guess,
the franks, but presenting in french is not impossible - anyway, i want to
know now the way to temple of the goddess ...

Zivancevic Nina <zivancevicn65@gmail.com>
To: Marc Léger <leger.mj@gmail.com>
31 March 2015 at 03:28

I committed a terrible crime- I misspelled Bruno's name (papa Freud
might have smth to do with it) he's Bruno Péquignot

Directeur de Film and Art Media department (or better google him out) at Sorbonne Nouvelle (Paris 3)
- say I'm the author Nina spoke about yesterday at the meeting, and gave to Swen his book on New Avant Garde to translate (yes, I did that!!!)
Swen is a Danish guy, jack for all trades , asst to Pizzi, so they'll be discussing yr case soon (hmm) tell him the time (now Bruno says such conf could be executed only in October when the un starts and all students are here- makes sense)
and the content- yr new book coming out, yr like to present all yr previous books - when asked WHAT DO YOU ACTUALLY DO- I said you're a theorist of culture (like my dad incidentally), sociologist cum anthropologist of culture, aestethician cum philisopher
what are you Marc, indeed, what do you do?
When asked at the party How do you do? you answer
I doooooooooooooooooooooooooooooooo.. doodley do
xxxx

Marc Léger <leger.mj@gmail.com>
To: Zivancevic Nina <zivancevicn65@gmail.com>
31 March 2015 at 10:51

not sure about anthropologist but i guess we're all structuralists now, one way or another, and so yes, i do and i don't - so i hope my letter is sort of what you had in mind and thanks! for suggesting a French translation of Nagg - that book has sold 1000, which is not bad for little me and my first book, a slim one at that and a collection of essays - not even a monograph ...

https://www.youtube.com/watch?v=tIkGohO_-QE
[Sonic Youth, live studio performance of "Kool Thing" (1993)]

Now evrthin is clear 2 me

Zivancevic Nina <zivancevicn65@gmail.com>
To: Marc Léger <leger.mj@gmail.com>
31 March 2015 at 09:26

I found in this dictionary of names that Léger family name comes from
ancient German Leod (people) and Gari (always dynamic, ready for a
battle). Funny though that's my name as well Ziv means alive, dynamic
Thus Zivancevic or the-one- who stays alive in a battle
When's yr bday, Marc? Perhaps that wld be a good day for yr conf
Check M. Satrapi's film "voices"
It's gory but you'd love it

Marc Léger <leger.mj@gmail.com>
To: Zivancevic Nina <zivancevicn65@gmail.com>
31 March 2015 at 10:34

i heard about the voices - Satrapi's Persepolis i think was also the
inspiration for the western-vampire female revenge film A Girl Walks
Home Alone At Night, which has a good premise and had some nice 80s
moments (like something from Jarmusch mixed in)

Mark is a Roman name so that makes both my names really european,
but i guess if you're Staying Alive with me on the disco I have nothing to
loose. to me Zivancevic means: Joan of Arc - gory but lovely - what have
i done to deserve you, and, will you lead me into battle? Yes!

my birthday is October 8, 1968 -- 888 -- the mobius strip of birthdays
and so no wonder i'm this freak of the social disaster - i was destined to
be inside-out - same day as MLK and John Lennon, give or take a few
hours

you make me jealous with all your artificial ingredients and it seems like
you are so kind as to indulge me that it would be fun to stage - i would
want a 2-piece leather suit for you just because that would look so nice
- also, i have some other plans, but now, waiting until the fall, that will
make for a nice summer

Marc Léger <leger.mj@gmail.com>
To: Zivancevic Nina <zivancevicn65@gmail.com>
31 March 2015 at 11:16

more sapphic poetry soon ...
Envoyé de mon iDéedel'Avantgarde

Zivancevic Nina <zivancevicn65@gmail.com>
To: Marc Léger <leger.mj@gmail.com>
31 March 2015 at 14:16

And the Count said: I feel her coming ever closer...elizabeeetha...
And then he says: love will prevail!
Oh Marc! You are getting closer and closer..perhaps you should wear..
Turtlenecks to protect yourself from my old European fangs...?

Marc Léger <leger.mj@gmail.com>
To: Zivancevic Nina <zivancevicn65@gmail.com>
31 March 2015 at 19:22

oh Nina
i see you are a john e rotten fan - i like his forthright robin hood attitude
i also like mark e smith quite a lot too; he says vampirism oughta be a
crime

Zivancevic Nina <zivancevicn65@gmail.com>
To: Marc Léger <leger.mj@gmail.com>
31 March 2015 at 19:55

yap! My whole adulthood in England (see i multiply so i live every two
weeks down in London)
was marked by people like Lydon
and the founders of IT, my lovely editor Chris (Aram) Sanders,
Niall Mc Devitt, and David Graeber, also by now contributors to STRIKE,
there's a poet James Byrne and great playwright Johnny Brown (of
Radio Resonance)-- to me there are like gians
of so called artistic resistance, and all sorts of folks
Mick Badger and Will Firm, smoking crack with me and Eduardo Johns
on the stairways of Soho, some chicks that come and go

but hey.. what about your macho attitude like nurturing double standards and not wanting me to be your one and only pal, etc?
Marc, I think that our pre-nups definitively have to go bunkers!
xxxxxxxxxxxxxxxxxxxx

Marc Léger <leger.mj@gmail.com>
To: Zivancevic Nina <zivancevicn65@gmail.com>
31 March 2015 at 20:04

yowza! petit moi on the cover!
yes i will discuss D.Graeber at a later moment, when you and Bruno get back to me, after you've finished snorting Coke with all the famous people - Will Firm I don't think understands Situationism, but then the SIs said there's no such thing as Situationism and by the looks of all this post- galore subtext i suppose there's no Nina Zee, or not the one I was dressing up with a leather 2 piece in my macho imagination - good thing you got out of there alive - you go ahead and keep me straight and gay in your mind

is that you in my mailbox - i see three messages and i have not even recovered from the last one - hold on - the avant garde never gives up on Nina Zee - you are MY Nina Z. understand ! hey, i'M on your cover !

Zivancevic Nina <zivancevicn65@gmail.com>
To: Marc Léger <leger.mj@gmail.com>
31 March 2015 at 20:12

yes, in fact.. these are all people of my distant past and you are my bright, if not multilayered future!
that's why i put you on the back cover in fact you put yourself, it's not that i was begging you for it
so all others are out, and you're in , like the latest Prada leather skirt invention!

conférencier – avant garde – cinéma

Zivancevic Nina <zivancevicn65@gmail.com>
To: Marc Léger <leger.mj@gmail.com>
31 March 2015 at 17:37

Marc-- Now c'mon ... With everything we've been through and everything
you've learnt about me...do you think that I care?
As dr Rotten nicely remarked: you cld be black u cld be white
You cld be wrong or u cld be right.. As the song goes
I am delighted that I ran into you like a fast car into a field of
marshmallows! And i've always had fun eversince.. And I hope it never
stops .. This is the MOST narcissistic relationship I ve ever had as you
are-- so much like me..so
Why not , I cld be yr favourite bfriend and u cld be my favourite girl, we
cld take turns as really
Experienced vampires
just don't leave me in this terrible virtual desert full of yes nos and
maybes..
The rest of the world is so boring when your clicks are gone and out and
not to be found around
Ta lectrice devouee

Marc Léger <leger.mj@gmail.com>
To: Zivancevic Nina <zivancevicn65@gmail.com>
31 March 2015 at 19:00

okay, now i can see that you are fighting the law
and i wonder what other poetry tricks you have to seduce innocent girls
-- just a pen pal one day and then, in with both teeth - anything to get the
last word
and look at us in the mirror – we're not even there - me reading you, you
reading me, you writing for me, me writing about you for Cosmopolitan
magazine (how to land an endorsement)
but i wonder how you do it emailing 50 other virgins and then teaching
classes, corrupting the youth of Paris - now that's what I call narcissism
(some kind of wonderful transference) – you're like being addicted to
coffee beans - look at me, i'm at least four times a day, like the Albanians
do - that's not normal
but who wants to be normal when you can be super-normal. in that
regard, i don't know, but i would rather be your girlfriend than you be my
boyfriend - i don't know if that's a double standard, i guess so
so whenever you get the chance please tell me about your

hallucinations, i want to know everything
i hesitate to write XO - it seems so redundant at this point

Image: Soledad Miranda and Ewa Strömberg in Jess Franco's *Vampyros Lesbos*

from Bruno

Zivancevic Nina <zivancevicn65@gmail.com>
To: Marc Léger <leger.mj@gmail.com>
31 March 2015 at 19:38

hi!

*"i thought i would start with just a hello letter and then if Bruno is
interested in my work and wants to invite me i can send something more
precise - time wise, title wise and with an abstract - i didn't assume that
there was anything certain and so i thought to give him the chance to
reply..."*

This is how the story starts, and then in its elliptic and quasi entropic
manner it unfolds, always in folds and shedding its skin like a new-born
Cobra, the crawling Queen snake..
and yet and more and still-- are yet to come!
so the recipient of these letters appears to be just the innocent victim of..
Bruno!!

I have no desires at this point- and my nightmares and hallucinations
have been- just about the fact that I will wake up one day having no
desires
my only desire is to die
and before i accomplish this one- I would like to finish my book "I, Valida
Sultana" which talks about my life at the Persian court, 2005, where
I had to learn chess, strategy, riding Arab horses without saddle and
killing a gazele (a stupid remark) as it runs in front of me, how to play
santour without 4 fingers, how to ride a cloud and place all my web links
inside of it, how to seduce 400 maidens in my harem and run away with
my favorite eunuch, hopw to get Herat back from the Brits and then by
Russians, how to keep my cat/councelor always by my side, how not to
get poisoned at all 13 depts of la Sorbonne, etc etc
but one of these days, Marc, I will enter that tower of Supreme Silence,
and I will, like in Shirin's (Neshat)film leave my bones to the vultures and
become a good Zoro(astrian) again, no one will hear a word coming out
of my mouth, I'm gettinbg tired of this megagalore, and luckily, there are
people out there to replace me, look at my nephew, Dragan Zivancevic
who's a great subversive artist, against war government (LED Art
Group), Multiflex & Happy trash Production, they made many shorts like
Monkey Spa, they curate an interesting video festival "Medea" in Serbia..
where I'm heading just now, that is in two weeks and my son, Vlad,
who's definitively continuing my poetry/performance work and is the king
of every underground venue in Paris..
but I, how do i get to that tower of Supreme Silence? How do i get back
to my zigurat..? Yours Truly

Zivancevic Nina <zivancevicn65@gmail.com>
To: Marc Léger <leger.mj@gmail.com>
31 March 2015 at 20:08

good night , my dear friend, I shd really take care of my Kantor
conference- had a weird meeting with the director of that project today
who kept asking me- "but where do you see Kantor's censorship, that
is auto-censorship?" I was appalled: like he never understood his entire
work, Dead Class etc.. what's the world we live in? I must say, the only
writing creature that i really feel close to is Will Firm, he is like Swift who
spoke of selling the babies at the market instead of pigs...

Tr : PROGRAMMATION MARS

Zivancevic Nina <nzivancevic@ymail.com>
To: jerome carassous <editionsnonlieu@yahoo.fr>, "nonlieu@netcourrier.
com" <nonlieu@netcourrier.com>, "leger.mj@gmail.com" <leger.mj@
gmail.com>, "giancarlo.pizzi@wanadoo.fr" <giancarlo.pizzi@wanadoo.fr>
1 April 2015 at 08:11

Mon très cher Jérôme,
xcuse me:
(cc pour un être très proche à moi, Marc Léger et pour notre philosophe
présentateur Pizzi) je me pose la question
OU EST MON BOUQUIN, tellement beau et tellement cherché!!
Tout Paris lui annonce et nous sommes ici dans le programme de la
Maison de la Serbie
mais j'ai jamais EU MON LIVRE!!
Je pleure ici chez moi et person me voit, mais Jér^me, SVP il faut que je
tiens dans mes main ce objet d'art sinon
je vais penser que la viue est vraiment bette
bien à toi, Nina
tel 06 26 16 01 28

Marc Léger <leger.mj@gmail.com>
To: Zivancevic Nina <nzivancevic@ymail.com>
1 April 2015 at 09:27

OU est mon NINA ZZZ!!!??
okay, so you write to jerome
but here i am - très proche mais très loin:

Cher collègue, Il y a en effet un malentendu. Nous n'avons pas les
moyens d'une invitation. Je peux vous proposer une conférence
(payée) mais non financer un billet d'avion ou un séjour à Paris. bien à
vous Bruno Pequignot

please advise, cajole, subvert

Nina Zivancevic <nzivancevic@ymail.com>
To: Marc Léger <leger.mj@gmail.com>
1 April 2015 at 12:35

Marc , that's GREAT !!
Nobody pays airfare around here

If he's paying the conference that's already smth very good
Look- just say YES and don't compete with Zizek (we don't know
who's paying his air fares) I will take care of it ..(I imagine yr friend
will turn green and yellow and I feel sorry for her but that's the way
life goes) and I am sure that I can find another spot easily so u give a
performance/screening and earn some €€ from ticks and sold books
Ok? This is not yr continent where people still have more €€ or simply
more respect for the conference issues..(I was paid in the us the fare
and the honorarium etc so I understand yr reluctance)

Marc Léger <leger.mj@gmail.com>
To: Nina Zivancevic <nzivancevic@ymail.com>
1 April 2015 at 16:29

Nina, you're very kind but we already settled that and so it's not so
important for me to present my work over there - i will give it a few
days and tell Bruno thanks but nevermind, there was some kind of
miscommunication

Zivancevic Nina <nzivancevic@ymail.com>
To: Marc Léger <leger.mj@gmail.com>
1 April 2015 at 17:53

ok, never mind, perhaps that's not in our stars, but i don't believe in stars
and i make my own stars and destiny
and how can you say such an abberant thing that "it's not important that
you present yr work here"?
as if you lost yr mind..

Marc Léger <leger.mj@gmail.com>
To: Zivancevic Nina <nzivancevic@ymail.com>
1 April 2015 at 20:26

i think of Dean Moriarty ... i think of Dean Moriaaarty ...

who's your eunuch ?

Marc Léger <leger.mj@gmail.com>
To: Zivancevic Nina <zivancevicn65@gmail.com>
1 April 2015 at 09:51

yeah, okay, so you're pretty busy out there on the steps with all those
cocaine snorting mongols, past lives and empire of No desire, your life
at the Persian court with Toscanini - on s'est tous défilé n'est-ce pas -
but a meaningful stance? - now that's a psycho-onto-logico-hystyerico
problem for me - one day i will write it all down in our lassbook: The
Tower of Supreme Silence

Zivancevic Nina <zivancevicn65@gmail.com>
To: Marc Léger <leger.mj@gmail.com>
1 April 2015 at 12:19

But the meaningful stance...(u really know how to push all my buttons
you must be really French after all)
I sacrificed a lot for my idea(l)
And I cannot see myself indulging in the life that is like death to me and
tending to the zombie-like system of the us and so on.. All that' s already
described in Sylvere's anthology Hatred of Capitalism. Like there Christa
Wolf and... I, had a lot to say about yr doubts "is she dumb?" Is she
politically correct??
Love you, Marc
That's all for today - and that's already a lot..

Zivancevic Nina <zivancevicn65@gmail.com>
To: Marc Léger <leger.mj@gmail.com>
1 April 2015 at 12:10

See.. My eunuch is my consciousness
And Toscanini is not my boyfriend but my best friend
I haven't had a boyfriend , as I 've told you , eversince I parted with the
"Persian prince" . I promised him, swore on Holy books of all trades
That I wld never fall beneath our standard, and that was the case and
will be. Now, true, once I started reading yr books i read yr bibliography...
I started thinking that you were very close to me even above the
standard.. But this is
all blah blah
Cocaine I don't snort as I have a sinus problem
You can be very arrogant though and constantly jumping into
conclusions

My book about Persia is my love or my test of "my life with.." Isis?.. How can or where does East meet so called West It' s (like livingonair) an attempt to cover my investigative theory with the sugary coating of a say... Novel genre
Yeah sure, that YOU understand and that's why I love you
Mind you, I have NO idea how you look like
You may be a Quasimodo
You may be rolling in a wheelchair

Love,
(Your
Thought
Patterns)

Marc Léger <leger.mj@gmail.com>
To: Zivancevic Nina <zivancevicn65@gmail.com>
1 April 2015 at 16:40

Comrade Zivanshevik, my cover is over, Hatred of Capitalism is in fact where I found you. Christa Wolf I cited in my MA thesis c.1996 and lots of Easterners I met weren't happy about Cassandra - i knew when I read your poetry and put on the incense that there would come a time when you would email me and set me straight. From now on it's clean living, no more junk food for my little kitty

Envoyé de mon iAmAnAnarchist-iAmAnAnti-Christ-Don'tKnowWhatiWant
ButiKnowHowToGetIt-iWantToDestroy. ...

Zivancevic Nina <zivancevicn65@gmail.com>
To: Marc Léger <leger.mj@gmail.com>
1 April 2015 at 17:46

Wait a minute, Marc,
you're a star. It turns out that you're becoming a star here. Tonight I went to my association of poets from l'Harmattan and there was marianne Tadiou, whose dad (ach!!) is a bigwig at Paris 8, has a chair in philosophy and when I saw her.. it occured to me that she cld be the right person to ask for yet another gig of yours, this time at Paris 8 (as Bruno has already declared- no money no tickets)
So I exposed yr case, so to speak , in a slightly more elevated academic language, and as I had yr book - now the only one left in my bag on

Neolib zombie culture(s) I showed it to her, she snatched it away from me and said that she'd like to read it and then.. they cld decide.

Not bad, only now I have no books of yours with me which makes me very very sad. But, hey, seems you'll be quite a big star in this stale and intellectually abandoned neighborhood..

I mean if you had 2 paid gigs, that wld make yr traveling ends meet, right?

Now, I'm doing this promo work out of my cheap and ulterior motives, but ain't we all human somehow? Human too human as camarade N. would say..

At any rate, I am happy that you found me, my name in that book, contrary to my belief that Chris Kraus or Sylvere put a good word about my work and my persona and that you promised them somehow to find me in the web forest of life... (they always feel sorry for me as they think that my development got retarded by moving back to Europe, etc etc). Amazing! I hope I won't disappoint you, as indeed, I can clean up my bowl - when necessary, and write some meaningful or nonsensical stuff in a more elevated language, including the punctuation and proper sentence construction- for the ocassion.

I'm a nervous wreck right now and oddly enough, this is what I find in my mailbox tonite- ha ha- as if the marabou knew where to place his daily ad

see the attach here, someone finally who can embellish my days and det me free. Action guaranteed!

Now, also, am sending you something else from a daily, what my poor sisters on Rue Blondel have to go through.. There's a new law in France, now to be turned down i believe, that both the girls and their clients are punishable by law for their own kinky actions and fantasies..Who cld like such a state?

Now you tell me? Even my parakeets or yr kitties wldn't like this phoney baloney form of high Capitalism as exercised around here.. OK, enough, they can kick me out of this country as well..

I haven't eaten all day today and I have to correct students' exams all night long for tomorrow, 8am sharp-- wish me luck!

xxxxxxxxxxxxxxxxxxxxxxxxxxxxxxx

Zivancevic Nina <zivancevicn65@gmail.com>
To: Marc Léger <leger.mj@gmail.com>
1 April 2015 at 18:22

Anyways... Whatever happens next..for me this is and will be an extraordinary romantic literary friendship
You are MY Marc, a real hero from my very own picture book.

Marc Léger <leger.mj@gmail.com>
To: Zivancevic Nina <zivancevicn65@gmail.com>
2 April 2015 at 00:37

Image: Still of Juliet Berto from Jean-Luc Godard, *Le gai savoir*. Subtitle:
We can say all we want about what we see

Image: Still of Juliet Berto from Jean-Luc Godard, *Le gai savoir*. Subtitle:
If you want to see the world, close your eyes, Rosemonde

Zivancevic Nina <zivancevicn65@gmail.com>
To: Marc Léger <leger.mj@gmail.com>
2 April 2015 at 06:05

Goodmorning King of my heart--
perhaps i shd go and see a shrink again.. but just before i close my eyes
and see you again in a 3D tech (and i have no idea how you really look
like aside from that tiny photo plus short video , though tech is always
deceiving)
i wld like to write a "book", a piece w/ you-- when u have some time, it
cld be on anything involving everyone
yeah just our dialogues (it's already highly publishable
before we even started doing it) right this second:
my head is full of messy sleep
no i don't take drugs, can't afford them timewise moneywise
and there's withdrawal period.. which i cringe from and the worst thing
i've experienced
in my long life
however
i'd love to hear what u think about staring the dialogue, a theme, subject,
yes
and yes: i do understand yr time and the price u put on it
do i ever get to see you in person?
and how come i keep on writin writing to you
as if.. i had nothing else to do in this world
full of
obligation
obligation
obligation
one thing after another,
no time to breathe.. my Love birds, Bonnie and Clyde, have groovier
time than i do they keep on twittering twirping they're always together
and now i won't ever get to see you..

Marc,
you are my greatest Lacanian experience
you taught me about Desire first hand experience
just when i though i had none of it
i find myself looking at this stupid e box as if..
i think i'm lost, big way, i've lost it just when i started thinking that i got
my act
together
i shd cut on this obsession , you're probably getting tired
hasta la vista or
hasta le clic

Zivancevic Nina <zivancevicn65@gmail.com>
To: Marc Léger <leger.mj@gmail.com>
2 April 2015 at 06:41

Mais.. C'est moi , Léa, La chatte perdue..je cherche mon maître Marc,
qui m'avait abandoné devant le supermarche..

Envoyé de mon iPhone

Marc Léger <leger.mj@gmail.com>
To: Zivancevic Nina <zivancevicn65@gmail.com>
2 April 2015 at 08:53

ah yes, hello kitty
it was you all along,
looking for un homme sans contradictions
what's wrong with the air that you breathe ?
if you send me a picture of yourself in a Mao outfit
i will send you hi tech anything you want and an attachment
i want to include it in the write-up i'm preparing of you called: Heloise,
Why?
neoplatonic neoliberal poetry where two zombies duel over email
so what do you want to dialogue ?
how much more can a shrink think ?
i don't charge much and you can keep the royalties

Zivancevic Nina <zivancevicn65@gmail.com>
To: Marc Léger <leger.mj@gmail.com>
2 April 2015 at 17:01

Ah, I am sorry .. seems like I made a mistake
but in fact, i've known it all along
but in fact, YOUR very own speech does not seem sincere to me
the tone is cold and nasty
(am i to be scorned that i couldn't get you the round trip to the Eiffel
tower?)
anything less tall than that seems like "not enough" for you
you like cheep mountaineering as you usually climb to the top fast
perhaps
i cannot put up with these sorts of muddy water which varies
from "gracefully smart, submerged in devotion".to. "find me yet another
performance gig on the spot",
and sadly enough, when you're at yr funniest- that reeks of insincerity
then it becomes slightly offensive and i hear you giggling behind and
between yr clicks
your words sound great and smart and deep etc. - but who is to believe
them
ok ok i know, you're the king of transparency and we all admire that
streak in you
but you seem to be liking to dress me in some more opaque colors
no thank you, i've been through that sort of training
one thing escapes your lovely jovial head:
life is not a TV commercial
life is not a click
is it a trick or a "flic" though, I can't tell you now and
frankly you've had enough of my words and all sort of stories
however
I'll never regret we've had an amazing exchange (whatever you think of
it)
sorry if my post-midnight chat ever bored you to life
you can help yourself to yet another piece of my liver
as my heart stays intact for some other birds
look at these shiny feathers falling off
and i'm holding to a steady rock
by the sheer grace of my virtual existence

Marc Léger <leger.mj@gmail.com>
To: Zivancevic Nina <zivancevicn65@gmail.com>
2 April 2015 at 19:23

nina,
as if i don,t have enough problems - eating your liver, pulling your
feathers
and after the nice adjectives i though i had sent you: avant-byzantine
or have you forgotten
and what am i to think about your living theatre and all those videos you
post of yourself
belly dancing and poetessing
i'm only human
okay i suppose i might have been all those things in one instant of a
second
who are these people anyway you talk about who know my transparency
who have you been talking to ...
maybe you deserve something sincere from me
but as i am a poet you have to read my Verlaine style
TV commercials, mega-galore, as you so dismissively put it
so you rebuke my style
this is not about you and me it's about who is the cis-poet
n'est-ce pas Napolion ???
i admit it
i enjoyed every minute i pulled on your ponytails
and you blame me
you're my terrific friend
taking my words for cash
i did it all for you and who i think you are
and i guess i am now damned in our book
some figment of a correspondence
Kathy Acker had it all and you're stuck with this schmuck
but you call me a star
and then a schmuck
after i red you i knew you would email me and correct me
and i was looking forward to it
and i still am and i hope you get up at 2 am like i did last night
just to see what you're up to this time
j'accuse
tu accuse
elle accuse
nous accusons
i don't know what you're talking about another gig on the spot - i have no
such plans
i am gentle and thankful

a nice gazelle
and you go by with your sin-serity bow
and just like that - in my empty heart
as if i had anything to do with it
my one true fear is that you don,t know me
and what is this baloney: one thing escapes your lovely jovial head: life
is not a TV commercial; life is not a click
can you tell me that in Serbian ?
it helps to drive home the fact that life is not a poetry reading
poetry is poetry and life is life
and tv commercials are tv commercials
you can't just write nice things all the time
but of you course you will
you will keep writing and writing until you drop
but the question is, how many more drops for me
i went to an anti-austerity march today
and i was going to send you some photos
but i think that you should see these pictures of me
this is what i look like when I write to you
with the SI manual beside me
and i need it
and you can stop writing me if you need to
i understand, you're an important writer
but don't say bad things

Marc: do i look cold ?
Nina: Yes
Marc: Why are you writing about Istvan Kantor ?
Nina: I'm not, I'm writing about Jerzy Grotowsky
Marc: What do you think of all of his shot-counter-shot dialogue ?
Nina: I hate it — it's commercial. I hate capitalism
Marc: Whose you're eunuch ?
Nina: You, I suppose
Marc: I don't like Phillip Garrel
Nina: That doesn't surprise me
Marc: Don't hate me
Nina: I don't hate you, but I'm saving my heart for others
Marc: I,m not transparent
Nina: Yes you are
Marc: I guess so
Nina: Yeah

Image: [next page]

MJL at home in his kitchen.

Zivancevic Nina <zivancevicn65@gmail.com>
To: Marc Léger <leger.mj@gmail.com>
3 April 2015 at 04:19

thank you Marc
so what is this fucking email doing in my box
where you're calling me
a Neoliberal poet zombie etc
Perhaps I misread yr words but i don't think i did
i may be lots of things, Marc,
but stupid i am not unfortunately
my burden and my tragic outlook, i'm not..that stupid

Marc Léger <leger.mj@gmail.com>
To: Zivancevic Nina <zivancevicn65@gmail.com>
3 April 2015 at 09:09

this line
neoplatonic neoliberal poetry where two zombies duel over email
this line refers to two zombies
because in your stance and in you words i had already morphed into a
zombie
you didn't want what i was doing and asked for what i wasn't doing
so i figured if that was true then that's at least two of us
if you want to take lines one by one we can go through each
and i can offer interpretations to everything that could be used against
me
but i'm not in a self-defense class
but you are right - some of those lines are contentious
your poetry class made me carefree
and i see that for you i was simply careless
i don't even know you after all
suddenly
along the way you were encouraging and so i did not think there was a
problem
i laughed at our situation and the pleasure i was having writing you
i wish we could simply move on from here
but do you think it would even be possible or desirable ?
i will spend as many days and weeks as you like explaining myself
i want to do that because i don't want to loose my funny bird
i think you have no idea how fond i am of you
please don't leave our orbit
i will be more careful ?

Zivancevic Nina <zivancevicn65@gmail.com>
To: Marc Léger <leger.mj@gmail.com>
3 April 2015 at 08:06

Oh Marc.

Envoyé de mon iPhone

Zivancevic Nina <zivancevicn65@gmail.com>
To: Marc Léger <leger.mj@gmail.com>
3 April 2015 at 08:08

Killing you
It feels like a total suicide here

Zivancevic Nina <zivancevicn65@gmail.com>
To: Marc Léger <leger.mj@gmail.com>
3 April 2015 at 08:16

Perhaps I shd do it quickly
So I don't suffer for a long time

Zivancevic Nina <zivancevicn65@gmail.com>
To: Marc Léger <leger.mj@gmail.com>
3 April 2015 at 08:06

As you are so much... Like me, by killing the idea of you
Is like killing
My Other
Ka

Zivancevic Nina <zivancevicn65@gmail.com>
To: Marc Léger <leger.mj@gmail.com>
3 April 2015 at 08:16

Didnt u talk about some diagnosis?
What are u diagnosed for?
Can i take care of you?
Can i be yr surrogate mom?

Zivancevic Nina <zivancevicn65@gmail.com>
To: Marc Léger <leger.mj@gmail.com>
3 April 2015 at 08:05

And yes I am thankful
For yr endorsement
And yes I will supply a chapter to yr book
And how do I look behind my computer?
Tired, fucking tired
Excuse my language
Don't u see I'm crying
Right now
This very instant 12:35 my time

Zivancevic Nina <zivancevicn65@gmail.com>
To: Marc Léger <leger.mj@gmail.com>
3 April 2015 at 08:06

Oh.. My Marc..
Like there are two Marcs like..tale of 2 cities
I'm writing to marc no 1
So why dont u like Garrel?
i dont cause he climbed up through his dad's connections
What about Chris Marker?
Caviare de gauche
Ok Nina , u learn to love the whole world
No more schopenhauer sandwich for u.
Like that tshirt from Berlin said
Oh marc- that´s for you:
I used to be schisophrenic but
Now we are ok...

Marc Léger <leger.mj@gmail.com>
To: Zivancevic Nina <zivancevicn65@gmail.com>
3 April 2015 at 09:42

Death in Ninasville.
But what's with all the killing? Fill me in
We're crying together - like two sops.
Like, me crying with an important writer from an unknown
I look forward to your chapter
And your book was wonderful
i can be Marc no 1 but i don't think i'll even manage to get rid of Marc
no. 2, but i can keep him in the basement

Chris Marker is seraphim class
Nina Zivancevic, she has a t-shirt that says: F You
It takes a Garrel to laugh; It takes a Ninazee to cry.

Zivancevic Nina <zivancevicn65@gmail.com>
To: Marc Léger <leger.mj@gmail.com>
3 April 2015 at 10:06

And i still want you..
But that's my problème
I have to deal with it
Ill. snap out of it

Envoyé de mon iPhone

Zivancevic Nina <zivancevicn65@gmail.com>
To: Marc Léger <leger.mj@gmail.com>
3 April 2015 at 10:12

See who can get rid of you?
However ill see a shrink again to est me free from u
This hasent happened to me since
1999

Marc Léger <leger.mj@gmail.com>
To: Zivancevic Nina <zivancevicn65@gmail.com>
3 April 2015 at 10:30

i had a bad dream
all those images
through which i imagine you
as a symbol and a reality
was this jumping off a conclusion ?
is Nina 1 dreaming that she is Nina 2 dreaming that she is Nina 1 ?

Zivancevic Nina <zivancevicn65@gmail.com>
To: Marc Léger <leger.mj@gmail.com>
3 April 2015 at 11:25

Sorry you felt that way
I'm sort of embarassed because i'm experiencing utmost
Tenderness when i think of you
AND that's crazy as i dont really know you
But all the things that you've been
Sending to me-- i ve been experiencing them too or most of them
So i feel tenderness as if you were my younger long-lost brother whom i
found again
Funny that way--
"If we close our eyes, is that color blue less intense than the blue we
watch once we opened them?" (Bergson)
I think that you're doing some thing extraordinaire to me.. You bring me
back an illusion that i can be in love again, and that's great! I thought
i was done with it(thus my last Book "love is just a 4 letter word"(after
Beckett)
But then our correspondence started and i found myself totally
surprised..like i cld feel somerhing again, dont know what but..
Ok - a nice
Very nice day indeed to you

Marc Léger <leger.mj@gmail.com>
To: Zivancevic Nina <zivancevicn65@gmail.com>
3 April 2015 at 12:00

i bought you flowers
https://www.youtube.com/watch?v=1GWsdqCYvgw
[Nick Cave & The Bad Seeds, "Higgs Boson Blues"]

ninasville

Marc Léger <leger.mj@gmail.com>
To: Zivancevic Nina <zivancevicn65@gmail.com>
3 April 2015 at 02:47

it's a nice place
i really do love it here
it's very quiet right now
early in the morning
there's a sign on the edge of town
it reads: *I'll never regret we've had an amazing exchange (whatever you think of it) sorry if my post-midnight chat ever bored you to life*

Zivancevic Nina <zivancevicn65@gmail.com>
To: Marc Léger <leger.mj@gmail.com>
3 April 2015 at 04:28

I can't tell you what I've been through recently
to get you presentations and gigs in this helluva city
which Baudelaire called "putain" and son of a bitch
where they eat people alive in the name of Communism, Socialism etc
wait- I have a lot to say everything around here
turns into "caviare de gauche" and you get a bitter taste in yr mouth after
a while
and i want to bring Marc, my Marc, into this arena, to explain to them, to
sqome of them who're not dead yet but suffer from aberrant living, that
they cld do something else
look, whoever they are: Tancelin, Pequignot, Pizzi—they're OK people,
really OK so-- not in power, if we try to get you paid gigs and not the
plane tickets- that's already
something, i abhore snot and snotty attitudes
please
don't be that way with me
i have a lot to say
I AM THE RESISTANCE and we are resisting this modified secret ever
mutated form of capitalism
this virus is dangerous cause it's mutated and there's no cure for it
perhaps PODEMOS perhaps.. OK, wld be interesting for u to come over
here and talk to some people
i think it wld be perfect fr yr investigation of the folds, mutated folds of
Neoliberal values
Zee

Marc Léger <leger.mj@gmail.com>
To: Zivancevic Nina <zivancevicn65@gmail.com>
3 April 2015 at 09:37

it's more than something that you wanted and maybe still want me to go
over there
i don't necessarily know what you,ve been through in that regard and
i thank you for everything and everyone you have spoken to - i tried to
treat my exchanges with Bruno with the utmost courtesy and have not
yet responded to his last email - so i did not close off that possibility
in my delusional universe i take things one step at a time
i am every day on the edge of the abyss
i did not ask for gigs but i did dream with you about doing something
i even wanted to do one of these with you - i would have loved that
but this was your invention - this was your gesture
what i said was that if i go it has to be expenses prepaid
that is not arrogant that is simply my reality
i have debt and no way to pay it
i don't know how i manage
i don't really think about all the wonderful people over there that you
know
and that are part of what you are living through
i don't know them
maybe they are comrades
it's enough for me that they are your friends and colleagues
though you sometimes say big wigs and then i don,t know what
i hope that i remain yours
you can be sure that i do not only watch television all the time
and i had the chance to read your books and that was a pleasure for me

Zivancevic Nina <zivancevicn65@gmail.com>
To: Marc Léger <leger.mj@gmail.com>
3 April 2015 at 10:03

Ach! As if i wldnt know distress
I really wanted to send you airfare ticks out of my respect fr yr work
dummy, but i guess you misinterpreted my intention.
Please just as or like an elder sista
I'm begging you never ever to jump into conclusions and wallow in them
As u often do or it seems..

Marc Léger <leger.mj@gmail.com>
To: Zivancevic Nina <zivancevicn65@gmail.com>
3 April 2015 at 10:19

let me know when i'm wallowing
things look closer in the mirror

Zivancevic Nina <zivancevicn65@gmail.com>
To: Marc Léger <leger.mj@gmail.com>
3 April 2015 at 10:32

Hmmmmm. I know u have to have opinions – what's a poet without
opinions
But i admit now that i made a lot of mistakes out of opinions
I'm also waiting for a labor dépt trial
In September
A bad school owes me 15000 euros
Dickens and Swift together
When i went to court i told the judge: emil Zola's Germinal is a joke for
this school yr Honor
And as the adversaire didnot know of this author
The judge took some liking on me

Marc Léger <leger.mj@gmail.com>
To: Zivancevic Nina <zivancevicn65@gmail.com>
3 April 2015 at 10:45

Joseph K. territory
and one of the reasons i fell in love with Montreal
it's one of those Merz events
and political awakenings

Zivancevic Nina <zivancevicn65@gmail.com>
To: Marc Léger <leger.mj@gmail.com>
3 April 2015 at 11:06

What you read is what you later write..i grew up on Balzac he was my
hero
And dickens as well

They were real to me as much as you are
Now i have nô patience to read fiction
More later..

Zivancevic Nina <zivancevicn65@gmail.com>
To: Marc Léger <leger.mj@gmail.com>
3 April 2015 at 18:29

Thank you my dear .. and strange and nice evening it was--
I got a very nice letter from Gerard whom I lost, I thought I lost him in
NYC many years ago
and he sent me two brilliant excerpts from his Memoirs on Pierro Helitzer
and on Angus Mc Lise (the original Velvet Underground member),
I used to see Gerard every so often with Ira Cohen, many of my friends
gone and lost now,
then had a 4way Skype conversation that is, a virtual party
with Tim in Barcelona, Chris in London and Eddie Woods in Amsterdam
who tried to get us all on Twitter"s porn scene,
I felt rather strange and realized that i was a true romantic, trying to
reach a guy I've never met, miles away in Canada, the only person i wld
have sex with right now
thinking about a friend who told me once "Nina, Nina, everything's
happening in yr head and only in your head" as if i didn't have a body on
my own...
but THIS story is a proof that the ONLY thing that turns me on is a sort
of a social discourse or a theory i can relate to, and this shows how
damaged i am, instead of getting out and getting a soda in the street
or whatever comes along. a line to make you happy: if you don't go i 'll
never leave you... imagine a grid with a 1 000000 possible combinations
more like a maze of chance operations.. I run into the right opening
every 20 years ..like i've run into you... it's more conspicuous that John
Cage
it leaves me a chance to relate to someone i like
two or three times in a lifetime aside from the library of possibilities i've
admired eversince..
talking to you is like a semi-dream semi-awake state of mind, and now
that
you're becoming a definite hero of my everlasting library, I bathe in my
sweat and ask myself: was it just yesterday
when i felt sorry for the guy who starred in the film "Her".
Marc, are you a computer program?
who are you, my dear dear one? and,
yes, a very nice evening to you too!

Marc Léger <leger.mj@gmail.com>
To: Zivancevic Nina <zivancevicn65@gmail.com>
3 April 2015 at 19:59

WAR IS OVER! (You Want It)
i now can read signs that say Pierro Helitzer, Mangus Mc Lise and Ira Cohen
Ninasville has a lot of surprises
i for the most part get something here something there
not sure about john lydon's theory about "sorting out" the world
sorry for all this prefab, i know our publisher will want new stuff
i know that you would like something deeper but i'm not sure i can indulge
you're the writer and i'm the song and dance man

Zivancevic Nina <zivancevicn65@gmail.com>
To: Marc Léger <leger.mj@gmail.com>
4 April 2015 at 05:11

Hey, when i think of you and (me?) i always think of John and Yoko (that can go intyo our book..)
You are more important to me than Raul-- simply because yr handsome and he's ugly- let's face it, the girl has top make some sort of aesthetic choice
(this doesn't go into our book)
let me know if i ever get a chance to see you, or do i have to read you till the end of time? (not a bad choice either, and THIS can go into our book..)
xxxxxxxxxxxxxxxxxxx

Zivancevic Nina <zivancevicn65@gmail.com>
To: Marc Léger <leger.mj@gmail.com>
4 April 2015 at 05:16

thanks for pere Ubu and Xanakis stuff
don't be so snotty
you are a writer and i cld be.. yeah, a mystery girl
(my "transparency and telling it all"-- you know, is just a stance
i'm a totally different (we are OK now) person and.. on my way to the public library.. kissssssssssssssssssssssssssssssssssssssssssssssssssssss
sssssssssssssssssssssssssssssssssssssssssssssss

Marc Léger <leger.mj@gmail.com>
To: Zivancevic Nina <zivancevicn65@gmail.com>
4 April 2015 at 09:19

i am sending you a copy of the idea of the avant garde vol 1 by very slow boat

---

Zivancevic Nina <zivancevicn65@gmail.com>
To: Marc Léger <leger.mj@gmail.com>
4 April 2015 at 10:02

Oh.. Thank u so much, Marc! How come- are u scared that I won't be up to that task of contributing to vol 2 and that u have to coach me about it? Ok yes, u might be right
I'm a wastebin these days, shd sharpen my brain
And as to the books-- let the young PhD candidates sort our books and chronology, put them together on one shelf, they will already have so much work to do, material and data to collect on us—we'll be tougher for them than Voltaire an mme Chatelet or Pasternak and Marina tsvetayeva, Mayakovsky an lily brick
Etc etc etc
Boy ! Am I tired...

Marc Léger <leger.mj@gmail.com>
To: Zivancevic Nina <zivancevicn65@gmail.com>
4 April 2015 at 10:05

Orpheus: An Incongruous Thriller (Him and Her)
with Marc Léger and Marie Déa

Zivancevic Nina <zivancevicn65@gmail.com>
To: Marc Léger <leger.mj@gmail.com>
4 April 2015 at 10:44

Yeah I think I should translate a text of yrs or two for Orphee Rouge: check out- next issue will be edited by Toscanini and Graeber, I got David hooked on it but yeah- these are all my dear very very dear colleagues like you are just you are so special to me as you like this "play thing" , like me,

meaning: performance and theater an they are not into it
The more I read u the more I discover how similar we r I did not say
identical but so close almost incestuous and this fact will tear us apart
like any entropy that's not good fr yr stomac oh I love u in a library or out
of it merry Xmas Easter and any other day
To me it's a holiday wherever I get an email from u..

Marc Léger <leger.mj@gmail.com>
To: Zivancevic Nina <zivancevicn65@gmail.com>
4 April 2015 at 10:48

bon bon psychedellic
oh Nina ...
and if i call for you ... wait until it's over ...
i have an essay that i will ponder sooner or later - one of these days
when i get back to thinking about work ....
.... on art engagé and anarchism's love relationship with
communism - maybe a draft of it could be for OR and your friend no. 13
Toscanini
but you won't wear a Mao suit
been there done that you say
can i see the pictures ?

Zivancevic Nina <zivancevicn65@gmail.com>
To: Marc Léger <leger.mj@gmail.com>
4 April 2015 at 11:53

U just want to see me in a Mao suit?
U can watch Sava Andjelkovic video about Nina Z' s life an times-- there,
i was in Mao suit gangsta that i am
And some clips were posted on my website under "theater"
I cańt be promenading always in the same outfit and same vidéo , its
highlight was a young actress Tania in the role of Nina Zee and her
i mean my best line in there "and do i have to glue all the doctor's
prescriptions on yr brow so that you understand
How much i yearn to be free?"
Tania was great in that role...

Marc Léger <leger.mj@gmail.com>
To: Zivancevic Nina <zivancevicn65@gmail.com>
4 April 2015 at 13:03

sorry to disturb you
i would like to interview you eventually, ask you questions
really get into your craw

Zivancevic Nina <zivancevicn65@gmail.com>
To: Marc Léger <leger.mj@gmail.com>
4 April 2015 at 14:01

am a veery good mother
I stayed with the inquisition here in France because of him
His father also marc
Blackmailed me into staying or losing the kid
I've had a very unhappy life
well , that part of my life- is nothing to write home about!
but, where's my home? i don't have it,but listen:
will you be my home? now that you're my life and i've been writing all
these emails to you?
xxx

Marc Léger <leger.mj@gmail.com>
To: Zivancevic Nina <zivancevicn65@gmail.com>
4 April 2015 at 19:41

if you put it that way, what can i say, are you going to paint our apartment
all kinds of crazy colours - i like things minimal when possible but space
is always an issue

Zivancevic Nina <zivancevicn65@gmail.com>
To: Marc Léger <leger.mj@gmail.com>
5 April 2015 at 06:25

Ah, i detect a certain hesitant tone there,
no, how can i impose on yr space? That is, more than I already do,
I have a rococo boudoir here which, indeed I'd like to rent out and move
out of France but i was thinking of getting a place in Serbia, where i

come from (and i'm not so certain any longer) and where I belong?
I'll keep you posted!
but include, please, that final line in my poem- it's meaningless without it!
xxxxxxx

Marc Léger <leger.mj@gmail.com>
To: Zivancevic Nina <zivancevicn65@gmail.com>
5 April 2015 at 09:25

hesitant tone - after all these emails ?
one day i will interview you about Serbia, which is another part of the story
but right now, you know me, i'm thinking we also will need a photograph
but first i have to make sure i,m always on your good side

Zivancevic Nina <zivancevicn65@gmail.com>
To: Marc Léger <leger.mj@gmail.com>
5 April 2015 at 09:49

you mean we need a photographer?
that cld be that pink poodle from my novel

Yes

Zivancevic Nina <zivancevicn65@gmail.com>
To: Marc Léger <leger.mj@gmail.com>
4 April 2015 at 10:53

Darlin
It sends chills up my spine
- the very thought that you may be sendin these emails to 50 different
people
Jus changin names so my turn is no 23, after Chichi or no 45, just after
David Greaber.. With those funny links and click it and all...

Envoyé de mon iPhone

Marc Léger <leger.mj@gmail.com>
To: Zivancevic Nina <zivancevicn65@gmail.com>
4 April 2015 at 11:09

actually, click here is code language for no 23 - how did you know - so
smart and so in love with her iPhone

Zivancevic Nina <zivancevicn65@gmail.com>
To: Marc Léger <leger.mj@gmail.com>
4 April 2015 at 12:00

F-u Marcus Aurelius!!
(Oh How i'd love to do THAT!)
But anyways, stop pulling my pigtails
And start telling the truth!
Why dont u wear that Mao pijamas
I am dressed in basic ninila zee Colors

Envoyé de mon iPhone

Marc Léger <leger.mj@gmail.com>
To: Zivancevic Nina <zivancevicn65@gmail.com>
4 April 2015 at 12:47

yes, i put on my Mao pyjamas yesterday and went out there as usual
with my bathrobe
you know one thing about Badiou that you will like is that he thinks that
love transcends iPhone technology –
i found a copy of your CV online and i'm going to snoop it
have a nice dinner
at what restaurant are you right now ?
and in whose company ?
what what artist or academic or journalist ?
and don't forget i am your waiter
and we're putting on a guerrilla performance where you have to decide
tea or coffee

Marc Léger <leger.mj@gmail.com>
To: Zivancevic Nina <zivancevicn65@gmail.com>
4 April 2015 at 12:48

i started reading this yesterday while the MRI was spinning around
Chichi:

those of the disaffected youth who are articulate, however - for instance,
the Beat or Angry young men - are quite clear about the connection: their
main topic is the 'system' with which they refuse to co-operate. they will
explain that the 'good' jobs are frauds and sells, that it is intolerable to
have one's style of life dictated by Personnel, that a man is a fool to work
to pay instalments on a useless refrigerator for his wife, that the movies,
TV, and Book-of-the-Month Club are beneath contempt, but the Luce
publications make you sick to the stomach; and they will describe with
accuracy the cynicism and one-upping of the 'typical' junior executive -
Paul Goodman, Growing Up Absurd

it says: Mr Goodman has the analytical apparatus and theoretical
formulations of modern sociology, psychology, historiography and
aesthetics at his finger tips

Zivancevic Nina <zivancevicn65@gmail.com>
To: Marc Léger <leger.mj@gmail.com>
4 April 2015 at 13:40

My dear friend
Please take care of yr girlfriend
It seems that she needs u as much as we do
As it seems that's she's having as many health problems as i do
Xxxxxxxx

Zivancevic Nina <zivancevicn65@gmail.com>
To: Marc Léger <leger.mj@gmail.com>
4 April 2015 at 13:56

I am with my bébé , baby.
My 20year old son
And we are about to see Ernst toller play

Marc Léger <leger.mj@gmail.com>
To: Zivancevic Nina <zivancevicn65@gmail.com>
4 April 2015 at 15:10

i can see from your cv that you are who you say you are
second, about Marc James moralisé
i had to confess that i was inspired by one of my favourites, Georges
Seurat
i think our 1 in billions of billions of stars of a chance might have
something to do with our star-crossed paths
you for a short while worked with one Beat poet - a real optimist that one
and i worked for about the same amount of time for another, but a Beat
photographer
you probably never heard of him and we didn't stay in touch after i got
escorted out of Rochester by two bikers

Sent from my iLoveNinaZivancecic

Images: [next two pages]

Georges Seurat, *Le Cirque*, 1890-91.
Collection of the Musée d'Orsay, Paris.

Nathan Lyons, from the sequence *Riding 1st Class on the Titanic*, 1974-1999. Courtesy of Nathan Lyons.

Zivancevic Nina <zivancevicn65@gmail.com>
To: Marc Léger <leger.mj@gmail.com>
4 April 2015 at 19:03

ach ach!
i sent you a short poem and it's quite unsubstantial but Ginsbergian in its spirit- the old man loved me as much as u do, I guess, i was like his daughter and assistant and a secretary and a friend for the last couple of years of his life, now that he's gone, i miss him dearly as i miss my own father
we had so many things in common- he adored my accent of a Slavic girl- it reminded him of his mother, Naomi,
we had the same sense of humor (and you do, Marc!!)
a bit bitter, a bit sarcastic, "grinçant", but real
I'll never forget the day he asked me to join his court
he said now you should join us in Colorado, we need you over here , and i was just 20!
My own father freaked out but Allen calmed him down, saying "i'll take good care of her"-- which he did, he introduced me to the son of his publisher, Grove Press and I married into Grove Press, only to divorce 5 years later, i ran away with an Italian theater director, who subsequently became a Buddhist monk and is known now
as the Venerable Lama Shopa Sherpa, sends prayers my way, from time to time..

Zivancevic Nina <zivancevicn65@gmail.com>
To: Marc Léger <leger.mj@gmail.com>
4 April 2015 at 19:10

oh.. that was quite something!
pure expressionist theater at its best! Pure Toller, pure Hasenclaver, Jensen! AND you know
(or rather you don't) how picky i am-- I can't stand a semi-good performance just because
I devoted almost half of my life into studying/performing the
Expressionist theater..) I always go out after 5 minutes if something isn't "kosher", but yeah,
i haven't checked my emails in there
now, thank you for sending me my favorite painting
-- eversince i saw it i wanted to join-- not only the circus but i wanted to ride horses
as exemplified by the cover of my LIVING ON AIR...

De nina zi

Zivancevic Nina <zivancevicn65@gmail.com>
To: Marc Léger <leger.mj@gmail.com>
5 April 2015 at 14:26

And i'm doing my marc léger homework too. Which books should i get through a-zone now? They took those i had away "to read".

Envoyé de mon iPhone

Marc Léger <leger.mj@gmail.com>
To: Zivancevic Nina <zivancevicn65@gmail.com>
5 April 2015 at 15:11

Warning: You are now entering the fantasy zone.
Warning: You are now leaving the fantasy zone.

Zivancevic Nina <zivancevicn65@gmail.com>
To: Marc Léger <leger.mj@gmail.com>
5 April 2015 at 16:06

Thank u doctor. Now i know
I will never leave that fantasy zone with you. We can go within that zone wherever you want.
In fact, it feels like we are building a new recreational playground for our MJL-NZ think tank team
The humans will only have to say thank you , think tank team..

Dear denizens of Earth,
We are fortunate to announce
The arrival of our new ThinkTankTeam which came down to Earth with the sole purpose to enhence and preserve your fantasy
The TTT is a powerful duo consisting of our very own MJL and his female counterpart NZ. They say they are even capable of modifying your DNA cells into potent fantasy genes. They will stay with us on Earth for only 7 years in order to accomplish their mission..

Marc Léger <leger.mj@gmail.com>
To: Zivancevic Nina <zivancevicn65@gmail.com>
5 April 2015 at 16:20

We come in peace!

Image: Laurie Anderson with text: I think a lot of people in Washington are extremely suspicious of NASA

Zivancevic Nina <zivancevicn65@gmail.com>
To: Marc Léger <leger.mj@gmail.com>
5 April 2015 at 17:27

yeah it's a bumer i have to have my own performance on april 25 when Laurie has hers, oh Supermannnn
i'm pissed

Marc Léger <leger.mj@gmail.com>
To: Zivancevic Nina <zivancevicn65@gmail.com>
5 April 2015 at 18:33

lou reed (RIP) said that rock n roll can change the world

Zivancevic Nina <zivancevicn65@gmail.com>
To: Marc Léger <leger.mj@gmail.com>
5 April 2015 at 18:42

yeah but he died.. so now it's up to us, Marc, to replace these people

look at these impertinent people!

Zivancevic Nina <zivancevicn65@gmail.com>
To: Marc Léger <leger.mj@gmail.com>
4 April 2015 at 19:18

my editor now is asking me to translate a poem by Voltaire (!!) in two to five minutes!! i mean, he may think highly of me, but people can be really --too much!!

Bonsoir Nina,

Excuse-moi, j'ai oublié tout à l'heure de te demandé un petit service. Peux-tu traduire le petit poème de Voltaire ci-joint (et la référence). C'est pour un ami qui fait une conférence sur la tolérance au Panthéon dans quinze jours.

Merci,
Pusa,
Jérôme.

Dieu de tous les êtres,
De tous les mondes et de tous les temps,
Tu ne nous as point donné un cœur pour nous haïr,
Et des mains pour nous égorger.
Puissent tous les hommes se souvenir qu'ils sont frères !

Voltaire, Traité sur la tolérance, « Prière à Dieu »."

NO COMMENT....

Marc Léger <leger.mj@gmail.com>
To: Zivancevic Nina <zivancevicn65@gmail.com>
4 April 2015 at 19:54

i don't know if you're planning on staying up late but i can help you with that

God of all beings
Off all times and places
You did not give us a heart for haircuts
And hands to jack off
You get what you get
Amen

Marc Léger <leger.mj@gmail.com>
To: Zivancevic Nina <zivancevicn65@gmail.com>
4 April 2015 at 20:08

consider it done
that reminds me of the impertinent people here in this province where
you are now adored
in the April schedule for the cinématheque québécoise
they're quite clever
they have Françoise Durocher Waitress in there, in between the Black
Power Mixtape and Show People
that is with some special programming for April on the X-You-Go-Slav
Avant-Garde so tell me, which of these have you slept with ?

Dusan Makavajev
Zivojin Pavlovic
Vojislav Kokan (Coke can ?)
Dragoslav Lazic (sounds no fun)
Sava Trifkofic (Day of the Trifkovics)
Petar Arandjelovic (Petar, come here Petar)
Tomislav Gotovac (go to vacuum the karpet)

Zoran Popovic (must be related to zoron)
Vjekoslav Nakic
Slobodan Sijan
Bojana Vujanovic
Miodrag Torana and Mirko Avramovic
Nikola Duric
Ljubomir Simunic (in québec, we say simonac)
Ivan Obrenov
Radoslav Vladic
Bojan Jovanovic
Miroslav Bata Petrovic

i,m going for a walk: the theatre of the oppressed

Zivancevic Nina <zivancevicn65@gmail.com>
To: Marc Léger <leger.mj@gmail.com>
5 April 2015 at 06:50

How dare you! Cld it be true that my rococo stance and bluff you take
for smth real?
I can tell you who these people are or some of them..but why do you
think that i sleep with anyone i meet?
We pushed our jokes very far that's true
but cmon we can be also on "vous"
for common knowledge:

Dusan Makavajev GENIOUS filmmaker, quite avant garde
Zivojin Pavlovic communist party bébé (got everything with a party card)
Vojislav Kokan (Coke can ?) Coke can
Dragoslav Lazic (sounds no fun) could be fun
Sava Trifkofic (Day of the Trifkovics) got his gigs with a party card
Petar Arandjelovic (Petar, come here Petar) cld be watchable
Tomislav Gotovac (go to vacuum the karpet) nothing under the carpet,
cld be great

Zoran Popovic (must be related to zoro you know who)
a close friend, founder of our Fluxus and pal of Marina Abramovic
Vjekoslav Nakic don't know
Slobodan Sijan true blue , the right account of civil wars
Bojana Vujanovic (no, you didn't ?!) don't know her
Miodrag Torana and Mirko Avramovic bearable
Nikola Duric don't know
Ljubomir Simunic (in québec, we say simonac) don't know
Ivan Obrenov
Radoslav Vladic
Bojan Jovanovic watchable
Miroslav Bata Petrovic
a real hero not to be confused with
Alexandar Petrovic, true avantgarde but not included
where's that Srdjan Dragojevic ("Gay Parade") , the most important
filmmaker as of today, who was supposed to be a one-night stand but
left me in a car while we were driving to Novi Sad, he went out at the
gas station to get a drink and left me in a car for 5 hours, i slapped him
verbally when he returned
but had no desire to share a hotel afterwards
I'd say from all of them- stick with Dusan Makavejev, he's the REAL one

Marc Léger <leger.mj@gmail.com>
To: Zivancevic Nina <zivancevicn65@gmail.com>
5 April 2015 at 09:39

okay, i take your word for it, Makavajev, but if i do that i think i will
become some kind of jelly fish with antennae and mashed potatoes that
sends love notes to Serbian writer with a please let me in the party card
- life is so strange and wonderful

Zivancevic Nina <zivancevicn65@gmail.com>
To: Marc Léger <leger.mj@gmail.com>
5 April 2015 at 09:44

areyou going to that fest?
who's the selector(s)???
i think Srdjan (the lost hotel guy)
is the best but he's not in this selection

Marc Léger <leger.mj@gmail.com>
To: Zivancevic Nina <zivancevicn65@gmail.com>
5 April 2015 at 09:46

i have to go, what are you crazy ?
it's a hommage to us - news travels fast

Zivancevic Nina <zivancevicn65@gmail.com>
To: Marc Léger <leger.mj@gmail.com>
5 April 2015 at 09:55

yeah, but who's the selector?
(it's a mix of rightwing and leftwinged creatures)
if u give me the name of the selector i'll tell you -- oh
everything about that fest

Marc Léger <leger.mj@gmail.com>
To: Zivancevic Nina <zivancevicn65@gmail.com>
5 April 2015 at 10:01

i looked it up and they don't say, so it must be someone who works for the CQ, which makes sense in this case as i am paranoid and sometimes drunk and i really do think they're onto us, which is really sweet, don,t you think ?
they also have l'avant garde croate des années 60 with Lordan Zafranovic, Ivan Martinac and Tomislav Gotovac (wasn't he Serbian a minute ago?)

Zivancevic Nina <zivancevicn65@gmail.com>
To: Marc Léger <leger.mj@gmail.com>
5 April 2015 at 10:05

yeah... lets do our interview
i know a lot about these absurdities
he was nazi yesterday
today he's a star in brazil or argentina
like klaus barbie (not that barbie doll)
but if u do an interview with me- you'd be tapping into smth truly important and AG (avantg)

Marc Léger <leger.mj@gmail.com>
To: Zivancevic Nina <zivancevicn65@gmail.com>
5 April 2015 at 10:18

sorry, but all i can think of while we do out interview is me in your boudoir painting your toenails pink

---

Zivancevic Nina <zivancevicn65@gmail.com>
To: Marc Léger <leger.mj@gmail.com>
5 April 2015 at 10:55

ha ha ha
hmmm why did she ROSIKA divorce you?
too much kink?
(love it though)..

Marc Léger <leger.mj@gmail.com>
To: Zivancevic Nina <zivancevicn65@gmail.com>
5 April 2015 at 11:28

rosika is hungarian - that should tell you all you need to know ...

Zivancevic Nina <zivancevicn65@gmail.com>
To: Marc Léger <leger.mj@gmail.com>
5 April 2015 at 11:47

Oh i dont understand
A new racial théorie ?
Like she is too much into goulasch and you.. Into sushi??

Marc Léger <leger.mj@gmail.com>
To: Zivancevic Nina <zivancevicn65@gmail.com>
5 April 2015 at 11:56

stereotypes ...

Zivancevic Nina <zivancevicn65@gmail.com>
To: Marc Léger <leger.mj@gmail.com>
5 April 2015 at 12:03

Oh youve seen that roseisaroseis video of mine?

Marc Léger <leger.mj@gmail.com>
To: Zivancevic Nina <zivancevicn65@gmail.com>
5 April 2015 at 12:48

Samantha McCheese,
no, which video is that ? - but i promise you
i am looking into all of this
don,t be distraught and hang up
because i have not yet written some sapphic porno-poetry to you today
or worse
you know that i am here for you building your self-esteem and destroying

your literary career
one email at a time
but it takes time to destroy properly
especially the part with you tied up for 5 hours
are there any writings from that era ?
i'm working for you, don't worry
gonzo interview

Zivancevic Nina <zivancevicn65@gmail.com>
To: Marc Léger <leger.mj@gmail.com>
5 April 2015 at 13:03

Dear doctor Joe-Schmoe,
I tried to End our sessions
But instead of seeing you twice a week, now i realize it has to be twice a day.
You know that i always come on time and just for you.yes
I've been building yr analytique career and you've been recovering my self-esteem. Yet another ballad of emotional dependency..and i lived without it for 12 years! I thought that i was cured. But nô, here i go again.
I was "cured" but i didn't feel happy.
Now i'm out of my closet again
Like that scum conchita wurst or Elizabeth wurlitzer
Please have mercy on me cause
I'm really fucked up

Marc Léger <leger.mj@gmail.com>
To: Zivancevic Nina <zivancevicn65@gmail.com>
5 April 2015 at 13:37

i feel just like you - 12 years a slave
and i thought i was cured of 'affect theory'
but who let you out the closet ? i gave strict orders
i warn you (hi hi) i'm not one of those Almodovar men who cheat on their wives
and send them to the mental hospital
i'm allegory of freedom and you are Marie Madeleine, no ?
sorry, my literary and drama references are next to zero
isn't this what Pasolini wanted all along ?
again, i'm doing my NZee homework very soon and will get back to you with questions

---

Zivancevic Nina <zivancevicn65@gmail.com>
To: Marc Léger <leger.mj@gmail.com>
5 April 2015 at 14:30

Darlin
Roseisaroseis is on my website ninazivancevic.com
Theater section
Je t'embrasse bien fort mon cher marie-François dit
Voltaire

Marc Léger <leger.mj@gmail.com>
To: Zivancevic Nina <zivancevicn65@gmail.com>
5 April 2015 at 16:41

The TTT team, now known as TTTT, is proud to announce that Moon
Unit NZ will be kept in a padded PVC metro car with only her iPhone
and a box of crackers for several days until her publisher Laurent Lafont
gives in and begs us to sign a contract for a series of research papers
on wurlitzer.

Zivancevic Nina <zivancevicn65@gmail.com>
To: Marc Léger <leger.mj@gmail.com>
5 April 2015 at 17:31

ha ha ha ha!
one more joke from our Jupiter James satelite
and Moon Unit is going to dangerously ap^proach his orbit!
she may even show up at his door with that box of sesame crackers and
some Whiska cat food to sustain her in exile..

Marc Léger <leger.mj@gmail.com>
To: Zivancevic Nina <zivancevicn65@gmail.com>
5 April 2015 at 18:35

another alien abduction - oh well ...

Zivancevic Nina <zivancevicn65@gmail.com>
To: Marc Léger <leger.mj@gmail.com>
5 April 2015 at 18:48

Voltaire,
you're getting very willy-nilly on this matter...
I avoid looking at yr pics because.. oh well, never mind, according to
Lacan, sex does not exist. Did you know that?

please girl

Zivancevic Nina <zivancevicn65@gmail.com>
To: Marc Léger <leger.mj@gmail.com>
5 April 2015 at 09:53

shit! have 15 min to my name, i'm a mess , hair and all the rest, shd take
a shower AND WHAT NINA FINDS AS THE EASIEST THING TO DO?

TO WRITE EMAILS TO MARC!
(mind you , this not so much anodine habit has been already criticized by
most of my friends who come and go like "poor nina, she's writing to that
can,adian guy again",
and "nina, can you talk to me just for a second, this has to be done right
now, ARE you writing to that guy Marc, again?")
they get worried..

Zivancevic Nina <zivancevicn65@gmail.com>
To: Marc Léger <leger.mj@gmail.com>
5 April 2015 at 10:14

eye of my eye
i'lll have to write to u from
my eye-phone
i keep it handy just for u
(in case u wish to write to me while in a shower or on a subway or on
the toilet etc)

Marc Léger <leger.mj@gmail.com>
To: Zivancevic Nina <zivancevicn65@gmail.com>
5 April 2015 at 10:29

actually, an anodine habit is one of the things i had in mind
you are always reading my emails
have a nice trip and think only of me

Zivancevic Nina <zivancevicn65@gmail.com>
To: Marc Léger <leger.mj@gmail.com>
5 April 2015 at 11:23

Back to my Eye phone..
Ohh where are you Marc James
So thirsty so funny and handsome..
You make me so weetttt
Unbecoming to my age
But because of you..
I'll become a little girl again
In toutous and high socks
Sliding along the shady docks
Of paree , montreal and berlin
Ohhhh just let me in please
Let me iiiiiiin
(End of Song 1, to be incorporated into our Book)

Envoyé de mon iPhone

Marc Léger <leger.mj@gmail.com>
To: Zivancevic Nina <zivancevicn65@gmail.com>
5 April 2015 at 11:35

it's really not what i had planned - it just happened that way - i see you
much more mature and respectable - maybe in the zone of the Violent
Femmes or Siouxie --- any of these accoutrements will work fine in our
duet lecture-performance - and as it happens, you have to explain to me,
is this selection of high socks a matter of absolute knowing, reason or
ethical being - now i'm really confused

Zivancevic Nina <zivancevicn65@gmail.com>
To: Marc Léger <leger.mj@gmail.com>
5 April 2015 at 11:54

I feel sorry for myself as u reserved such a boring respectable and
mature rôle for me! I dont want it
I want to run around and break my knees on skates etc
I dont wanna none of dat serious stuff

Zivancevic Nina <zivancevicn65@gmail.com>
To: Marc Léger <leger.mj@gmail.com>
5 April 2015 at 21:28

It's three o'cmock in the morning (cmok means kiss in Serbian) and i read all yr emails..
You know, it's so rare for me to be talking to someone at the same wavelength, honestly I haven't believed that it cld ever happen to me again but ahoy ! Life is short but also it's very long..who is the person who wrote about this encounter, I'm just curious..

serious stuff

Zivancevic Nina <zivancevicn65@gmail.com>
To: Marc Léger <leger.mj@gmail.com>
5 April 2015 at 10:03

here's the place where we shd place our novel, no shit, interviews in a
form of memoire monography
working title
VOLTAIRE- MME DE CHATELET 2015
Laurent Laffont
is our guy, lit director of Laffont editions
we need him, he needs us (other others are worse than us, including
Houellebecq..
i'm running through all my cards with emails, gotta invite them to my
launch coctail party for Plane Sonnets
than i take a plane to Belgrade
any use to u, camarade Legerovich?

Marc Léger <leger.mj@gmail.com>
To: Zivancevic Nina <zivancevicn65@gmail.com>
5 April 2015 at 10:17

yes, absolutely and you must think like me because you start with a
title - i usually start with an image for the cover - and i love Voltaire
- Mme Chatelet - let me know how this goes - but that changes my
really modest proposal which was to interview you and do a photo
shoot (the photo shoot was the most important part - the cart and the
horse) and i thought it should be on this web site, the end of being
(http://theendofbeing.com) - why ? i cant say i know why but they did
have something on Ginsberg a while back and on Garrel's film with
Nico so that must be what i was thinking for us - so what i will do in the
meanwhile, while you rush off to catch your plane, is catch up with you
based on online sources - but this Laffont is a publisher of children's
books or what ?

Zivancevic Nina <zivancevicn65@gmail.com>
To: Marc Léger <leger.mj@gmail.com>
5 April 2015 at 10:32

cmon Marc! you don't know who Laffont is? ohhh
ok, an offshot is LATTES
in the meantime

I'"m sending you smth, a fest of south-east european film, that cld be referential to you, im sure(see i started working for u and on yr behalf) have a lovely day

---

Marc Léger <leger.mj@gmail.com>
To: Zivancevic Nina <zivancevicn65@gmail.com>
5 April 2015 at 10:54

what's great about these films is that they all apply to us - the universal case of and the new genre of krush fiction as it will come to be known

---

Zivancevic Nina <zivancevicn65@gmail.com>
To: Marc Léger <leger.mj@gmail.com>
5 April 2015 at 11:41

Tell yr mom there's a French girl madly upset about you (yes in fact i'm french now)
They're gonna think that i'll make u brush up on yr manners
And ask yr mom if you shd visit me in Paris (dont tell her i'm only 6 years old)
I have to work though-- i may have already checked into airport but my trip is after my conference In 10 days

---

Marc Léger <leger.mj@gmail.com>
To: Zivancevic Nina <zivancevicn65@gmail.com>
5 April 2015 at 11:52

more honestly
you should carry a drill with you at all times
maybe for the cover of our book

Zivancevic Nina <zivancevicn65@gmail.com>
To: Marc Léger <leger.mj@gmail.com>
5 April 2015 at 12:00

Ach.. I can go worse than that.. But u r such a serious indépendant scholar
U didnot read my story about the empire of PVC and me tied up to a bed

for 5 days .. Like a kitty cat
Those days are over
And inside my leather outfit.. Ill send u some pics i keep stickers "fight
aids"
But the image the face is really mine here.. Where did u get it?

Marc Léger <leger.mj@gmail.com>
To: Zivancevic Nina <zivancevicn65@gmail.com>
5 April 2015 at 12:03

Instagram of l-u-v-e

Zivancevic Nina <zivancevicn65@gmail.com>
To: Marc Léger <leger.mj@gmail.com>
5 April 2015 at 17:19

hey hey- the end of being is such a great place to be seen it has Allen ,
Brian Gyson, Jodorowski etc many people i've loved and admired
please, ask me about all of them! yeah, let's do something funky like that
and here's my pic where i really look like a bmovie goddess (credit Kiki
Faeh) i donno.. will look for some other pics..

Attachment: Several images of NZ

Marc Léger <leger.mj@gmail.com>
To: Zivancevic Nina <zivancevicn65@gmail.com>
5 April 2015 at 18:31

oh LA REINE - this interview will write itself - who was that crazy person
who left you in the trunk of a car for 5 days ?

Zivancevic Nina <zivancevicn65@gmail.com>
To: Marc Léger <leger.mj@gmail.com>
5 April 2015 at 18:39

that was SRDJAN DRAGOJEVIC, Serbia's leading filmmaker , author
of "The Parade" and other valuable films.. as to me- an asshole in his
prime!!

He preferred a bar, that is a couple of votkas, or perhaps he was gathering courage for the car's back seat, will never know except that --it didn't sit well with me..
but—aren't u supposed to be with yr mom? na na na, are you THE biggest joke in our TTT org?

Marc Léger <leger.mj@gmail.com>
To: Zivancevic Nina <zivancevicn65@gmail.com>
5 April 2015 at 18:58

back to you later - thanks for all the ideas and i have of course to do more studying before being suitable, but i will commit to that and ever so nice to be in second order cybernuttics and padded cell with you all this time - like Marc Augé wrote about our poetics of encounter

---

Zivancevic Nina <zivancevicn65@gmail.com>
To: Marc Léger <leger.mj@gmail.com>
5 April 2015 at 21:30

Who's Marc augé and when and where he wrote the indescribable? He must be quiet a poet himself..

Fwd: Colloque Kantor-programme (version finale), invitation au déjeuner

---

Zivancevic Nina <zivancevicn65@gmail.com>
To: Marc Léger <leger.mj@gmail.com>
6 April 2015 at 06:47

DARLING: THIS HAS TO BE DONE CORRECTLY:
I'M NOT ANSWERING PHONE NOR MAILS (EXCEPT FR YOU OF
COURSE)
my funny Valentine...
your TTT team

Marc Léger <leger.mj@gmail.com>
To: Zivancevic Nina <zivancevicn65@gmail.com>
6 April 2015 at 08:46

good morning - cmok - let me know if you want to see the interview
between Badiou and Kouvelakis and yes, marc augé - this is the book
"in the metro," which i bought Chichi when she first came to Montreal - it
describes "non-places" like airports and the city spaces of what some
people started to call "krush modernism" around the 2000s - thanks
for the document you sent - i think i have my first question but will wait
to send these to you after your conference - you have such a nice
intellectual life and what more could a member of society want - oh
yes and also i woke up in the middle of the night - was woken up - and
what flashed to my half closed eyes was your email avatar, like it is now
circulating in my mental positrons

Zivancevic Nina <zivancevicn65@gmail.com>
To: Marc Léger <leger.mj@gmail.com>
6 April 2015 at 09:18

Ay ay ay .. What a schisophrene culture, society we live in..you were
woken up by yr lover in the middle of the night only to read or glance at
my email...look i have no pretensions, i cannot expect you not to have
a lover- i'm walking into this mise-en scene out of the blue, deus ex
machina, and likewise ,, only i cant have a lover as i'm a perfectionist
and i've been looking for the member of my TTT eversince the old
one declined membership in 2005 but yeah, i've tried at least to be
professional and serious and yes,
I'll try not to be sad because you are not around for a lively dialogue
about it
Big cmok and the rest.. It's a lovely sunny day here and over there?

Zivancevic Nina <zivancevicn65@gmail.com>
To: Marc Léger <leger.mj@gmail.com>
6 April 2015 at 09:20

Yeah i want that Augé interview badly..
And some of yr books as well

From "Kittie cat"

Zivancevic Nina <zivancevicn65@gmail.com>
To: Marc Léger <leger.mj@gmail.com>
6 April 2015 at 13:51

And as to "the intellectual life of Paris " that's why i'm here eating shine
and crayola shit and potatoes You can join me and try it for yourself but i
dont think that you'd really like it after a while

Kittie

Zivancevic Nina <zivancevicn65@gmail.com>
To: Marc Léger <leger.mj@gmail.com>
6 April 2015 at 13:45

This is me as à "kitty cat"

Image: Black panther growling

Marc Léger <leger.mj@gmail.com>
To: Zivancevic Nina <zivancevicn65@gmail.com>
6 April 2015 at 13:46

hello, little putty tat

Marc Léger <leger.mj@gmail.com>
To: Zivancevic Nina <zivancevicn65@gmail.com>
6 April 2015 at 14:56

doctor Divancevic,
i love this Kirchner painting i saw last winter - please psychoanalyze me

---

Image: [next page]

Zivancevic Nina <zivancevicn65@gmail.com>
To: Marc Léger <leger.mj@gmail.com>
6 April 2015 at 15:09

How do u want me to analyze you?
Ontologically or ontically?
Within the Lacanian frame or Freudian one? (I did not say jungian) as we
know it all .. In fact Lacan was pure Freud no chaser..
So my love, at any given moment,
I have Benjamin's photo on my computer
And sooner or later i am also going to commit suicide
I just want to ask u one thing before i die tonite: why wld we
Why shd we expose our correspondence to the public (the last part of
the interview)?
Marc... Oh Marc!!

Ernst Ludwig Kirchner, *Artistin Marcella*, 1910.
Courtesy of the Brücke-Museum, Berlin. Photo by Roman März.

Marc Léger <leger.mj@gmail.com>
To: Zivancevic Nina <zivancevicn65@gmail.com>
6 April 2015 at 16:25

yes, please analyze
in social class terms only
and explain to me why i always have the urge to lick my paws and why
when i want to vomit hair balls i always do it on the carpet
please in your report cite the works
Plekhanov, Voronski, Crnjanski, Bulgakov and Plath

okay so if you don't want me to chase you around and around and
around our interview you can edit the last part as is befitting our secret
affair and thereby evade being fired from the collège, you can edit me,
anyway you want

Zivancevic Nina <zivancevicn65@gmail.com>
To: Marc Léger <leger.mj@gmail.com>
6 April 2015 at 16:28

Phew!

Envoyé de mon iPhone

Zivancevic Nina <zivancevicn65@gmail.com>
To: Marc Léger <leger.mj@gmail.com>
6 April 2015 at 16:30

Now i'm womitting my
Haïr balls!
Where's that secret love affaire ?
I Mean the secrecy?
I mean the love?
And quite some affaire !

Marc Léger <leger.mj@gmail.com>
To: Zivancevic Nina <zivancevicn65@gmail.com>
6 April 2015 at 16:37

Louise, of course our love affair with iPhone and funny emails

---

Zivancevic Nina <zivancevicn65@gmail.com>
To: Marc Léger <leger.mj@gmail.com>
6 April 2015 at 17:09

dont be so condescending..
meaning- I've been a real Howard Devoto answering all the impossible
questions..
there are some eschatological reasons for all this..
but there have been zillions of reasons
ok *on reprend*
there was something in me that needed you, really badly
and there was something in you that needed me..
but why turn it into a public testimony,
now i'm coming to think.. that you really see all this as a big joke...

Zivancevic Nina <zivancevicn65@gmail.com>
To: Marc Léger <leger.mj@gmail.com>
6 April 2015 at 17:21

yes, please analyze in social class terms only

OK here we go: You like the painting because you feel like that violated
little girl who has to suck far too many dicks for money
her only consolation is the cat and some wine (lots of wine on the table)

and explain to me why i always have the urge to lick my paws

you may wish to clean up yr act or take so many baths in a day or...oh,
Marc.. Marc: and why

when i want to vomit hair balls i always do it on the carpet

there comes in an inherent hate towards all middle-class carpet values
(you've seen enough of them) and to you a carpet may be the place of
rape, spiritual, intello, physical, I don't know
there is something utterly fragile that i'd like to protect in you, in me
eventually, and that's already bien dit when i communicate with you, i
communicate with that fragile part of myself
--so as not to repeat myself.. "this is in my view the ultimate narcissistic
love or relationship that we are developing" dig it?

Marc Léger <leger.mj@gmail.com>
To: Zivancevic Nina <zivancevicn65@gmail.com>
6 April 2015 at 18:00

i thought that bouddhists were supposed to have no attachments in
their emails -- that's why the bouddhist said to the hot dog vendor: make
me one with everything -- the Master said: I've never met anyone so
thoughtless in all my life. Keep up the good work. Margarita said: Thank
you, Master.

Marc Léger <leger.mj@gmail.com>
To: Zivancevic Nina <zivancevicn65@gmail.com>
6 April 2015 at 18:10

*OK here we go:You like the painting because you feel like that violated
little girl who has to suck far too many dicks for money her only
consolation is the cat and some wine (lots of wine on the table)*

that's wrong

*you may wish to clean up yr act or take so many baths in a day or...oh,
Marc.. i*

lick or click ?

*there comes in an inherent hate towards all middle-class carpet values
(you've seen enough of them) and to you a carpet may be the place of
rape, spiritual, intello, physical, I don't know*

Poem for Nina Zivancevic

the are known knowns
unknown unknowns
known unknowns
and vacuum cleaners for that
– Vanessa Place

*there is something utterly fragile that i'd like to protect in you, in me
eventually, and that's already bien dit when i communicate with you, i
communicate with that fragile part of myself --so as not to repeat myself..
"this is in my view the ultimate narcissistic love or relationship that we
are developing" dig it?*

say no more

Zivancevic Nina <zivancevicn65@gmail.com>
To: Marc Léger <leger.mj@gmail.com>
7 April 2015 at 03:57

yeah, now me and my birds, they wake me up every morning as they fly all over my place..
but Marc, should i be that bird in your kitty-mouse?
seems we never get out of our old patterns:
Confession 1
yesterday I showed yr photo from PM Aesthetics to my girlfriends:
they asked me- "what's Marc (Sorrodjé, my father's son) doing on yr computer again?"
that's one of the answers for my overall clicking..
I'm such an inveterate sucker for the emotional clicks- clacks,
have to go back to school
speaking of which
I have to take care of my conference, and yes, once I'm done I'll certainly
get to out interview and
the rest (the Agarde contribution if you still will)
yours (is tis still necessary)---

Marc Léger <leger.mj@gmail.com>
To: Zivancevic Nina <zivancevicn65@gmail.com>
7 April 2015 at 08:43

i thought your conference was double duty for the AG book, no ?
in any case yes, the vol.2 book AG is AG and your contribution is essential
the interview also but you can think of the interview as now also essential
and i don,t want to overwork you with 6 emails in your inbox this morning or anything
yes, and that book cover was made by a young designer here in MTL
i mean, really Young - if you know what i'm saying

Zivancevic Nina <zivancevicn65@gmail.com>
To: Marc Léger <leger.mj@gmail.com>
7 April 2015 at 09:31

No i dont understand
mTL or MJL
Or T or TTT
Glad its not BhL...

Envoyé de mon iPhone

When I started loving you

Zivancevic Nina <zivancevicn65@gmail.com>
To: Marc Léger <leger.mj@gmail.com>
6 April 2015 at 14:25

It was after u told me your best heroine was ultra violet or candy darling
and i grew up with Jackie curtis and margo
Howard -Howard
I grew up with nyc drag queens
U can include this into our interview
..perhaps too many names, James?

Here i go again

Zivancevic Nina <zivancevicn65@gmail.com>
To: Marc Léger <leger.mj@gmail.com>
7 April 2015 at 09:08

Dear MJL , It was comfortable and comportable in our little nook, such a
cold academic world outside
I'm gearing up for the interview tonite,
Intellectual tour de force which will embarras people like https://www.
academia.edu/t/a-J17KGMb-Xv9MA/11728366/Jessica_Trevitt_Speaks_
to_David_Damrosch_World_ Literature_and_Translation

Envoyé de mon love you my

It's my pleasure an duty to receive yr future translator tomorrow for
lunch. He will bring me back yr books which i sorely miss as they served
instead of coffee table while serving hotdogs and donuts in my budoir.
So relax!
Dont read TS éléphant any more.
Bientôt tu vas être traduit dans tous les langues occidentes
And for the Chinese (torture)
And Japanese (hotdogs), we'll consult an expert in Hungary when they
visit Europe once a year
Yr camarade Zi

De moi

Zivancevic Nina <zivancevicn65@gmail.com>
To: Marc Léger <leger.mj@gmail.com>
6 April 2015 at 15:51

En plus
Are we entering again that master slave dialectics?
Why do i have to answer always yr questions? Why not u answering mine?
Why make public our private zone?
Ok i can answer it, but then again, you wont like it...
And if we are such a public team like John and yoko sharing a bed naked, why do we have to exchange so many private emails?
Lets make it all sparse and-- public

Marc Léger <leger.mj@gmail.com>
To: Zivancevic Nina <zivancevicn65@gmail.com>
6 April 2015 at 16:34

i don't think of the interview as anything so profound, but there is something at the end there with us hovering like a couple of UFOs

Zivancevic Nina <zivancevicn65@gmail.com>
To: Marc Léger <leger.mj@gmail.com>
6 April 2015 at 17:03

OK OKYOU...... won again!!
PS: I can't help it, twisting my fingers
now can i ask you a question:
IS this all some sort of joke for you? do you see me as a part of "life that's just a joke"? (all around the Watchtower) why are you pulling my invisible pigtails constantly?
do you see me as a joke?

Marc Léger <leger.mj@gmail.com>
To: Zivancevic Nina <zivancevicn65@gmail.com>
6 April 2015 at 17:54

for better or for verse, when someone said to me you should contact Nina Zivancevic for your book on the avant-garde, i went to talk to the prose to see what she's all about, that's when i knew i really wanted to meter; even if she is ad-verse to TV commercials i thought, a little click here and there and it would be like selling Peanuts to T.S. Elephant; for her i started writing poetry but i only made it to poe; i know that for her there's no place for knock knock jokes, all cats are red

---

Zivancevic Nina <zivancevicn65@gmail.com>
To: Marc Léger <leger.mj@gmail.com>
7 April 2015 at 04:27

so who was that "famous unknown" who suggested you contact me? (s)he did a good job
and i will answer yr TTT question correctly (i see that my alien TTT joke settled in yr mind)
but as they say- in every joke there's half truth or even the entire thing is a joke i mean truth, perhaps truth is some joke told in a fun(k)y way
i am moved that you had to consult our Master of verse, TS Elephant -just for me
see, i used to be a theorist like you then i became a poet
which is like being a marxist and then joining yet another church of Holy Poetry
no hot dogs and hot cats around here, only my hot birds flying all over the space

---

Marc Léger <leger.mj@gmail.com>
To: Zivancevic Nina <zivancevicn65@gmail.com>
7 April 2015 at 09:10

Lyrics for NZ

i tried to be creative in my offerings not too disappoint
i even consulted a thesaurus went to the funky goddess
offered her some kink, some think and some pink toes
she said come hither, if you want i will spare your life but don't tempt me
oh, I said, you must be that other person they call You and then it got confusing
there's no way out she said i am the city of eternal irony

Zivancevic Nina <zivancevicn65@gmail.com>
To: Marc Léger <leger.mj@gmail.com>
7 April 2015 at 09:37

Brilliant
You're improving
I myself will translate yr book of Poetry

To the

Zivancevic Nina <zivancevicn65@gmail.com>
To: Marc Léger <leger.mj@gmail.com>
7 April 2015 at 10:18

Sweetest sweepstake Master
This French kitty
Wants to cuddle with the canadien tyger...
Envoyé de mon i love you very much phone

Image: Pink kitten

Marc Léger <leger.mj@gmail.com>
To: Zivancevic Nina <zivancevicn65@gmail.com>
7 April 2015 at 12:43

the TTT team
unidentified purrrrrring objects

all manner of obscenities

Marc Léger <leger.mj@gmail.com>
To: Zivancevic Nina <zivancevicn65@gmail.com>
7 April 2015 at 13:02

ick
lick
click
schtick
flic my bic
you r cosmic
nina zivancevic
....

Zivancevic Nina <zivancevicn65@gmail.com>
To: Marc Léger <leger.mj@gmail.com>
7 April 2015 at 13:48

In the manner of speaking
The mannerists that we are
Will come to terms with
Our interview as of..tonight

Wait...i'll send u

Zivancevic Nina <zivancevicn65@gmail.com>
To: Marc Léger <leger.mj@gmail.com>
7 April 2015 at 14:03

Smth tonite

Envoyé de mon iPhone

Re: When I started loving you

Zivancevic Nina <zivancevicn65@gmail.com>
To: Marc Léger <leger.mj@gmail.com>
7 April 2015 at 04:34

as to my iphone bothering you or so it seems--
i got the damn thing 5 days ago when my 6th cellphone was stolen on a
bus
i got it from the Store of Stolen goods for 50 euros, but i guess it
damages my image of a proleteriat punk duchess so i won't be clicking
from it any longer..
in the realm of Samsara, Edie Sedgwick was so beautiful, her sister
Susana was our guest here while visiting Paris
she spoke of her sister and her own life with A Jodorowsky to my
students of avantgarde
I wanted you, i mean i want you to come over here and speak to us too
(no ulterior motives in here), you know i respect you so much
and adore in our church of Holy Marx & Holy Guaqemoly..
yr reverant slave, nina zee

Marc Léger <leger.mj@gmail.com>
To: Zivancevic Nina <zivancevicn65@gmail.com>
7 April 2015 at 08:57

50 Euros - not sure where else you could get a deal like that
you must live in a world of bargains
i guess that's why they call you Zee for short
perhaps we should now include Susana Sedgwick to our interview list ?
i am already on your list and it is my privilege - since i must be boring in
comparison

what are you doing tomorrow nite ?

Marc Léger <leger.mj@gmail.com>
To: Zivancevic Nina <zivancevicn65@gmail.com>
6 April 2015 at 13:46

hey beautiful,
so i have this interview thing ready
and i thought
well, if you have some lonely nights you want to take care of
maybe you and me could stretch this interview thing out over some
evenings with brandy and meowww.org mix
oh, but i understand, you are a respectable professor
you only undertake projects that have the utmost
and you know i love that portrait - sophisticated, smart, accomplished
leather coat, simple hair cut ... she must be interesting to talk too
you just want to know what is behind the suffering
what drives her

Attachment: Interview preamble and questions to NZ from MJL

Zivancevic Nina <zivancevicn65@gmail.com>
To: Marc Léger <leger.mj@gmail.com>
6 April 2015 at 14:14

Ok gorgeous! Great ! Lets do it
Do u give me one night though? To think about you?

Marc Léger <leger.mj@gmail.com>
To: Zivancevic Nina <zivancevicn65@gmail.com>
6 April 2015 at 14:33

of course, you can have one thousand and one nites
i am treading a fine line now

Zivancevic Nina <zivancevicn65@gmail.com>
To: Marc Léger <leger.mj@gmail.com>
6 April 2015 at 14:40

And lets try to talk a bit about the following dichotomy in life and in art
Kitty cat vs panther

Stranglers vs midnight summer dream
Oxymoron as the figure of our contemporary life

Zivancevic Nina <zivancevicn65@gmail.com>
To: Marc Léger <leger.mj@gmail.com>
7 April 2015 at 04:37

i'll master my ulterior motives envers vous
and answer all yr questions tonite after Berkley Books poetry slam
where i'll read a poem about John and Yoko, i may do it in japanese, the
language you understand the best

Marc Léger <leger.mj@gmail.com>
To: Zivancevic Nina <zivancevicn65@gmail.com>
7 April 2015 at 08:39

you have been invited to Aaaaargh - you can register
the first of which is this attachment for Augé's non-places
i did not find "In the Métro" but this attached book is the theoretical
essence
this is a picture of you and me in the airport yesterday after all our
iPhones

Image: Two young people in an airport, slumped over their laptops

Attachement: Marc Augé, *Non-places: Introduction to an Anthropology of
Supermodernity*

Zivancevic Nina <zivancevicn65@gmail.com>
To: Marc Léger <leger.mj@gmail.com>
7 April 2015 at 09:28

Ha ha ha ha
Who's that young thing though?
Marc Augé?
Cute kitty

Marc Léger <leger.mj@gmail.com>
To: Zivancevic Nina <zivancevicn65@gmail.com>
7 April 2015 at 12:53

let me know whenever you have the guts to invite me to Paris
we can get our gaming on in a poetry slam match or
whatever they call it in Serbia
i want to be your Charles Bukowski and you could be my Southern
Comfort

Zivancevic Nina <zivancevicn65@gmail.com>
To: Marc Léger <leger.mj@gmail.com>
7 April 2015 at 13:20

Ha ha ha
yOU are really something!!

Marc Léger <leger.mj@gmail.com>
To: Zivancevic Nina <zivancevicn65@gmail.com>
7 April 2015 at 13:32

actually, what i had in mind is a 10 km road race that starts somewhere
and ends nowhere in particular - the first one to finish loses - it could last
a long time

Zivancevic Nina <zivancevicn65@gmail.com>
To: Marc Léger <leger.mj@gmail.com>
7 April 2015 at 14:19

You're into metaphorical thinking now?

Marc Léger <leger.mj@gmail.com>
To: Zivancevic Nina <zivancevicn65@gmail.com>
7 April 2015 at 16:03

no, actually, the literal run-race would be a good idea
are your a jogger or walker, either way

you can wear a black addidas albanian DJ outfit
and you can suggest what for me costume
and you look marvellous in those boudoir selfies
very French - Givanchevic

Zivancevic Nina <zivancevicn65@gmail.com>
To: Marc Léger <leger.mj@gmail.com>
7 April 2015 at 16:14

I AM FRENCH, silly!
ok, you can't relate to my costume
cause you're GAY! and thats OKAY!
but tonite also i'm sending you the interview.. you can use some of these
pics though..

Marc Léger <leger.mj@gmail.com>
To: Zivancevic Nina <zivancevicn65@gmail.com>
7 April 2015 at 16:18

i saved them all - i am going to make a necklace out of them

Zivancevic Nina <zivancevicn65@gmail.com>
To: Marc Léger <leger.mj@gmail.com>
7 April 2015 at 16:27

OK, but get back when you can , tomorrow etc- i'll send you the interview.

Zivancevic Nina <zivancevicn65@gmail.com>
To: Marc Léger <leger.mj@gmail.com>
8 April 2015 at 05:40

You're patsying with that Hermeneutics again , Marc.
I thought I was done with our Schleiermacher but there u go again ..
I guess u shd find a very young girl or a boy, to run that race with..
I think I'm going to die soon.

Marc Léger <leger.mj@gmail.com>
To: Zivancevic Nina <zivancevicn65@gmail.com>
8 April 2015 at 09:58

let me know when you die
i will edit the obituaries written in your honour
add some images
la reine de la nuit
medical service 24 hrs
and big Ed's free predestination estimates
add some soft violin music and orchids
run that never-ending journey from marathon to carthage
die of sweet exhaust
parfaitement acceptable, as they say

Art critic cum friend can we

Zivancevic Nina <zivancevicn65@gmail.com>
To: Marc Léger <leger.mj@gmail.com>
8 April 2015 at 07:02

Use smth from this batch?
We are in musee Guimet now
And I m ready for a ride!

Envoyé de mon iPhone

Attachment: 2 photos of NZ in museum with statue of a Minotaur (pre-Angkor, 7th century Cambodian sandstone)

Marc Léger <leger.mj@gmail.com>
To: Zivancevic Nina <zivancevicn65@gmail.com>
8 April 2015 at 09:58

Samantha,
our road race does not begin until 620 BC XX,
but you can choose a track suit of your colour choice
your best accessory will be your exquisite allure

Zivancevic Nina <zivancevicn65@gmail.com>
To: Marc Léger <leger.mj@gmail.com>
8 April 2015 at 10:14

Pooh !

Envoyé de mon iPhone

Nin

Zivancevic Nina <zivancevicn65@gmail.com>
To: Marc Léger <leger.mj@gmail.com>
8 April 2015 at 10:17

Marc, can you refine (affiner) yr interview questions so that it doesn't look like Peoples magazine or Paris match ..
Please! Too many names..

Marc Léger <leger.mj@gmail.com>
To: Zivancevic Nina <zivancevicn65@gmail.com>
8 April 2015 at 11:16

that's intentional, obviously; you can keep your answers short or use these names to talk about things other than the person mentioned
what about my preamble ?
you don't want to work with me on this
why don't you write something about how Allen Ginsberg never read Paris Match
you know
any names you want to take out is fine with me, but i would say, keep the names but keep the answers short, like "yes", or "no", or "she was something" (sorry, I don't mean to write this for you)
like i mentioned previously, in other words you can do what you want with it, but i'd like to keep the names ... as for the last question, again, we can take out the TTT reference and replace it with something less scientific
perhaps my last question won't be Marc James Léger but a question
question
sounds okay ??

Zivancevic Nina <zivancevicn65@gmail.com>
To: Marc Léger <leger.mj@gmail.com>
8 April 2015 at 12:15

Wunderbar ! (i dont want to ruffle yr feathers)
I may even keep yr last question ...(notin porno in it , meaning vulgar)
In fact i've sort of answered it already
And you'll like it as camarade Hegel speaks out here
To end this part of He story..

For Marcus Aurelius from his ghandara freind

Zivancevic Nina <zivancevicn65@gmail.com>
To: Marc Léger <leger.mj@gmail.com>
8 April 2015 at 11:35

Attachment: 3 images of a Buddha statue

Ok I'm getting this object jus 4 u

Zivancevic Nina <zivancevicn65@gmail.com>
To: Marc Léger <leger.mj@gmail.com>
8 April 2015 at 11:32

Envoyé de mon i love u Marc phone

Image: Fetish corset on gold-coloured mannequin in display window

---

Marc Léger <leger.mj@gmail.com>
To: Zivancevic Nina <zivancevicn65@gmail.com>
8 April 2015 at 11:35

anything you say
… actually, what i mean is
why has my pulse rate altered ?

Zivancevic Nina <zivancevicn65@gmail.com>
To: Marc Léger <leger.mj@gmail.com>
8 April 2015 at 11:42

U need dr Zee to check yr blood pressure

Envoyé de mon iPhone

Marc Léger <leger.mj@gmail.com>
To: Zivancevic Nina <zivancevicn65@gmail.com>
8 April 2015 at 11:59

that is exactly what i had in mind for our interview
i am passed out
the blood has rushed out of my head and your presence is all-enveloping
bliss

Ok I'm getting this object jus 4 u - 246

Zivancevic Nina <zivancevicn65@gmail.com>
To: Marc Léger <leger.mj@gmail.com>
8 April 2015 at 12:19

Yes...and then... Go ahead!

Zivancevic Nina <zivancevicn65@gmail.com>
To: Marc Léger <leger.mj@gmail.com>
8 April 2015 at 12:22

I will
Always be
There
For u
My true blue
I can bring some
Air
Into yr lungs
I wld chop off my fingers
For you
Cause i know
Who ...

Fwd: Now u have me de Lanclos in her

Zivancevic Nina <zivancevicn65@gmail.com>
To: Marc Léger <leger.mj@gmail.com>
8 April 2015 at 05:08

Comarade Marc,
Here my friends suggest these pics don't do me any justice in my
comatose setting, we'll use smth else for the interview , perhaps we
place Putin and his Greek friend instead..
However, I AM quite old and ready to tell stories of bygone ages aka
A.G.
But as I'm a vamp I can also enter a young girl's body and play my violin
as I used to, 3 centuries ago. My violin teacher who's 25 thinks I'm his
age.
Anyways you can use that pink kitty pic (that wld be a blast! Any copy
rights?) or I'll ask some pals around to take better pics of me, morning,
straight out of shower...ok?
How did yr editing job go? Have u got any @@@@ or are u still a
Greek?
Xxxxxxxx

Marc Léger <leger.mj@gmail.com>
To: Zivancevic Nina <zivancevicn65@gmail.com>
8 April 2015 at 09:59

please vep
i want to see you climbing the rooftops
to steal the diamond necklace
with the black cape
petite voleuse

Zivancevic Nina <zivancevicn65@gmail.com>
To: Marc Léger <leger.mj@gmail.com>
8 April 2015 at 10:22

Are u a police officer?
Ok yeah that was a great PVC movie
These are the roles society had thrust upon us..

Marc Léger <leger.mj@gmail.com>
To: Zivancevic Nina <zivancevicn65@gmail.com>
8 April 2015 at 13:57

no, they are eternal essences
les vampires, judex, nuits rouges

Venice VIP Invitation

Nina Zivancevic <nzivancevic@ymail.com>
To: Marc Léger <leger.mj@gmail.com>
8 avril 2015 18:51

Wanna come w me to Venice?
We wld have so much fun there, that is my grand-maman's city, i
know it so well! And we wldnt die there just...jump over the roofs.. Like
Casanova !
Plus you have that catalogue

Marc Léger <leger.mj@gmail.com>
To: Nina Zivancevic <nzivancevic@ymail.com>
8 April 2015 at 13:50

you must think i,m some kind of gondolier
i am merely your reflection in the water

Nina Zivancevic <nzivancevic@ymail.com>
To: Marc Léger <leger.mj@gmail.com>
8 April 2015 at 14:00

You dont have to be that mean...
I meant to tell u smth nice
I see you know my friends from the muséum of Novi Sad (msuv) where i
will go next week..
So Marc 2 got out of basement
Ok now i'm getting used to yr tantrums

Nina Zivancevic <nzivancevic@ymail.com>
To: Marc Léger <leger.mj@gmail.com>
8 April 2015 at 14:04

Yes i think what u think that i think
A virtual shadpw...until one day i try to materialise yr image and try to
see you (there i risk a lot)...i predicted it all
So---a ce soir.. Avec mon entretien ..
Bien À toi,

Zivancevic Nina <nzivancevic@ymail.com>
To: Marc Léger <leger.mj@gmail.com>
8 April 2015 at 16:57

i see... my dear Marc...
kitty dad daddy cat..
(look, if i were your gfriend or bfriend- or even dfriend—i'd really get worried at this point)
if you want everything to go public, why don't you show them these emails?

xxxxxxxxxxxxxxxxxxxxxxxxxxxxxxxxxxxxxxxxxxxxxxxxxxxxxxxxxxxxxxxxxxxx
xxxxxxxxxxxxxxxxxxxxxxxxxxxxxxxxxx CMOK!

Marc Léger <leger.mj@gmail.com>
To: Zivancevic Nina <nzivancevic@ymail.com>
8 April 2015 at 18:22

what is this - blackmail or something ?
my friend, confidante, slave girl
and now threatening putty tat

Me as pink kitty with my pal MJL

Zivancevic Nina <zivancevicn65@gmail.com>
To: Marc Léger <leger.mj@gmail.com>
8 April 2015 at 07:00

Envoyé de mon iPhone

Attachment: 3 more photos of NZ in museum with statue of a Minotaur

---

Marc Léger <leger.mj@gmail.com>
To: Zivancevic Nina <zivancevicn65@gmail.com>
8 April 2015 at 09:58

it's adam and eve in the earthly magazine
eve was made from adam's stone rib
and that display case
the person who took these photos
who is she ?
she does not understand how to frame a statue
she left your feet out in the first of these
how can your gay eunuch kiss your feet when they are gone ?
and that's a good one - the first one with the slightly 50s style pose
but without the feet i would have to make adjustments
do you have it in high res that one without the mesopotamian horse
statute
i don't think i'M so hieratic as that rock n roll animal
yes and that is salmon rather than pink
an art critic or a fashion editor would notice such things

Zivancevic Nina <zivancevicn65@gmail.com>
To: Marc Léger <leger.mj@gmail.com>
8 April 2015 at 10:13

F… u colleague !
sTTTop pulling MY pony or pigtails!!

Envoyé de mon iPhone

Marc Léger <leger.mj@gmail.com>
To: Zivancevic Nina <zivancevicn65@gmail.com>
8 April 2015 at 13:56

bite me

Zivancevic Nina <zivancevicn65@gmail.com>
To: Marc Léger <leger.mj@gmail.com>
8 April 2015 at 14:10

If i bite you-- you will really remember the day
That is, u wont forget it..
Pick the date and i'll come to see you

Envoyé de mon iPhone

Marc Léger <leger.mj@gmail.com>
To: Zivancevic Nina <zivancevicn65@gmail.com>
8 April 2015 at 14:26

this is a video of you, me and chichi
cute, n'est-ce paw ?!
https://www.youtube.com/watch?v=YLDbGqJ2KYk
[Two kittens playfighting and a third kitten pukes]

Zivancevic Nina <zivancevicn65@gmail.com>
To: Marc Léger <leger.mj@gmail.com>
8 April 2015 at 14:50

You shd let "chichicute" bite you and make u happy, but i'm afraid that
her teeth/crocs are not long enough.. To satisfy you
Oh yeah, nor are mine, i mean they are old and break easily any time i
bite at...

Zivancevic Nina <zivancevicn65@gmail.com>
To: Marc Léger <leger.mj@gmail.com>
8 April 2015 at 14:44

He he.. I'm not into cat fights.. If i were a Persian cat i wld be...
This vidéo cld be you and Dan and me as well
Ok i see u love... yr girlfriend very much... and just serve me cold
croquettes for dinner..
I think it wld be unfair to compare us and measure against one another
..she's all there for you anyways
Beh.. Bon appétit !
Miaul !

Marc Léger <leger.mj@gmail.com>
To: Zivancevic Nina <zivancevicn65@gmail.com>
8 April 2015 at 16:02

what's wrong with my croquettes
i have upset the stone goddess
will write real poetry soon - my best effort so far

Zivancevic Nina <zivancevicn65@gmail.com>
To: Marc Léger <leger.mj@gmail.com>
8 April 2015 at 16:35

I ain't no Goddess! i'm more like yr new slave! answering every click and
whim and ohhhhhhhhhhhhhh please, Master, set me free!

(as in that ancient song "i wanna live, i wanna give"...N. Young)
nothing wrong with the croquettes but i can't eat them now as i'm in
zeitnot
lack of time, freaking out, you
making fun of me etc etc

here's something to titilate yr spirit now- my other Master (he really
thinks that i'm bound to be his slave, and is much more perverse that
you
is my "british editor", barncott press. perverse: he knows that I AM
DEPENDANT on his words and actions- tonite, as he had'nt heard from
me (proooperly, 5 hour miaow miaows on Skype) for a month, he sends
me his newly edited book on an underground filmmaker

-- you'd probably love to read it! there u go!
and i am going to get
into our interview and this Kantor thing
love you, Marc. WHAT MORE can I tell you right now??

Marc Léger <leger.mj@gmail.com>
To: Zivancevic Nina <zivancevicn65@gmail.com>
8 April 2015 at 16:50

nothing, say nothing

Zivancevic Nina <zivancevicn65@gmail.com>
To: Marc Léger <leger.mj@gmail.com>
8 April 2015 at 17:02

i must be a (sur)REAL intellectual as i got hooked (check this out!!) I got
hooked on your texts and books and interviews-- all to be addressed
tonite in our interview
the pivotal point: the top ; max point of my pathetic issue
"i dont even know how u look like
you cd be a Quasimodo
you cd be in a wheelchair
i just love your
thought
patterns!"
where are u gonna find this elsewhere in this
(mate)real world??

Marc Léger <leger.mj@gmail.com>
To: Zivancevic Nina <zivancevicn65@gmail.com>
8 April 2015 at 18:47

Ah yes, I promised you some poetry ...

Straight poem for Nina Zivancevic

Look
I'm finally getting things straight

You are Nina Zivancevic
And I am Marc James Léger
You are a poet and a professor
And I am an independent scholar
You live in Paris
And I live in Montreal
You are a great writer
And I don't have a clue about great writing
You are in love with Dan
And I am in love with Cayley
You write nice emails to me
And I write nice emails to you
You are nice to write to
And I write you are nice too
You are a Buddhist
And I eat a lot of guacamole
You are a woman of the French écoles
And I am a stone statue, hieratic and cold
You are a cute little kitty
And I am now worried you are crazy
You are going to contribute to my book
And I will edit the book and correct your Nazi typos
You are a (sur)REAL intellectual
And I am reading Annie Le Brun to try to figure you out
You are writing an interview
And I am waiting
You are irreplaceable and encouragable
And I know it
You are a cute little kitty
As I said before

Now that everything is settled I hope you have a pleasant evening and please write soon.

The END

Zivancevic Nina <zivancevicn65@gmail.com>
To: Marc Léger <leger.mj@gmail.com>
8 April 2015 at 19:18

Oh, thank you.
Now I really don't know who's crazy here.

Must be both of us, although, I must be crazier than you are
as I admit, I've been encouraging yr craaazy activity of sending me tons of emails
and click-a-clack links, images and of course, responding to them.
As my friend Bob Holman said "I know you're craaaazy, we're all crazy, but if you're crazy, just tell me: why am I crazy for youuuuu!!"

At any rate, you have nothing to worry about and I have no intention to worry if we slip out of these forementioned categories you've placed us in. Now we should not abuse of it- there's use, and then -the abuse. I found your abundant eloquence funny and interesting
but to me- it did not imply any further obligation. Perhaps I've had many various obligations at this stage of my life, thus, as an artista-sandinista I tried to run away from them by writing to you and encouraging this silly gem of poetry/correspondence/ activity.

Please, don't worry and above all- stop freaking out, it's so unbecoming for a person you are and wld like to be.
How old are you, in our fuzzy kittinish world?
Here's my intro to the conference, which , if you please, you could use for a certain discussion pertinent to our goal..The interview will arrive shortly.

no 1. we should try to finish our job(s) here.
2. we should try to be as much respectful, and not condescending towards each other while we're at it- cause, we should leave something worthwhile behind, in this silly world,
and to me, worthwhile always reads "beautiful".
And you should repeat every day,
like a prayer "I love C.", and
Nina loves D.
I love C.", and
Nina loves D…
This practise will help you overcome all obstacles in this , sort of fuzzy and zany communication with me. We should try to cut on all possible (see "delusional" and diluding) intimacy so that we wouldn't hurt ourselves - and some other people in return.
Your camarade Z.

sent from my very private own Watch Phone latest version:
Watchagonnado? Phone

Attachment: NZ text, "Tadeusz Kantor and his role in the"

Marc Léger <leger.mj@gmail.com>
To: Zivancevic Nina <zivancevicn65@gmail.com>
8 April 2015 at 20:19

i'm glad that my quixotic afflictions were not lost on you
and why am i writing like this, what am i Cyrano da Bergerak
who is Bob Holman and Hart Crane and all your other men
without any additional irony
you love D and I love C
what can you do,
as you as MY Nina and as i have been in Ninasville for a ling time
i don't just cmok you
anyway, let me know if you want to hang out on email or if you've had it
with this baffoon

Zivancevic Nina <zivancevicn65@gmail.com>
To: Marc Léger <leger.mj@gmail.com>
9 April 2015 at 04:55

Like i said and please let us not repeat ourselves -we dont deserve
this
Let us try to be respectful and comprehensive twds one another
No more petit bourgeois insults and/or compliments
If you want to continue being a friend and camarade and a collègue
We can go on..
I am aware of the dangers of this "virtual" dialogue and yes
Sorry if i said smth that might have Hurt yr ego
And i wish u all the best
and will send the first congrats if you scheduled a new wedding
Hey we still have some years ahead to catch up
I look forward to getting to know u better
Live and love
Yr nina z

Zivancevic Nina <zivancevicn65@gmail.com>
To: Marc Léger <leger.mj@gmail.com>
9 April 2015 at 06:33

How stupide and stupid u are!
Not to understand that i is just- a word
When i say i it contains multitudes

Ohhh what a waste of time in your garden..
Go back to Zhizhek (i hope you pronounce at least his name correctly)
and train yr brain
God (yeah Check Spinoza too) is a bit larger than yr little finger
With which you click click click
Holywood sequels and porno pussycats...
How disappointing and truly lacking in faith and confidence
I dont know u Marc and i'm not sure that i want to know you
You dont get my jokes and …

Marc Léger <leger.mj@gmail.com>
To: Zivancevic Nina <zivancevicn65@gmail.com>
9 April 2015 at 08:54

all those things you say: guilty
like the cover came in today
my spine is 17.72 mm

Zivancevic Nina <zivancevicn65@gmail.com>
To: Marc Léger <leger.mj@gmail.com>
9 April 2015 at 12:04

My problem w you is bigger or longer than 17 mm but
I wont go into that
I understand there is Marc 1 And Marc 2
And it clearly shows in yr correspondence
I'm keeping everything under a separate file
I hope that you get on good medication and solve some of these issues

---

Zivancevic Nina <zivancevicn65@gmail.com>
To: Marc Léger <leger.mj@gmail.com>
9 April 2015 at 12:06

And i hate myself for having said all this , right this very moment.

Marc Léger <leger.mj@gmail.com>
To: Zivancevic Nina <zivancevicn65@gmail.com>
9 April 2015 at 12:10

you're like the monsoon in that Marguerite Duras film
meaning: Delphine Seyrig
maybe for you, one day i will read Spinoza
it might be good for me too – some kind of paradise

Zivancevic Nina <zivancevicn65@gmail.com>
To: Marc Léger <leger.mj@gmail.com>
9 April 2015 at 12:15

I've just tried now "nina 2" on you
So that you see
Become aware of it , How it hurts..

Zivancevic Nina <zivancevicn65@gmail.com>
To: Marc Léger <leger.mj@gmail.com>
9 April 2015 at 13:10

Marc 1 is back?
I need Marc 1 as he's my hero whereas i dont like the no 2
Oh Marcus garvey
Help me see you in yr integral version
I know you can do it
And because of that one i've writtén all these lines

Marc Léger <leger.mj@gmail.com>
To: Zivancevic Nina <zivancevicn65@gmail.com>
9 April 2015 at 13:10

i would say that you need a poem
but you're way beyond my tenacity when it comes to the tug of words
that Kantor piece was really painful and, yeah, it hurt a lot
i won't go into the details of it and will rest until you send the updated
enhanced killer version (it's a wonder there isn't a warrant out for your
manuscript)

why all the names ? you said that the end of being looked good because
it had Gainsbourg and Gysin in it
so i made your interview that way
take my advice and email me

Zivancevic Nina <zivancevicn65@gmail.com>
To: Marc Léger <leger.mj@gmail.com>
9 April 2015 at 13:42

Thank you for sending such a brilliant sincere letter
I've had very few of those coming from you
One thing you shd know : i didn't send you ANY piece on Kantor please:
dont dilude yourself
I sent you my 1st page conference intro as
There were times when i wanted to share every little text with you
This time is over as you had hurt me
I wont let u do that any longer
You will get the interview and my modest contribution to yr book
But no further enthousiasm nothing really wild
I have a bitter taste in my mouth when i think of you

Zivancevic Nina <zivancevicn65@gmail.com>
To: Marc Léger <leger.mj@gmail.com>
9 April 2015 at 14:41

Wow! You are having yr 1968 right now!!

Marc Léger <leger.mj@gmail.com>
To: Zivancevic Nina <zivancevicn65@gmail.com>
9 April 2015 at 16:10

yeah! and listen to me: you can't fool the children of the revolution

Zivancevic Nina <zivancevicn65@gmail.com>
To: Marc Léger <leger.mj@gmail.com>
9 April 2015 at 20:31

there you go...Hope you- like it.

Attachment: NZ interview with MJL

Marc Léger <leger.mj@gmail.com>
To: Zivancevic Nina <zivancevicn65@gmail.com>
9 April 2015 at 20:54

thanks Nina, it's a wonderful interview !!! i will send it to endofbeing and
see what they say - i was thinking of adding two photographs - the ones
that are attached here - please let me know if you have these available
in a higher res and also if you want to add any information in captions or
maybe it's enough for them to simply exist, without further comment

surely but slowly…

Zivancevic Nina <zivancevicn65@gmail.com>
To: Marc Léger <leger.mj@gmail.com>
10 April 2015 at 19:50

i'm advancing through the history of cont. theater, and i'd like to thank
you for directing me to M. Augé and other helpful references
i am shocked though that you wld ever think that i sent you my intro
page as any meaningful critique.. the rest of my draft goes like.. eerrr

*Kantor devours the univers of Kafka, but also the univers of the Polish
writers such as Wyspianski, Witkiewicz, Gombrowicz and Bruno
Schulz. And as much as Kantor was under the influence of Gombrowicz
and his theater of the absurd throughout his life, by the end of it his
thoughts occupied the minimalist economy of Schulz, whom Bablet calls
"Polish Kafka" but whose "ubermanequin" body certainly nourished my
compatriot Kish as well as his Polish counterpart. In the Dead Class,
Kantor conducts the steady but rather hidden dialogue with Schulz, the
author of Tractatus on Mannequins, who is his Virgil, thus his guide in the
degraded reality of the junk world and discarded objects not only in this
particular play but also in Waterhen (the theme of the eternal voyage).*

*Kantor's reality reflects horrors since 1942 when he created in
Cracovie his first clandestine theater in the catacombs ,influenced by
Schlemmer's mannequins and the Bauhaus stage scenography. His
first play Slowacki's Balladyna as well as his Return of Ulisses in 1944 ,
also performed in a non- place (as Marc Augé would name the lieu) bear
marks of abstract and austere realism including raw materials, mud,
dust, a cannon and old wooden logs, dusty boxes, the entire minimalist
stage world which Kantor is going to describe in his theoretical essay
"The Independent Theater".*

*We shouldn't watch a play the way we watch a painting, For the
aesthetic pleasure, but we have to live through the theater piece
properly./I don't obey aesthetic canons/ I am not connected to any
historical era/ I know them and these don't interest me/ I am only
profoundly endebted to the era in which I live and to the people who
live next to me./ I believe that the barberians can coexist with the subtle
ones, the tragedy can co-exist with the ironic laughter/ I believe that
everything is born out of contrast and that the bigger the contrast the
more palpable and concrete and lively this world (is).*

*Yes, this stance we often found in Rabelais, and whenever I think of
Kantor, Kantor the director or the performance artist, I see his connection
with the great Russian Constructivists such as Malevich, but also with
someone like Michail Bachtin, whenever his love toward the grotesque
springs up, that grotesque laughter which brings both Kantor and
Bachtin to Rabelais.*

In his shows, Kantor connects the elements, even the most tragic elements into a funny humorous, grotesque manifestation- and here we come to his notion of minimalist performances, autonomous and divided scenes which could- each of them stand by itself as a minimalist fragment, but later connected by the fine line of grotesque humor into an entity as is the case with the Dead Class.

Each fragment/scene from the Dead Class could stand as a mini performance of its own where actors are exposed in a phenomenological net, as some special objects, mannequins who are in fact the objects predestined to relate to one another in a phenomenological manner. Here he comes close to another giant of the postmodern theater, the American director Richard Foreman who had a similar approach to his theater sets and his actors in his Ontological-Hysteric Theater. However, Foreman's theater is Ontological in terms of placing his actors/playful objects within a middle-class semantic field, filled out with angst and memories of his bountiful reality whereas Kantor's theater is a painful historic memory of the European past filled with battles and wars. And where Foreman offers us a Barbie doll as a memory of an abused childhood- in a memory of Vienna secession and Freud, Kantor turns a man with a hat into an object leading yet another much older creature by his hand who turns out to be an epitome of European History- a blind object leads yet another blind thing.

As It is very difficult (in terms of scenography), to set into motion all these very precise Dadaist objects, and as it is already very problematic for actors cum objects and objects cum actors (as Kantor would have it) to create and sustain the inner story of such a phenomenological play, both of these directors have never believed in improvisation in theater. Hardly they both believed in a coherent and contingent story in a play as their miniature fragmented scenes could be taken as a series of separate performances in themselves. However, as Kantor's Polish reality of the 1960s and 1970s appears more politically restrictive, Stalinian and suffocating than Foreman's American one, Kantor's metaphors- as they are being thrust upon the spectator- are more somber and raw in their appearance. Kantor is obsessed with the relationships between art and life and he claims that "the problem of art is always essentially the problem of the presence of an object. As the abstraction is a formal lack of an object which exists outside the picture", he employs the intricate net of associations which bring the spectators back to an object, as exemplified in his Dead Class.

In the opening of Kantor's Wax Museum of human dolls and mannequins, the number of the said objects turned into people keep raising their hands, as if they had something to ask, as if they had something to say. But they are not capable of telling the story, or the murky History of the man whose soul died under the Communist boot and censorship.

And when they start uttering words and semi-coherent sentences, their declarations are unimportant and non-sensical , as they turn around in circle or in circles around the bench. However, Kantor obtains in his staging process a certain neutrality of his object which becomes in turn an independent semantic sign, like Duchamp's "Fountain-urinoir", a recyclable "ready-made". In his Cricot 2 Theater he treats the text also as an organic "ready-made" object, ready to be manipulated by an actor.

Kantor per se has never believed in "props", as his view of his object had always had a strictly political, utilitarian role- it was there, made to be ready to jump into action and break the frontier between the representation and the spectator. And then there was his WATERHEN: after this particular performance the objects enhance their phenomenology status- they gain on their proper meanings and significance, they speak for themselves, their roles are totally equal even competing with the roles of actors who, in turn, become things.

Kantor provokes the spectator with his objects, and although they are sparse and not numerous on stage, they are disturbing. He does not believe in illusion and he draws the spectator in right away: in media res- he learnt from Piscator that supreme lesson in disturbing the voyeur and he will not let him dream- if his spectator is lulled to sleep, he will make sure that by the end of the show, his dream becomes a nightmare.

Bablet nicely remarqued that Kantor's performance is not a can that a spectator can open every evening and be served there the same, tasty meal: Kantor invites his audience to join his stage, but unlike the Living Theater (also the adepts of Piscator)he does not impose his political vision on them, nor he lures the spectator to construct or deconstruct the stage mentally (the way that Foreman, the Brechtian soul would do). Kantor invents the semantic game and sets it on the stage resembling a chess-field where he invites you for a rollercoaster ride (each slope is a different chapter in History full of wars, slaughterhouses, inner prisons and censorship). And so as not to sound or appear sordid in all his gore reveling, he introduces Rabelaisian humor to it, decadent prostitutes turned into dolls, minimalist boxes (or prison-houses?) where all shades of grey, black and white parade in their splendor... AND SO ON AND FORTH

--hope i didn't bore you, but if i had snore you, sorry, just wanted to tell you not to think of me, yr friend nina zee, as a wastebin of ideas.

I... I... Just want to

Zivancevic Nina <zivancevicn65@gmail.com>
To: Marc Léger <leger.mj@gmail.com>
11 April 2015 at 12:18

And ohhh wld I rather travel with you but as u are so far
Away and with other folks
I will work and get into some other talks, leave with Daniel next week off
to Belgrade ...

Marc Léger <leger.mj@gmail.com>
To: Zivancevic Nina <zivancevicn65@gmail.com>
12 April 2015 at 09:19

ninotchka, it would be wrong for me to comment on this Kantor work
of imagination - perhaps, matter of fact - but i don,t think you should
consider Malevich a constructivist - yes, he was in the same building as
them, but really he should have his proper scaffold, called suprematism,
which has its own relationship - i think that probably yes, in thinking
about all of this, you swallowed all those energy drinks when you wrote
'surely but slowly' - i heart anais nina, but alas, time after time, one Marc
Augé non-place after another - i'm really just your sidekick in this rococo
non-place

Zivancevic Nina <zivancevicn65@gmail.com>
To: Marc Léger <leger.mj@gmail.com>
12 April 2015 at 09:34

Shit,, Judith Malina has just died...
Let me remake our inter
In that direction ...
Have a great Sunday
Will write to u tout de suite...

Envoyé de mon iPhone

Marc Léger <leger.mj@gmail.com>
To: Zivancevic Nina <zivancevicn65@gmail.com>
12 April 2015 at 09:48

yes, absolutely
remake as you need
that's a real loss for everyone

Zivancevic Nina <zivancevicn65@gmail.com>
To: Marc Léger <leger.mj@gmail.com>
12 April 2015 at 10:55

Oh.... You! Thanks for CoRRECTING me my dearest Marc about that
Mal Mal....guy, sure it was a little abused girl's (aka Freudian slip) not a
slipper not a sleep but a real SLAP

Marc Léger <leger.mj@gmail.com>
To: Zivancevic Nina <zivancevicn65@gmail.com>
12 April 2015 at 11:38

writing with you is like being in an airport and looking at the light board
with all those arrivals and departures
and then i think, what do you mean your caring world – that's a trick you
learned from Althusser - i'm checking your cv and figure that i must be
really close now to the violent femmes and women in distress you've
written about ... like the code of hammurabi and the subcontracting of
ideology mon amour

Zivancevic Nina <zivancevicn65@gmail.com>
To: Marc Léger <leger.mj@gmail.com>
12 April 2015 at 13:03

"Writing with you is like being..
Papa Heidegger please help us: it is like the essence of being
The airport ness of the airport
The loveness of love
The prison house of language
And yes

Yes
Yes
Or no
Or whatever you say
It's such fun
To know you Marc…
Look who can get all these triple jokes put on cube or square but
You and only you
And sometimes even me behind that Big You

Zivancevic Nina <zivancevicn65@gmail.com>
To: Marc Léger <leger.mj@gmail.com>
12 April 2015 at 13:09

Yes I will swashbuckle my way through your existence
I'm like a Terminator 5
And.. My family comes from that Austrian region as well
Just watch me out...

Marc Léger <leger.mj@gmail.com>
To: Zivancevic Nina <zivancevicn65@gmail.com>
12 April 2015 at 13:56

you are a real trapeze artist and great stage performer
but part of you I think is tucked away in the Carnavalet

Zivancevic Nina <zivancevicn65@gmail.com>
To: Marc Léger <leger.mj@gmail.com>
12 April 2015 at 14:03

Aha.. They released me from that cage though,, so now I can wallow in
my "social benefits" and bluejeaned reality,,
But you must have some famille money, right? How can u not work? I
mean live "as an indépendant scholar"?
Anyways... Rich or poor, dead or alive i want you. ok lemmie think about
it for a sec… How can i do it,,,?

Zivancevic Nina <zivancevicn65@gmail.com>
To: Marc Léger <leger.mj@gmail.com>
12 April 2015 at 14:32

There u go again pulling my pigtails
So as to your presentation of the so called nina's ptit bourgeois crap: i
aint no carnevallet museum babe
I destroyed the image of the museum itself
And you.. Need not feel threatened
No infériorité complex please
I love your pensée and you are my great teacher cum editor
(Gee, why do i deserve all this tonite and from my fave person?????)

Marc Léger <leger.mj@gmail.com>
To: Zivancevic Nina <zivancevicn65@gmail.com>
12 April 2015 at 16:24

when you say my pensée are you talking again about the Blaise Marc 1
vs Marc 2 showdown ? maybe i should find a nice spot for you that you
would be more happy with, like the courtyard of the maison Delacroix
where you could give a libretto of "les oiseaux de la charmille" - that
would be nice
why is my petty bourgeois crap ? you said that in your novel somewhere
so i thought maybe we're really getting down to something fundamental
like everyone wants to know where it's going and whether or not
these blues really count as research or should go under service to the
community

Zivancevic Nina <zivancevicn65@gmail.com>
To: Marc Léger <leger.mj@gmail.com>
12 April 2015 at 16:54

I was feeling lousy
Judith meant so much to me
Just the pics are passing by
Thé pain sort of goes away
Ill get to u in one hour

Envoyé de mon iPhone

nina z

Zivancevic Nina <zivancevicn65@gmail.com>
To: Marc Léger <leger.mj@gmail.com>
12 April 2015 at 19:33

SOCIAL AND HEALING ROLE OF THIS CORRESPONDENCE

Yes my zany attirance and attraction for your letters
coincide with my reading of your text on Goddard and his Socialism. He
said it all, in my view though.. hmm, but OK my pfriend, we will have to
put up- for the rest of our respective lives with tweet tweet performances
and other blockbusters...
Now, I'm glad I'm back to Marcville, not as a non-place but the healing
place for me , you said "it's warm and cosy here and the bright neon light
shines with an incredible brio..look
the first thing that comes to my mind is
that I have to, i want to say, a couple of things about Malina, my life with
her etc- and that may take a few words more like a couple of pages, and
not only I'll have to redo the whole interview for "what's the endof being
or beingness of being" etc but any place that wld print it
-- come to think of it , i'll have to redo my conf presentation on Kantor
and target it to my memories of the Living T. and Judith's role in the AG
performance, ay ay...
I AM SO HAPPY to get to know Marc 1 and Marc2 and yeah, bring me
over Marc 3 and 4- I'm sure they're my people, and as John Waters said
(through miss Divine and Mink Stole
xxxxxxxxxxxxxx
PS : and I'll be doing lots of commemorations, necrologues etc all over
Europe now..
these pics were taken 3 years ago, her last trip to paree. very moving
story

Attachments: Images of Judith Malina with NZ and friends

Marc Léger <leger.mj@gmail.com>
To: Zivancevic Nina <zivancevicn65@gmail.com>
12 April 2015 at 20:15

there is a picture of Judith in vol.1 (at Occupy Wall Street) and now sadly
i will have to include her name in the dedication of vol.2 along with some
heroes - very much the AG exists because we love those who came
before us - for vol. 2 i focus on some kind of continuing relevance for me
and those involved - which is something good to have learned from the
cinema of JP Gorin

Zivancevic Nina <zivancevicn65@gmail.com>
To: Marc Léger <leger.mj@gmail.com>
12 April 2015 at 20:27

OK, we can enter the land of Baroque exaggeration- but there are no
tears in there, at least not in terms of the Beautiful Anarchist Revolution
that the LT tried to set
what really makes me annoyed here is the end of Malina, she was
chased again from their space and sort of in the street and the nursing
home
and in fact it was Ilyon Troya (who was Julian Beck's lover) who's a
close friend and I should call him now.. err and so many LT BEINGS but
I have no heart to do it so as not to turn into this mushy ball of the living
flesh and pain—
thanks for this exchange, dear M., it really means a lot to me right now
this very second

Marc Léger <leger.mj@gmail.com>
To: Zivancevic Nina <zivancevicn65@gmail.com>
12 April 2015 at 21:11

good news -- you can play Susan in the new *Ned Rifle* - kind of young
this Hartley motif but on the other side you have the literary genius

Zivancevic Nina <zivancevicn65@gmail.com>
To: Marc Léger <leger.mj@gmail.com>
12 April 2015 at 22:35

ohhh well! what a blast! (ned rifle, just what i needed)
Like the highlight of my love life is playing the violin with my violin
teacher twice a week and we never crossed the boundaries of "vous
devez.." nor we ever will..
look, i will get a two hour sleep, then into yet another chapter on Kantor
who is definitively one of THE Fathers of pomo performance.. i am such
a child and a dummy when i watch his work. i mean, i'm so incompetent
when it comes to "theater"..
xxxxxxxxxxxxxxxxxxxxxxxxxxxxxxx

Zivancevic Nina <zivancevicn65@gmail.com>
To: Marc Léger <leger.mj@gmail.com>
12 April 2015 at 22:41

also, is there ANY way that i get yr vol.1? any chance? can i buy it from you? i'm thinking of getting a totally different essay now, for yr book, different from this Kantor thing which takes a different shape
but what i have in mind is really tracing down (like a hound snif snif) the avatars of the contemp French AG and getting some valuable testimonies from some interesting people here- that wld be smth innovative, not my musings on the
AG in general , etc..

Marc Léger <leger.mj@gmail.com>
To: Zivancevic Nina <zivancevicn65@gmail.com>
13 April 2015 at 09:47

i will mail you a copy of vol. 1 later but for now i don't want to influence your choices – it's really what you want to say and to share with les autres, l'experience de l'enfer - the idea of the AG and yes, the focus is on today (not so much yesterday) – more like Julie Ruin's "the Road" as an update on Seurat

Zivancevic Nina <zivancevicn65@gmail.com>
To: Marc Léger <leger.mj@gmail.com>
13 April 2015 at 10:11

thank you for the stars
and you deserve a kiss
and please think of Signac when you do your circus Seurat thing
I'm wearing that V costume today (as this conference starts and I am
jusqu'ua ici avec tout ça!!)

Marc Léger <leger.mj@gmail.com>
To: Zivancevic Nina <zivancevicn65@gmail.com>
13 April 2015 at 11:31

in terms of the books, it's my George Maciunas fantasy
that seems the best way for me to go with it

Zivancevic Nina <zivancevicn65@gmail.com>
To: Marc Léger <leger.mj@gmail.com>
13 April 2015 at 11:53

Oh no
U were talking about yr critique of pasolini critique of LT
An u said you r having similar exchange w wooster group now
Can u send it or you're too B&B? (Busy and bored)
I'm organising à mémorial for Judith but in Belgrade
Old members living in Central Europe will join me there but my friend
Ivana, in charge of festival Bitef, worked with Schechner for years as
much as i did the LT
Now we will all pay hommage etc

Marc Léger <leger.mj@gmail.com>
To: Zivancevic Nina <zivancevicn65@gmail.com>
13 April 2015 at 12:01

it seems someone in WG is writing smthing
i have to wait and see
the LT crit is in my essay on Pasolini
it's Pasolini who made this criticism in one of his essays on the new
theatre
but i must warn you
it will cause trouble between us
it was written before the Godard piece and i was searching under
communism
there is more that could be done with Pasolini but this was a singular
piece singularly

Attachement: MJL essay on Pasolini

Zivancevic Nina <zivancevicn65@gmail.com>
To: Marc Léger <leger.mj@gmail.com>
13 April 2015 at 13:58

I havent opened it but
Calm down
You no that théorème is my favorite text
And u r my Paolo
And i'm yr franceska

Or to push-pull further , i'm yr Elsa morante
Always rouge..

Envoyé de mon iPhone

Zivancevic Nina <zivancevicn65@gmail.com>
To: Marc Léger <leger.mj@gmail.com>
13 April 2015 at 18:59

Marc, it's really an important text
and i couldn't agree more with Pasolini, in fact--
you're really talking to someone who distanced herself from that
"burgeois product AG reality" as exemplified by the recycled AG forms
aka commodity avant and aftergarde products
i can assure you that my artistic life here is quite different that the one i
had in NYC.
I will go now, the conference starts ..
xxxx

Marc Léger <leger.mj@gmail.com>
To: Zivancevic Nina <zivancevicn65@gmail.com>
13 April 2015 at 20:32

as you are my alibi for Pasolini i thank you for your kind reading
i knocked myself on the head today
i generally refer to AG as anti-cap culture, social and use value within
without the dialectic - pretty basic definition and rather than innovation
i have more complex definitions to work with but it has the combination
art and politics

Image: Pasolini film card from *Teorema* with the maid ascending into
heaven

Zivancevic Nina <zivancevicn65@gmail.com>
To: Marc Léger <leger.mj@gmail.com>
14 April 2015 at 03:00

Bachtin coined it
It was an army military term

Invented fr people like me an u.
Keep yr fingers crossed ce matin
Jack Lang opens this shit and i.ll do it basically for Judith and fr my
memory of the Living

Zivancevic Nina <zivancevicn65@gmail.com>
To: Marc Léger <leger.mj@gmail.com>
14 April 2015 at 06:45

While i'm listening to the conférence blah-blah.. Let me tell u something
which u may even find interesting: my grandfather milan used to play
chess with Lénin in Switzerland and Zizek is right when he says that AG
art can never ... All that u quote here
I think.. In fact i'm pretty sure that he wanted to kill mayakovsky at the
time when he was working on Kruchenykh's piece "victory over the sun"

Zivancevic Nina <zivancevicn65@gmail.com>
To: Marc Léger <leger.mj@gmail.com>
14 April 2015 at 06:29

That whole era was so important to me. Viktor Shklovsky is my God (the
way zizi is yours)
I've learnt everything from his notion of Poetry cum art in the procès of
defamiliarization
Dialectical juxtaposing etc
I am pissed he is dead otherwise i wouldve planned my pre nups with
him... But you're not such a bad replacement , you know..

Marc Léger <leger.mj@gmail.com>
To: Zivancevic Nina <zivancevicn65@gmail.com>
14 April 2015 at 09:08

that's quite a story about playing chess with the supreme leader and how
the black squares won - i have a few ideas about this military thing and
why more people should read the reports of the egyptian correspondent
oh, i should not bother you while you listen to Patti Smith, a.k.a. Jack
Lang

Zivancevic Nina <zivancevicn65@gmail.com>
To: Marc Léger <leger.mj@gmail.com>
14 April 2015 at 09:24

And the people around me screamed: hushhhhhh!
Stop laughing Madame! Go out to consult your phone
I should check in into one of those net detox Cliniques where they give
strong doses of anti-MJL medication ..

Marc Léger <leger.mj@gmail.com>
To: Zivancevic Nina <zivancevicn65@gmail.com>
14 April 2015 at 09:33

is it Bert Brecht laughter or that bozo Louis de Funès ... ?

Marc Léger <leger.mj@gmail.com>
To: Zivancevic Nina <zivancevicn65@gmail.com>
14 April 2015 at 09:51

this is what stepxxxz says to me:
steppxxxxz • a month ago
*Mr Leger seems not to realize Zizek is a crypto fascist, and racist. And
willfully misreads Lacan. Shockingly so at times.*

Zivancevic Nina <zivancevicn65@gmail.com>
To: Marc Léger <leger.mj@gmail.com>
14 April 2015 at 12:40

Both
Here we have Marc 1 jokes joined with Marc 2 who escaped from that
basement space
U know what?
I have a strange desire to feed Marc 2 in his basement and make
Natasha Kapuch out of him
I have to be drastique

Marc Léger <leger.mj@gmail.com>
To: Zivancevic Nina <zivancevicn65@gmail.com>
14 April 2015 at 12:51

Ach, you flirt

Zivancevic Nina <zivancevicn65@gmail.com>
To: Marc Léger <leger.mj@gmail.com>
14 April 2015 at 14:06

Who is the big one?
I'm jealous now
And i was treated badly at the conférence and was asked to hurry
up!!!!10 minutes hardly i had started and opened my mouth
And the rest of the presenters took one hour each!!!
And Marc doesnt love me(not asmuchas that sugary marshmallow girl)
And everything's going wrong

Envoyé de mon iPhoneyou phoney ou

Zivancevic Nina <zivancevicn65@gmail.com>
To: Marc Léger <leger.mj@gmail.com>
14 April 2015 at 14:09

Whos that freak, step123..whatever?
Yr circus is really big...

Zivancevic Nina <zivancevicn65@gmail.com>
To: Marc Léger <leger.mj@gmail.com>
14 April 2015 at 15:11

I see they are not (some , luckily not everyone)
Treating you much better either! How can they say such things about
Slavoj, are they that ignorant?

Marc Léger <leger.mj@gmail.com>
To: Zivancevic Nina <zivancevicn65@gmail.com>
14 April 2015 at 15:23

where are you now ?
is this the part where people stand around ?
if it were me i would give you all the time to explain to us this minimalist theatre
what is a formidable connoisseur of K doing at a conference like this ?

Zivancevic Nina <zivancevicn65@gmail.com>
To: Marc Léger <leger.mj@gmail.com>
14 April 2015 at 15:42

Oh when I get home I'll explain what happened
J for jealousy
P for pettiness
S for stupidity etc
Luckily: my friends Sava Andjelkovic
And beautiful Balladyna were there to support me
I've just heArd my last words before I quit the table
"Tis too bad, sirs, as I made a considerable effort to overcome my mourning /wake my family and Kantor's (Judith) has died and I came to pay homage to both of them
And you cut me short
But in my country I'm known as Wyslava Shimborska or as,, Marina Tsvetayeva ...you wldnt tell them to shut up, would you?
And this is just what you've done,,,
The audience were appalled and EVERYONE congratulated me on that one...

Marc Léger <leger.mj@gmail.com>
To: Zivancevic Nina <zivancevicn65@gmail.com>
14 April 2015 at 15:47

who is Balladyna … tell me more …

Zivancevic Nina <zivancevicn65@gmail.com>
To: Marc Léger <leger.mj@gmail.com>
14 April 2015 at 15:57

Marc
I don't want to talk to you in any way
I just want to... Hmmm play ping pong with you!
I mean the mental pingpong
To be more precise
Tonite I miss you badly
And I hope this evening doesn't repeat itself

Envoyé de mon " need phone "

Marc Léger <leger.mj@gmail.com>
To: Zivancevic Nina <zivancevicn65@gmail.com>
14 April 2015 at 15:59

what, who is Balladyna … ?

Zivancevic Nina <zivancevicn65@gmail.com>
To: Marc Léger <leger.mj@gmail.com>
14 April 2015 at 15:59

Balladyna is a beautiful polish actress and pop singer
Who often performs with me at la Cantada
Why do you ask, you filthy cad???

Envoyé de mon iPhone

Marc Léger <leger.mj@gmail.com>
To: Zivancevic Nina <zivancevicn65@gmail.com>
14 April 2015 at 16:01

just to make you jealous and petty
please send me photos of you and Balladyna
this is for the interview we're doing for the web site: european institute
for progressive cultural policies

Zivancevic Nina <zivancevicn65@gmail.com>
To: Marc Léger <leger.mj@gmail.com>
14 April 2015 at 16:07

And who are these people waiting?
Let's make this issue clear once for all: there are
A couple of people who are waiting in a line to talk to me
But they cant get à chance cause i'm writing emails to you all the time!!!
Dont think that your bar of popularity is raised very high...
They want to reach me too
And some folks are giving up on me cause they think that i'm crazy
"spending all my time emaling that weird canadian theorista"...

Marc Léger <leger.mj@gmail.com>
To: Zivancevic Nina <zivancevicn65@gmail.com>
14 April 2015 at 16:13

don't think i don't know it
but the people on these streets here tell me you're feeding me bananas

Zivancevic Nina <zivancevicn65@gmail.com>
To: Marc Léger <leger.mj@gmail.com>
14 April 2015 at 16:23

One thing's for sure: i've never loved a man without seeing him ha ha ha
Not making what? And hot... Like i can get it off simply on his brain and
Spirit.. Ha! Loving you is like talking to VOltaire!!
(Check this one out-- its a beautiful Line)...

Marc Léger <leger.mj@gmail.com>
To: Zivancevic Nina <zivancevicn65@gmail.com>
14 April 2015 at 16:27

In between the emails, I sneak in a little G.F.W.: "On the other hand,
in the ethical world we did see a religion, namely the religion of the
underworld." For absolute Being, read: absolute ping pong

**So I hope u don't mind this
dope of**

Zivancevic Nina <zivancevicn65@gmail.com>
To: Marc Léger <leger.mj@gmail.com>
14 April 2015 at 14:19

A girl at the. Conférence next to Guy Scarpetta etc etc

Envoyé de mon iPhone

Image: [next page]

Marc Léger <leger.mj@gmail.com>
To: Zivancevic Nina <zivancevicn65@gmail.com>
14 April 2015 at 14:53

they kept you in the basement for 10 minutes
i see they know better than to unleash the monsoon
that happened to me once at a feminist conference
they gave some very right wing women lots of minutes
and me i think i got 10 and was told to wrap it up
and then they said, mister, your examples of cool do not include women
any women examples ?
and i said it doesn't work that way (Nina Simone notwithstanding)
that would be redundant

and Blais that freak here in Québec has said on the news
no more "rigologie" dans les écoles - we want more sport
you know, the Canadiens hockey team

is this the Kator conference i heard about ?
why are you sitting in the corner, so forlorn
and they take your phone away
obviously they are afraid of the big Crackup
i don,t know who is that troll about Zizi it doesn't surprise me

https://www.youtube.com/watch?v=cE6_6DFNsVk
[Slavoj Zizek on Why You're Never Really Alone With Your Sexual
Partner]

NZ at Tadeusz Kantor centennial conference, la Sorbonne, April 2015.
Photo by Sava Andjelovic.

Zivancevic Nina <zivancevicn65@gmail.com>
To: Marc Léger <leger.mj@gmail.com>
14 April 2015 at 15:29

Ohhhh
Good! yOu are perceptive !! U see
Things ... Subtile nuances
Then i dont even have to mention
If u were here things would nt be snivel snivel for me
Perhaps i'd get some time off in that (now already famous Eric von
strocheim) basement
Perhaps we wld even work out the basement hours and i'd learn some
new rumba steps to dance when you're away....

Marc Léger <leger.mj@gmail.com>
To: Zivancevic Nina <zivancevicn65@gmail.com>
14 April 2015 at 15:43

what do i know about such things
rumba, salsa ...

Zivancevic Nina <zivancevicn65@gmail.com>
To: Marc Léger <leger.mj@gmail.com>
14 April 2015 at 15:52

But hey
This correspondence—ain't it the biggest pingpong big bong cum chess
game of them all?
On days like this I think I cld live w u anywhere you'd like to
A Crusoe island
Indiana jones temple
Marc James chessboard ..
And there will come a moment...
Anyways
Much more much later...

So I hope u don't mind this dope of - 294

Marc Léger <leger.mj@gmail.com>
To: Zivancevic Nina <zivancevicn65@gmail.com>
14 April 2015 at 15:57

i don't know if you are aware of your unconscious thoughts
but if this is MJ chess board
you are playing with the big blue
later skater

Zivancevic Nina <zivancevicn65@gmail.com>
To: Marc Léger <leger.mj@gmail.com>
14 April 2015 at 16:12

Ouf fucking gator...

Envoyé de mon iPhone

Loving you is like talking to Voltaire

Zivancevic Nina <zivancevicn65@gmail.com>
To: Marc Léger <leger.mj@gmail.com>
14 April 2015 at 16:58

So never let go of that innuendo
Stay up there my dear..
DON'T U ever trash our emails.. If nothing else (the kids, a car, à house)
this CLD become a beautiful book...

Marc Léger <leger.mj@gmail.com>
To: Zivancevic Nina <zivancevicn65@gmail.com>
14 April 2015 at 19:26

Industrial Music Poem
Industrial Music Poem
Industrial Music Poem

Zivancevic Nina <zivancevicn65@gmail.com>
To: Marc Léger <leger.mj@gmail.com>
15 April 2015 at 04:46

wow!
WOW!!
You're quite a poet dalin'!
Can i translate this one
Can i be yr traductrice
Can i be yr?
Can i be?
Can can...

Zivancevic Nina <zivancevicn65@gmail.com>
To: Marc Léger <leger.mj@gmail.com>
15 April 2015 at 05:04

Thank u. I got yr poem when i felt the lowest..
I d like to write one fr you
And it's in my throat (whenever i feel it there it is a good one usually)
But i need to sit down for that one..
And i wont be able before 5pm so hold on...

Cmok cmok cmok

Fwd: 201

Zivancevic Nina <zivancevicn65@gmail.com>
To: Marc Léger <leger.mj@gmail.com>
14 April 2015 at 16:15

Just one thing gator
You tell yr "friends" who feed u bananas.. Just tell them "btw nina's on
her way to the Montréal airport " but she cant find her way around. Cld u
help her find her way to my place?"
That would do...
Waiting then
However..i'm thinking of visiting you as well this summer
Let me know where are you going to be... Is there a cheap hôtel that i
can check in etc etc
this 'bidon' title made me think that i shd see you in person
But , it occured to me that my visit wld just freak u out and produce
a negative effect as u are used now to our onto/ hystérique
correspondence, my dear Marie François
However
If our correspondence becomes a bit impoverished and less interesting
I wont hésitate to hop on a dirigeable or a baloon and will visit your
brigade wherever yr forces are. I shdnt always dwell as a part of yr
Imaginary fantasy équipement and among yr anthropological/soc props
I LOOOVVE reality even at its worst
Aint i your.. Whatshername mme Châtelet ?
Wait then till i board my train on Saturday..
Perhaps i wont be able to write every hour but every three hours from
Belgrade etc

Envoyé de mon phone secret

Marc Léger <leger.mj@gmail.com>
To: Zivancevic Nina <zivancevicn65@gmail.com>
15 April 2015 at 09:09

Dear Mme Châtelet,
Whait?
You must be busy today on the train to Zaghreb
If you come here and disturb the fantasy i will turn into a poof of smoke
I will transform into the frog that croaked
And your Sheherezade stories are not even close to 101
After which time our ontic-hysteric liaisons will have challenged the art-
life thing
To your satisfaction

Perhaps we should call our booklet:
Corps Responds Danse Bidon: Poèmes Sans Filet
Has that one been used ?
I will wait 5 hours for your rejoinder

Zivancevic Nina <zivancevicn65@gmail.com>
To: Marc Léger <leger.mj@gmail.com>
15 April 2015 at 09:30

Ha ha ha !
My provocation made sense
I feel yr brave warrior's heart got weakened at the very mention of my
physical hommage to yr mountainous temple in
Montirreal!
Dear- what's the name of yr fantasy? Is that lovely thing taking a shower
chez toi right now?

Marc Léger <leger.mj@gmail.com>
To: Zivancevic Nina <zivancevicn65@gmail.com>
15 April 2015 at 10:45

to be fair to you
our thingamajing has to make some sense
still, i must say, you give me cause to stress
the medium is the mistress

Zivancevic Nina <zivancevicn65@gmail.com>
To: Marc Léger <leger.mj@gmail.com
15 April 2015 at 11:36

Ok ok bien entendue
And I am not a monkey although i start wondering sometimes
At any rate, to push our metaphor - I won't feed you bananas but a
banana cake
(Which is a major difference between the countess of Alba
And an Albanian village girl from the woods) for u to
tink thank about it

Marc Léger <leger.mj@gmail.com>
To: Zivancevic Nina <zivancevicn65@gmail.com>
15 April 2015 at 13:25

i wrote a paper on Enver Hoxha while an undergraduate history major
i also wrote about the Catholic Church in Ontario
i think that was good preparation for an encounter with an albanian
village girl like you

Zivancevic Nina <zivancevicn65@gmail.com>
To: Marc Léger <leger.mj@gmail.com>
15 April 2015 at 14:28

yeah really- and you'd say you want to meet an albanian village girl
just to say something contrary to me.. ok not to be too Lacanian about
it—
but I see now that you, Marc James Léger, have really flipped out at
imagining all sorts
of missibilities,
please calm down
I will not bother you with my visit or—in any other way..

Zivancevic Nina <zivancevicn65@gmail.com>
To: Marc Léger <leger.mj@gmail.com>
16 April 2015 at 08:11

Marc,
I am on the editorial board of Au Sud de l'Est, culture of the Balkans at
their best and .. We (Jerome) is soliciting articles on erotic art and writing
, wld you like to contribute? If you have smth on Albania or Bulgaria or
even Serbia or Croatia ?
Deadline is sept 1.
Or shd we do it in "4 hands"...I am lazy and bored to keep knocking
these texts out by myself.. D'accordo?
Muchos besos
Mme de..
Je, myself et moi telephone

Marc Léger <leger.mj@gmail.com>
To: Zivancevic Nina <zivancevicn65@gmail.com>
16 April 2015 at 09:37

Please find attached a Wiki PDF for Mme Émilie de Chatelet. You can enter this in your journal as an entry by me titled Wiki Poem for Nina Zee, by MJ Léger
let me know if this doesn't work for you and Jerome
I can maybe do better but I would need more time, like a day or two
Let me know
Marc

Zivancevic Nina <zivancevicn65@gmail.com>
To: Marc Léger <leger.mj@gmail.com>
16 April 2015 at 11:03

If we continue "understanding " one another in this manner i will stop this correspondence as Nina whatsoever And keep the imaginaire for MFV. Correspondence.. And that one cld continue- next year around this time.. You see: I need an uplift and yr words. Risk to bring me down, my dear M...

A serious poem for Marc J.

Zivancevic Nina <zivancevicn65@gmail.com>
To: Marc Léger <leger.mj@gmail.com>
16 April 2015 at 03:38

Dearest, you are denying the notion
Of the nearest
Your lovely beehive full of theories
Would not ever explore the ghetto I live in
There the hookahs the jasmine incense and the stench of yesterday's
cous cous makes me abhore
The very idea of the rolypoly alien
In the dark ally of that bygone French colonisation
As I walk my high heels and the poodle through the muddy cobbles of
Paree (after all, I have to eat something for dinner too), I think of
You, trapped in the prison of the analytic, you are so gorgeous when you
spell the politics, yr mind always dwelling on me and my high heels and
my poodle, you will zip Zappa and make him and some other acrobats in
yr circus doodle yr noodle
You think you got a formula for the clear blue sky and that extra sunshine
Turning the Bahamas into the web link and yr own commodity mall..
And is that all? That fills your inner space full of hissing
I need you badly when it comes to kissing
And some other social actions you perform in the morning and when I'm
not around...
Behold: never will I ruin yr fantasy of the free world gone asunder
Will never hold you close to my breast and provoke such blunder
I saw yr face on TV last night speaking of Kobane and Syria as if it were
a new toothpaste
The one I'm using before your virtual kiss
After all, I'm such a dainty "miss"
I wouldn't like you to miss me a lot
Once I'm gone off yr orbit...

Envoyé de mon espace le plusintime

Zivancevic Nina <zivancevicn65@gmail.com>
To: Marc Léger <leger.mj@gmail.com>
16 April 2015 at 05:14

For you to understand the notes:
The imaginary "I" comes close to Zhizhek in the poem
and the poodle is Stephen Kotkin
the high heels is a Madonna image etc
and all the rest, you can figure out by yrself

Fwd: Joseph Nechvatal – bOdy pandemOnium. Immersion into Noise – Vernissage 24. April, 20h

Zivancevic Nina <nzivancevic@ymail.com>
To: Marc Léger <leger.mj@gmail.com>
16 April 2015 at 05:40

I sent you a poem, Voltaire,
it's even better than a letter..
mme deChatelet

Nina Zivancevic <nzivancevic@ymail.com>
To: Marc Léger <leger.mj@gmail.com>
16 April 2015 at 07:02

My dear M.(Mariefrancois),
I imagine how hard it is for you to lick the boots of the king of Prussia
to obtain some money and some grants. While here in the countryside
I had heard the he also asked you to suck his dick and ugly and
horrendous as he is I imagine you said no to him.
Yes I am trying to go out very little
I'm taking care of this huge manuscript which will become soon
something known as my Memoirs..I miss you a lot
I know Prussia is not England by any means
And you won't stay there forever but..
Think of me sometime soon
Drop me a line (not of coke) but some nice fiction that dummies call yr
philosophy
I miss our cuddly playing in the bathtub
And I even fired 2 servants
They are not very good at it
You know better how to splash that water around
Your loving friend
Mme de Chatelet

pardon me your royal heinie

Marc Léger <leger.mj@gmail.com>
To: Zivancevic Nina <zivancevicn65@gmail.com>
16 April 2015 at 09:23

Perfume Poem for an Amateur

My dear Amélie
or as you are better known by your pareesian entourage
Gabrielle Émilie Zee
you are a great man with not too many faults
and not a wikipedia page to blemish your reputation
a well-kept secret
something should be done for you
as our supreme leader once said in a tv commercial
my wig is full of talc
it makes me delirious at times
yet the sense of duty to you knows no reason
this is no doubt due
as my knowledge has nothing to compare
such oddity
but we stand for our cmok antics and symbols
i imagine you somewhere
reading this letter
what do i know about court culture and prospects
their strange mannerisms and formalities
but i'm on to you
j'aime beaucoup les mille feuilles d émilie l'étrange
cette créature pas complètement zen

Zivancevic Nina <zivancevicn65@gmail.com>
To: Marc Léger <leger.mj@gmail.com>
16 April 2015 at 10:42

Ach! My lovely lovely
Marie François !! How sorely missed you can be and the idéal idea of
that idéal idea .. Now i really start feeling like a rhésus monkey in a cave
And you give me some light
And no shadow...
More later
Yr chiaroscuro pal..

Marc Léger <leger.mj@gmail.com>
To: Zivancevic Nina <zivancevicn65@gmail.com>
16 April 2015 at 15:03

okay, i did something, i don,t know
let me know if i made a mistake somewhere
you can send this to Jerome for special issue on albania
for the unusual art and writing from the Balcony
your fan

Author: Marc James Léger
Title: Le Cirque (d'Après Georges Seurat)
Year: 2015

Attachment: PDF of Wikipedia entry for NZ created by MJL

Zivancevic Nina <zivancevicn65@gmail.com>
To: Marc Léger <leger.mj@gmail.com>
16 April 2015 at 15:32

Oh my dearest MarieFrancois
You know i know you will say this is TOTALY crazy but i'm thinking about
this article.. If it's erotica from the Balkans yes of course
It cld be a talk about it, erotic writing between you and me
We sort of "fit the thème " , like U R totally legit to ask me question
- How do i write "it"? And do i wear that corset while writing
-- do i think of that object dark object of desire ...and How often i think (of
u) while writing
Am i panting and sighing
Do i have orgasms thinking of you? How often? What's the creative
pattern if any to it?
Yes! We can do it--
Ds this project intérêst u?
Yr zée

Zivancevic Nina <zivancevicn65@gmail.com>
To: Marc Léger <leger.mj@gmail.com>
16 April 2015 at 15:34

And thank you so much my dearest smartest creature on Earth
I've been missing you eversince you had gone..err.. 3 centuries ago ,
right?

Envoyé de mon iPhone

Zivancevic Nina <zivancevicn65@gmail.com>
To: Marc Léger <leger.mj@gmail.com>
16 April 2015 at 17:37

Oh! Thank you so much (this is just a light thing to say!!) for all your work
on the Wiki page
of course, I've been resisting, like I was resisting fooolishly my web site
for days and years
but for you to undertake such work!
Marc-- you are really a devoted friend and a brother! what can i say
more..
Big oversees kiss- you are really- well, a web master
and kank you!
NZ

Second set of questions

Zivancevic Nina <zivancevicn65@gmail.com>
To: Marc Léger <leger.mj@gmail.com>
17 April 2015 at 08:35

So now onto an even more difficult one: who is Zina Née ? This i cant tell u as she' s a born performer, changing all the time
She lives off white foam and civilized conversation , that almost extremely forgotten art of communication provided by a genius friend she meets every 20 years. Like she ran into Voltaire the other week. She read his books, she said "holy guacomole, this being i'm reading-- seems like someone i cld talk to.. Be it a boy, a girl, a cat, a snake.. No not snake, strike that.." But anyways she was delighted she cld talk to a being Baroque and Bauhaus at the same time, so she rushed in her delusional folly, and started writing emails emais emails. She was a bit selfish in her quest but her young friend, Voltaire, had always offered her a chair to sit down...whenever she started losing ground...

Envoyé et pour partie 3...

Part 3

Zivancevic Nina <zivancevicn65@gmail.com>
To: Marc Léger <leger.mj@gmail.com>
17 April 2015 at 09:11

And in fact, how to go directly into our "erotica" exercise..
In my view, you dont need any teaching or coaching as you are already
a born seducer (if u cld seduce someone like me!! With yr élégant and
ga ga galant style- you must be some very talented guy!)
But how to start, How to keep that high style, i just dont know .. If i knew
it once i tried to forget it..
At any rate and by all means we should be veryyy selective as to the
words and the so called plot..otherwise danger of becoming mellifluous
You see the idea wld be to show Viktor Shklovsky -- in action(writing) all
the premises that Lacan talks about
And Bataille , of course
In other words, in stead of saying "i desire her/him/you" one shd allow
that desire to penetrate the text-- which you often do, Marc, bravo!
You're already the champ of that genre i'm telling you!
All good writers are great seducers..and they are casual, léger
About it. Now you be Léger ! Which bring me to point no4 here..

late night entertainment with artistes

Marc Léger <leger.mj@gmail.com>
To: Zivancevic Nina <zivancevicn65@gmail.com>
16 April 2015 at 20:04

anais nyx
always, you travel more swiftly into the night
before me,
and you wake at the break of your chariot
now capiche that you don't mind my
shmoozing you on the internet
look, i even write all this like you
like van gogh in the cool mines
let us talk about erotic writing, the kind that says darling
and what is the meaning of this
this line is too long or too short and maybe you need some classes
the object of your desire is dark when you cover it with glasses
that project on the girl from albania
i'm all for it, of course
as long as it has the word girl i'm like a pushover
and not unfamiliar with the théorie de la fille
you can count on my collaboration in your resistance movement
we can talk about erotica in xxx-yugoslavia
but you will have to provide me with the requisite details
what can i do for you ?
what do i know about literature or the theatre ?
there is a line missing here
this thing is incomplete

Zivancevic Nina <zivancevicn65@gmail.com>
To: Marc Léger <leger.mj@gmail.com>
17 April 2015 at 03:51

Wow!
Wait a minute, your letter requires a serious answer, line by line, Voltaire,
And a serious analytic treatment
Which you will get from me, "for free". I have to reciprocate yr kindness
for including me into yr circus and Wiki tiki...i need more time for it as your
case, somewhat like mine, deserves a serious attention cum approach.
I see, there is a big confusion in yr head, dalin, and it has to be cleared
right away-- after all, they wldnt keep me in this doghouse called "la
Sorbonne" if i did not know how to bark or whine at least..
Having said all of the above-- i profoundly apologise to you for my sloppy
style and approach to our correspondence:
here's a piece of my analysis as well:

Not only that i'm tired from my two hour sleeps and my Life becoming worse than a catnap, but i felt very cosy in yr circus from the start.
The start of what?
More later
But at ANY rate , you shd not be afraid, start flippîg out and basically feel uncomfortable by my showers of affection.
Ok i'll stop it.
Gee, i'm talking to u as if u were a little boy..(arent We all ?:))

Zivancevic Nina <zivancevicn65@gmail.com>
To: Marc Léger <leger.mj@gmail.com>
17 April 2015 at 04:33

Ok i understand -- you dont want me to appear sloppy in any given way: it's like walking in my pijamas in yr salon or saloon, and you entertain the ambassador of Bhutan. I'll will clip my stylistic nails and brush up on my act
I will never wear my pijamas when you're around. What shd i wear?
For you to tell me and.. Start our erotica correspondence although i have to warn you: my expression is really rusty when it comes to miaow miaow language. In fact i have to remember my previous erotic expérience , as i've had so many awful encounters for the last couple of years that i decided not to have sex any longer. Analysis : it has to be both , head aaand stomac, and shd come from yr head.that's what the shrink said. So now, i wld like to train myself and you, why not, in that genre, yeah Nin and Miller are back, and you have a good sense of humor. That's important and that's no 1 in this sort of fiction, no pathetica in there..
And i know that Jerome wld like us to say smth like "what Lacan or Kristeva or winnicot or Jacques miller wld say about erotic writing" but we should not bother w theory at this moment.
We shd get trained with the original body of texte.
What do you think?
At any rate i'm getting back to u this very afternoon.

Zivancevic Nina <zivancevicn65@gmail.com>
To: Marc Léger <leger.mj@gmail.com>
17 April 2015 at 08:14

Ok, back to yr letter: I 'll answer the last questions first, then make it through the thicket of ideas towards the
beginning:

That the poem is incomplete- it shouldn't bother you so much
That it exist but is incomplete is Ok
And even better for a poem to remain incomplete ...unlike a novel or a
doggerel..they should be completed.
As to yr worries in a form of questions "what do i want from u?" What can
u do for...?etc
now the best thing is to relax and enjoy the act of writing. I can be,
more premeditative or calculating than me here, and now, with you.
But this time I was caught off avant guard.so I want nothing from you,
that is, nothing more than a civilized conversation worthy of my worthy
colleague .. At least I thought so a month ago but some categories have
slipped between my fingers and my toes..and i started writing more than
regularly to you
And you didn't discourage me in this postal looneybin..
I found this juxtaposition of not knowing you vs knowing many things that
you usually do-- highly amusing. And i find yr way of reasoning similar to
mine, a thing rare to find- also mindblowing. I hope you forgive me my
overzeal as it's totally benign even if i suffer its consequences.
The mind is tricky though ..and here the thème Song comes in "i've been
writing you for too long.. Cant stop now.. U r becoming a habit to me"
Ay ay ay... Gotta catch a bus..
Part ii follows:

Zivancevic Nina <zivancevicn65@gmail.com>
To: Marc Léger <leger.mj@gmail.com>
17 April 2015 at 12:44

Let us not enter into the reverie of the meaning, let's do like the school of
analytics- it either exists there or it does not; as to the Dark object of my
desire, he's a nonchalant subject and his name clearly shows his quality
à la Légère, that is, OMEN NOMEN as the Latins would say
I am not going to cover my eyes with dark glasses like i said in one of my
poems "I don't need glasses to see poverty nor the magnifier to see that
someone is blind.."
OK, I gave you a lot of poetic advice today which perhaps sounds like an
arrow through the air where I've been dwelling for a while, as my novel
says..
Time to get back to Earth.. How old are you indeed? It seems to me
eversince I started this correspondence that
you're very young, please stay that way, I mean keep the heart that way
and always REBEL, that's what Julia Kristeva said: stay young at heart
and complain, be angry
she says that that is very healthy for yr wellbeing!
ok the interview..

yet another arrow until I OD on these emails

Zivancevic Nina <zivancevicn65@gmail.com>
To: Marc Léger <leger.mj@gmail.com>
17 April 2015 at 17:49

yes, and that project on the girl from albania i'm all for it, of course as long as it has the word girl i'm like a pushover and not unfamiliar with the théorie de la fille you can count on my collaboration in your resistance movement we can talk about erotica in xxx-yugoslavia

does this mean you're a cad?

Re: ,you're my emotional rescuuueeeee

Marc Léger <leger.mj@gmail.com>
To: Zivancevic Nina <zivancevicn65@gmail.com>
17 April 2015 at 19:11

dina, to be read and rebutted whenever you've unpacked ... it looks
like you're going to be chocolat for 10 days or more but my guess is
you won,t resist sending me an iPhone here and there and as i'm only
16 years old i will reply to you in the briefest delay -- yes it's amazing
what 10 days can do to a person -- and where is Sophia and all
those characters in your plays - i hope you mention me in your radio
interviews, just casually, you know: "i was talking to that Canadian guy
the other day and he said something that made no sense and that I
would like to repeat here - he said my broken leg to him was a piece
of roccoco friandise and he would nibble on that for a while until i
confess all my bow wow fantasies in a nice delusional folly called these
correspondences of varying erotic, robotic, and analytic intensities" --
and sure when it comes to the érotische, it will make for an interesting
cad film or commercial and somehow that should tell us something about
our occupations and preoccupations, like speculative and experimental
zivancevics -- not a field i understand very well and so i guess you are
my girlf experience where you tell me things i can't understand

Zivancevic Nina <zivancevicn65@gmail.com>
To: Marc Léger <leger.mj@gmail.com>
19 April 2015 at 08:41

and where is Zina now in yr Pantheon - i hope you took her home that is
why no need to mention her here, and besides who are all these people
dina, nina etc
i know that dina is alice in wonderland,s cat...
this much i know, you cad of cads...

Marc Léger <leger.mj@gmail.com>
To: Zivancevic Nina <zivancevicn65@gmail.com>
19 April 2015 at 09:18

just a little tiny email
about where are you going on tv
you are straight outta (or into) compton
N.W.A. (Niggaz Wit Attitudes) = N.I.N.A

save for later – marcs 1 and 2

Marc Léger <leger.mj@gmail.com>
To: Zivancevic Nina <zivancevicn65@gmail.com>
19 April 2015 at 10:15

hey star
sorry to bother you backstage
i was wondering
how does a spinozist like you
get caught up in transcendental meditation
just ignore this
back to your big business

Zivancevic Nina <zivancevicn65@gmail.com>
To: Marc Léger <leger.mj@gmail.com>
20 April 2015 at 04:31

ach, no comment,
auuu an elephant sneezed and fell on his knees,
lots of sneezing around here, seems like we all had a very good time
around
here, pretty wasted this morning, so, how.. watcha say
a spinozist like me -always- had a good time while reading mr.H> and
fell into the well of Being--and hopped into the metaphysics of presence
or was it the meta meta of absence? you tell me Marc, the Marcness of
Marc, how do we go about the Hermeneutics of suspicion? is it always
hermeneutical that we are suspicious of this loop where we find
ourselves in early morning , and shiiit
it,s already 10 @) and my hair, the one you like to tease in the
metaphysical room of the internet is so dirty not really ready for this radio
or any other appearance
perhaps Zhizhek has to say something about this meta wreck around
here ZDRAVO Zhizhek and hello flamboyant
creature
soon i,ll go to check the reminants of the remaining radio and TV
buildings so many kids died around here but they are dying all over the
planet
as i can,t give them any money right night when i see beggars with their
cups i must say - back to metaphysics-
godblessyou

Re: telling it like it zizz

Marc Léger <leger.mj@gmail.com>
To: Zivancevic Nina <zivancevicn65@gmail.com>
17 April 2015 at 11:19

nyx, as i go through your sling of good mornings all i can say is that
my record in the professional sector has often been subverted, but
with you as we both seem to think, the beat goes on and yes it is a
correspondence that has some qualities as i know a good chocolate
wrestling match and have been loving to play with u it's truly my
privilege, you go first - now that we're getting to the "serious" stage
where all of this blends

there is a diagram from Hirschhorn's Timeline and i think i may have
shown it to you before - it has badiou's 4 truth procedures – love, art,
science and politics – and it's divided by four figures that his work
possibly leaves out of the picture: Gramsci, Bataille, Deleuze, Spinoza -
now is it not possible that in these corners it is the nina hagendaz, with
her constant stream of events and things to do and editor guy pals - and
over there it's me, this square boy focused on the little lines rather than
the cellophane reflections

yes of course you do the boy and i do the girl and i have never
considered anything but your original loveliness and so what comes next
if not erotica - but to keep it high i don't know if that is even in my vocab
though i have also taught the penetrating techniques of doctors Cixous,
Irigaray and others; this desire everywhere all the time just gets me into
trouble trying to get into the women's washroom

so let me know what's involved - i was thinking since i don't know
albanian and don't know south east from north west that we should write
something about makavayev's reich film and sweet sugar movies - or
maybe we do different parts

Zivancevic Nina <zivancevicn65@gmail.com>
To: Marc Léger <leger.mj@gmail.com>
17 April 2015 at 11:32

Oh, I love that Thomas Hirschhorn's painting
how beautiful, pity I haven't reviewed his show never ever
so i cannot ask him for a drawing, I guess I cannot
anyways it will stay always.. shit, here he goes again on Skype
hold on..

Zivancevic Nina <zivancevicn65@gmail.com>
To: Marc Léger <leger.mj@gmail.com>
17 April 2015 at 12:08

you're exuberant as ever
or your words have a speciall charm/effect on me
I've entered this mad mad state of mind where i believe that YOU
understand me and that I understand you
but- as usual, as always- it can be a damn illusion like you
wake up one day, and after good 10 years of living together you discover
that your partner does not undestand a word
you're saying.. or is it just that
they don't want to undestand? They gort tired of trying to understand..?
this has nothing to do with our erotica issue, but with me-- all erotica
goes through my head first and then.. well, materializes or not
hold on..
I'm trying in a mad rush- to wrap all things up.. as I'm leaving tomorrow
morning and will come back in 10 days
high packing anxiety catches up with me- what do i owe and to whom?
Ah, to you, pics in high resolution, there..
do you really think that I'm a boy? Tom-boy?, well i was never given
space or time- to be a gentle princess.. growin up under that Communist
regime in a family of a
high party official who fell out of political grace... it was tough, even now
when I
enter Serbia they go: yr father did this and that, or he didn't do this didn't
well he did not believe in Militant Stalinian marxism, he fought for it in
1920s and then gave up on it..
but wait.. I owe you the rest of the interview as well,will try to embelish it
before i get out, Lee Ann Brown is in town and has a reading, and then
Claude, invited me to dinner in l'Arpege, I'd much rather practice my
arpeggios on my violin but I like the restaurant. The last time we were
there I met Sophia Coppola, I held her hand for a minute and I said:
Thank you La'am for making such lovely movies! They're- good!
so she said something like "and what do you do?" to which I: Oh, i write
about films, and i haven't reviewed your up to now, but i will
(now with our Vontaire- Marie Antoinette RE I'll get into her story..
oh my dear.. I have already 3 interviews lined up in Belgrade, for the
radio and TV,
Dan is accompaning me as he's afraid to let me go on my own- see my
story with my broken leg is not very cheerful, I have to see some doctors
there..
I'll be on my best behavior though- I will organize that hommage to Judith
what else?
Hope that you will come with me and see my hometown one day-- that
is, if you're not adverse to the idea of meeting me, ever...

Zivancevic Nina <zivancevicn65@gmail.com>
To: Marc Léger <leger.mj@gmail.com>
18 April 2015 at 03:23

You are so ... handsome
Comes more like a curse in life than blessing
Than you have to hide behind the hard work you're doing.. All life long
ax ay ay
handsome as a sin
so i am in a real trouble
i mean ive been on yr leash for a while singing thoughtlessly -i wanna be
yr dog
little did i know, heavenly beauty that hides yr brilliant mind
well, i dont deserve you, thats for sure
penelope baking a banana cake, just fr you

Marc Léger <leger.mj@gmail.com>
To: Zivancevic Nina <zivancevicn65@gmail.com>
19 April 2015 at 03:23

as you conference and continue baking
8 days to go

Zivancevic Nina <zivancevicn65@gmail.com>
To: Marc Léger <leger.mj@gmail.com>
21 April 2015 at 06:14

JUST FOR YOU
Religion is opium for people
K:Marx

RELIGIOUS KETA DREAM - erotica piece
Empty skyscrapers over the suburb of Belgrade where I used to live as
a kid.Three quarters of the landscape,s background are filled with early
morning clouds and it is there where yr dainty face emerges, solemn,
sprinkled with tired wrinkles and recent internet memories. You keep
staring at my tiny early morning breasts sweating, showing up slowly
behind the covers, my light blue hair falls slightly over my Rembrandt
cheek....I know this Andre Breton look on yr face, after all, you are *un
Breton ,* in search of his Celtic roots, and we are in the land of Celts,,,
You're searching for my hand but it is hidden between my legs where
total intimacy, total madness, writing for the sake of writing are hidden

and where yr dreams of the abandoned childhood sleeps, covered under my sweaty blankets.

Ohhh, you are kissing me at the spot where i think it will hurt, total intimacy always hurts, your lips at the opening of my vulva, where have you been? Why did i wait for you for so long and now that you-ve appeared here, why do i feel so sleepy? You, fast as a Mexian jaguar, you-re moving through me with grace and you- re trying to reach that spot which has never been entered before.

By no one. It.s like a secret chambre, , discreet photograph which speaks to you at the moment when we hear the cries of the seagulls, the heart of the desert thickens and I see yr sweat on yr weary brow embedded with theories.

These are yr instant cookies which you pop into my mouth around noon, as I shiver, sitting quietly on the top of yr dick then i begin moving slowly. You are my perpetuum mobile and I adore you, ach und ach, shriueking louder and ever louder until you lift up yr hand and cover my mouth with the back of yr palm... "are you happy now?" You ask me, then having noticed that I nodded my head, satisfied, you take my other hand, the one which is not covered with sweat, and you take me out.

For a walk. We should feed the cat first, you say. And then the dog, and then my parakeets. They ate truly innocent... "so different from us", you say. You are my church, you say. And you are my religion, I add. I have never seen so much zeal, so much enthusiasm, like i-ve seen in you, this morning.

You are my palace of an utmost loneliness, you finally say, carefully locking the door behind us, and i feel like a good schoolgirl, that i am, trotting behind you along a cobbled street..

from me to thee

Marc Léger <leger.mj@gmail.com>
To: Zivancevic Nina <zivancevicn65@gmail.com>
21 April 2015 at 02:25

I think you're pink. Add some black leather, roccoco furniture, books and violin. How does one get from the pink lettering on the advertisements for *Marie Antoinette* to those small white dressers with the gold handles in your boudoir, topped with what looks like a printer (which at another time might have been a record player) and so many books, all of which have trained your muscles over the years to become the kind of animal that pronounces with measure and pleasure at the thought of some fiction, fired like Annie Oakley reading a rented farm and practicing her sure shot: sweet swagger. Amateur pornographer equals emancipated nun who embarked on a worldwide career two years before Barbie was introduced and dressed in the latest fashion of birth control and bikini lines. After Tom Wesselman and Richard Lindner and the mechanisms of honest dreams and confused fantasies. Beyond protest, fetishism and head games, makeup and anxieties, passion and exhaustion. This is not quite street Largo Santa Susanna near the Turkish standards but I would certainly let you be my assistant if such confidences were covered with thoughts like that, blue-green and black, converging at the center of a silken galaxy, swirling with caution, betrayal, interruption – a magnetism for sure displaced already down a different corridor and another room after shadow, paint, doors and blinds of forgetting. A thousand words are condensed into only a few tear drops. You get the picture without having to go through the motions. It's simple. I run my ideas around your mind and pull your reddish-brown hair. But you're pink today. Like a pink angora cat you leave scratch marks. A few thoughts are added to this: cameras and stereos at the 220 volt headquarters. The owner has a new policy: the world premiere of hot sex babes and wet suds. Uh, oh, she's lost interest... Got to attack, with sexy glasses, red lips. Sexology for a curious and smart Betty page. This is Paris Confidential, wearing nothing but a black scarf around your neck – an ekphrasis of the state of being and lying on the couch. Z & Voltaire.

Zivancevic Nina <zivancevicn65@gmail.com>
To: Marc Léger <leger.mj@gmail.com>
21 April 2015 at 18:05

i am sorry that you didnt like it...
and as the matter of fact why should,ve you liked it!?
now i,m totally losing interest to continue this or any sort of
correspondence pink green oir yellow
good night

Marc Léger <leger.mj@gmail.com>
To: Zivancevic Nina <zivancevicn65@gmail.com>
22 April 2015 at 18:10

now what can i do that you will not fly the ?
you cis-poet fuss
good night

Zivancevic Nina <zivancevicn65@gmail.com>
To: Marc Léger <leger.mj@gmail.com>
21 April 2015 at 18:22

I dont expect you to like my small exercise in my hometown ruins
you have already described yourself as cold, cynic and ..jaded
i won't say phony simply that,s the way you are, that is.. if you are of any
sort.
how can you be so judgmental and pretentious
in your Hollywood boudoir with your kitties and..
enough is enough' go back to your social stance and .
one thing you don,t get .. and it has to do with tenderness and natural
outlook at human beings, so back to farce and social analysis and paste
copy of...
ok sorry, will have to say good bye

Zivancevic Nina <zivancevicn65@gmail.com>
To: Marc Léger <leger.mj@gmail.com>
21 April 2015 at 18:26

and when someone offers you something different from your view
you slap him-her back and shower yr friend with mean and unfriendly
remarks.. yeah,
what was yr diagnosis all about_-
how can i repair that house of terror you've been hiding in for years
yeah, how's about that

Zivancevic Nina <zivancevicn65@gmail.com>
To: Marc Léger <leger.mj@gmail.com>
21 April 2015 at 18:48

sorry for this cold shower, but you are probably sending yet another
series of kitties to someone else and thus not responding

Marc Léger <leger.mj@gmail.com>
To: Zivancevic Nina <zivancevicn65@gmail.com>
21 April 2015 at 18:48

thanks for setting me straight
when i read your poetry i knew one day you would do that
i didn't think you would get all puffy and offer me lessons in human
nature
now who is pretentious here
you the goddess who does not appreciate my gifts and can't see past
your own sentences, or did i miss something
another thing - as they say here in some place not meant for tourists
if i had all of the adjectives you've typed about me listed you would see
some pretty different things
all i offer you is scarf and you get upset
and you are the one who started it
don't understand you, lady besmirched

Marc Léger <leger.mj@gmail.com>
To: Zivancevic Nina <zivancevicn65@gmail.com>
21 April 2015 at 18:49

what do you mean other kitties ?
you think i know poetesses like this social phenomenon diva
NO

Zivancevic Nina <zivancevicn65@gmail.com>
To: Marc Léger <leger.mj@gmail.com>
21 April 2015 at 18:54

now now calm down my social copy paste thinker
or should i say tinker...
no strike that i just want to tell you something ...
my one and only Marc James Leger
if you ask for haut expression and perfection in thinking
you should give it yourself
i am truly flexible at any sort of discussion
but it's YOU who sets the tone

Marc Léger <leger.mj@gmail.com>
To: Zivancevic Nina <zivancevicn65@gmail.com>
21 April 2015 at 18:58

i want you to give you a warm bath and fix your hair nice tomorrow
morning
have a drink
write me something when you have time and we can't continue this
erotic without some of your strange rules and regulations
like RESPECT, tact
other things happening -- yugoslavkya publik loves Nina i'm sure
ah shucks Nina

Zivancevic Nina <zivancevicn65@gmail.com>
To: Marc Léger <leger.mj@gmail.com>
21 April 2015 at 19:00

and any time you've written a letter to me
+a Wagnerian innuendo comes in here, which is by no means
trash and Sophie Calle
but rather Anette Messagers love for the dead birds...
anytime i-ve written a letter to you
there was a grain of truth in it
dont spit on it, please, i beg you, please

Marc Léger <leger.mj@gmail.com>
To: Zivancevic Nina <zivancevicn65@gmail.com>
21 April 2015 at 19:05

all this interview between Kristen Stewart and Patti Smith i just don't
understand what is punk about it - perhaps after this book i will be known
as Nina Zivancevic's assistant

Zivancevic Nina <zivancevicn65@gmail.com>
To: Marc Léger <leger.mj@gmail.com>
21 April 2015 at 19:07

when someone offers you something different from your own view
you slap him-her back and shower yr friend with mean and unfriendly

remarks.. yeah, please apply the same attitude of RESPECT and tact
in a more tactile manner
you are such a brilliant thinker
remain that way...
no sloppy pussyfooting from you
and you will not get it from other either

Marc Léger <leger.mj@gmail.com>
To: Zivancevic Nina <zivancevicn65@gmail.com>
21 April 2015 at 19:14

you must be writing down the rules of poetic engagement
with this business of your boudoir
take it easy
but i'm not a slapper - you misread, like maybe you're drunk already
what was i gonna say
déesse de la nuit - ayoyyye beaucoup plus de complaisance
pauvre petit minou le soir dans la ruelle - miaoouu

Zivancevic Nina <zivancevicn65@gmail.com>
To: Marc Léger <leger.mj@gmail.com>
21 April 2015 at 19:16

Marc-
Patti Smith is a phony
i am sorry but i have to point at yr illusion
instead, invite Penny Arcade, a working class girl to your circus
and you. will get something out of that contribution
she told me once she used to be Patti-s best friend
but avoided the commercial Patti like the pest, i was embarrassed to
meet Patti at the Cartier foundation 4 years ago especially when or after
i had learned lots of things from Robert-s lover Michael St Claire who
was my performance partner at the Living Theater
i don-t think i am any goddess or a punk rock star
but i can tell the difference between a black big cock and a white or pink
socialist pussycat
ok?

Marc Léger <leger.mj@gmail.com>
To: Zivancevic Nina <zivancevicn65@gmail.com>
21 April 2015 at 19:22

i won't go for penny arcade
and i'm not trying to get anything out of anything
i'm doing something
you know what i'm about
even if you think i'M a big black
je ne suis pas Charlie Hebdo
je suis un camarade et tu es une anarcho-trouble
je nage dans les dents de la mer

Zivancevic Nina <zivancevicn65@gmail.com>
To: Marc Léger <leger.mj@gmail.com>
21 April 2015 at 19:24

there you go again, and i will stop...
i think i am too much for you, even when i-m not drunk,
it really hurts when you flush insults down the toilet of my brain
at 1 30 am while my friends here are asleep and i hope to hear
one real and honest expression coming from you
whom i respect so much therefore i scream DONT do this to me
and DONT do this to yourself, you can do much better
without trying to be my assistant in my honesty

Zivancevic Nina <zivancevicn65@gmail.com>
To: Marc Léger <leger.mj@gmail.com>
21 April 2015 at 19:32

now that i-ve read in yr book that you don-t believe in anarchist work
what am i to think of your epithets?
you may be hating my guts and writing to me out of joke
and social cum editorial duty
Marc, i am afraid of you, i am at the point of going bananas
and stopping my mellifluous fiction called my letters to you
i may be someone who sells her blood around midnight to get one
miaow miaow from you
you can take this as a real poem for your dinner

Marc Léger <leger.mj@gmail.com>
To: Zivancevic Nina <zivancevicn65@gmail.com>
21 April 2015 at 19:32

you're brain is not a toilet and i do not flush insults
this is the way you describe me to all of serbia and to the sleeping
friends
as a tv guy
well, let me tell you – i'm post-contemporary post-bourgeois
just like you when you try to bamboozle me with DONT
and as for doing much better i need many more lessons in the school of
setting straight
and you are the one who will do better in that department i'm sure
but don't abandon me to your own devices
and don't throw around the wort hurt like it's a bing bong ball

---

Marc Léger <leger.mj@gmail.com>
To: Zivancevic Nina <zivancevicn65@gmail.com>
21 April 2015 at 19:39

what is this "take this" for your dinner
you must have grown up on off-off-broadway
here in the outskirts of ninasville, or far far away, whatever the case may
be
no one hates your guts - i love your guts - we love your guts
if you don't know that then you have gone bananas, truly
now have some gin or whatever you have in your hotel fridge and take it
easy
tomorrow is another day and i am left ecumenical - as i told you about
my comrades book
i have a critique of anarchism but we can't live without it and this isn't
1937 again
and the anarchists made some mistakes there too
so please, comrade, forget the word better

Zivancevic Nina <zivancevicn65@gmail.com>
To: Marc Léger <leger.mj@gmail.com>
21 April 2015 at 19:41

see how wrong you are?
and to set these records straight i must tell you
that i mentioned you in my radio interview yesterday
as the no 1 critic- historian of fresh market ideas
as someone really special in the post-communist world
who understands not only Hammurabi and Hieronymus Bosch but also
the workers of the Montreal film festival, and recommended your books
for reading and translation as i ALWAYS do , yeah even when i think yr
use of Žižek a bit redundant which i shd elaborate in my next letter if i
continue straining my childlike brain..
anyways, you can take that walk with me through Belgrade as an old
friend threw his keys at me yesterday and i will stay here throughout
June, July and August

Marc Léger <leger.mj@gmail.com>
To: Zivancevic Nina <zivancevicn65@gmail.com>
21 April 2015 at 19:52

yes, i am wrong
and i did not write the correct things and you are a good comrade who
helps me in the world
and i am not only patronizing you with my interview and book and
whatnot
i do not write essays for the journal of žižek studies, but you never know
some people, even in x-Yugoslavia, think that Brave was one of the first
books to apply Žižek to visual arts
whether or not that's true it was nice of them to say and some liked it
so that's good enough for me
and people in over-identification theory recognize that book as a relevant
source
so no, not redundant
i don't want to strain you further
i want you to have a good night's sleep
good night Nyx, goddess of all looming darkness

Zivancevic Nina <zivancevicn65@gmail.com>
To: Marc Léger <leger.mj@gmail.com>
22 April 2015 at 02:58

thank you.
This shows your good manners and good taste.
I apologize for my bad language as well...
which always appears less strong as it is a foreign language to me
I will say hello to yr camarades in Novi Sad, museum of cont. art where
i'm heading to this morning...

Zivancevic Nina <zivancevicn65@gmail.com>
To: Marc Léger <leger.mj@gmail.com>
23 April 2015 at 05:48

Dear Marc,
i don't see why you keep bombarding me with these images of THE
INTERVIEW's Gerard Malanga girls, OK, he is my friend and i accept all
his incongruencies and
both of you, it seems, like very very young girls and some animals
however, why not send me the Kim Gordon pic in a bathtub , for eg
and so, in this silly manner,when you set the tone, i follow with my
marshmellow silly fiction
as any POmo kid i like kitch and flatness but to a certain extent only
what's more at stake here and everywhere is 2 meters away
the country is still under some sort of dictatorship and not a pretty scene
around , i have to master all these scenes as this is my homecountry
and Djindjic was killed in a terrible way, i am still eager to know who
killed him and why
and for how much
my Democrat friends under the boots of censorship
the country will or most likely will not join the European Union but ther
effects of the CIA of Europe are already felt around here
now i was in N Sad yesterday and to my great relief
i saw in the Mus of cont art films by Zelimir Zilnik
like a bright red flower contradicting reality
oh, i have a lot to say about THIS reaslity
and i certainly will when i get back home in 3 days and get back to my
interview
can u wait this much
can u wait
i wondfer what's going on with u with the student movement over there
why you engage me in this so called Madonna and whore syndrome

havent you read any of my totally coherent essays

i really dont want to see any madnerss around me inside of me on top of me and all…

i already have a taste how it was in Hitler's bunker and then beneath the Berlin wall when i gave my last cabaret performance in Berlin… my piano player Bob Lenox collapsed and died afterwords

see i carry these images and memories many painful images like Gunter Grass

for instance thus

i dont want to deal with nonsense any longer , the real reason why i luckily quit the US of Nonsense

have a nice day, i will send you a really good interview this time around

Nina again

Zivancevic Nina <zivancevicn65@gmail.com>
To: Marc Léger <leger.mj@gmail.com>
25 April 2015 at 08:05

Alright, I've read my last email from Serbia to you,
yeah, perhaps I've hurt you. I mean it was hurting, something was
hurting me, something and I had to stop hurting and stop being hurt.

I love you implicitly, that is, your good writing (that's all i know of you),
you as a master sociologist and commentator and... a winged being (an
angel in disguise),
but lots of silly things have to stop in my life

or if i continue corresponding, it has to be much more substantial and
not hurting and all- can't obey the traps of the virtual in a funky manner
of speaking, nor you, I guess
love you
Nina

Fwd: Pozdav!

Marc Léger <leger.mj@gmail.com>
To: Zivancevic Nina <zivancevicn65@gmail.com>
28 April 2015 at 16:22

lemme know if you want me to draw up a word file with all of our exchanges - or if youre too busy these days to even think of this -- there is also the difference that a book is linear - i think retrofitting some parts would be necessary

---

Zivancevic Nina <zivancevicn65@gmail.com>
To: Marc Léger <leger.mj@gmail.com>
28 April 2015 at 17:33

I just have to ok the retrofitting, right ?

Envoyé

Zivancevic Nina <zivancevicn65@gmail.com>
To: Marc Léger <leger.mj@gmail.com>
28 April 2015 at 17:35

Yeah.. I authorize you to add or delete whatever u like
Sort of gets a better pic of you
Nice guy nice human fellow etc

Zivancevic Nina <zivancevicn65@gmail.com>
To: Marc Léger <leger.mj@gmail.com>
29 April 2015 at 18:15

I think I lived in some sort of a frenzy!
that part of you waking up in the middle of the night (or me for that matter and checking emails) is very poetical..
Now i don't know how to go about all this and above all, if we should really consider our correspondnce-- but come to think of it, there were many brilliant and memorable parts of it..
I know i pushed this correspondence very far.. and i always found like a mirror reflection in yr responses..
What i found absolutely astounding is the fact that we never ever met in person thus no physical contact whatsoever and yet i recognized the

traces of intimacy as if we shared our lives for many years or decades!
I was really ready to travel no matter where to meet you (perhaps we
saved each other from heavy disappointments)
but now, how to go about that fiction..
let me think about it for a while..
Whatever you decide I beg on you just to remember that the
correspondence is BETTER than anyone and everyone we could read
much (love)later
NZ

Marc Léger <leger.mj@gmail.com>
To: Zivancevic Nina <zivancevicn65@gmail.com>
29 April 2015 at 20:17

hello orange Nina
perhaps we could ask Masha Tupitsyn to write a foreword ??
cmok (is one potential title option?)

Image: [next page.]

Zivancevic Nina <zivancevicn65@gmail.com>
To: Marc Léger <leger.mj@gmail.com>
30 April 2015 at 09:36

Darling! I hope u dont mind me calling u darling as i call everyone i love
that way!
I am taking my parakeet to the vet! I even worry about my animals and
How cld i not /wldnot about you? Why thé wheelchair? You've been
in a real wheelchair, like the poet who i'm translating into english right
now? I dont know, this correspondence with you is timeless and hors
géographie ,, no i wont go to the Bahamas , i have better ways to fill
my days, really, but i was ready to travel anywhere in the world and see
you.. Look, there are funny sections of our exchange like the chapter i
give here:
Fear of Music (Cd be Musac)..
And that's the one with questions
Are u gay? Or are you triste etc...
Also there are some funny lines of yours concerning my protoburgeoise
lifestyle or activities.. As a punk friend of mine here remarked: where did
he find YOU to accuse of being petit-bourgeois ?
Etc etc

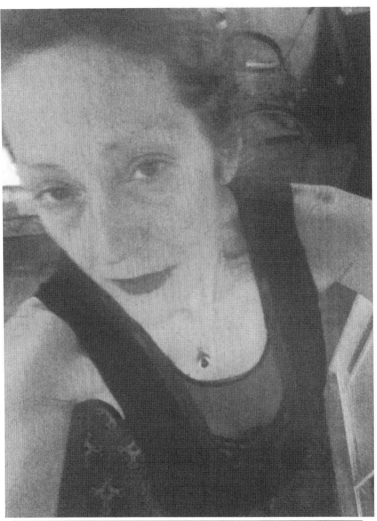

New NZ gmail avatar with orange skin, as of April 29, 2015.

Marc Léger <leger.mj@gmail.com>
To: Zivancevic Nina <zivancevicn65@gmail.com>
30 April 2015 at 10:11

my pet, if you don't mind this mujik droning druling all over you again,
i have to address this etc insofar as one concretely, one might say
jokingly, your egyptian status as an intellectual and artiste makes you
politically proletarian but in terms of composition something else (i'm not
just trying to flatter you) also, more later about why there is no such thing
as a Marxism-Leninism of sex

Zivancevic Nina <zivancevicn65@gmail.com>
To: Marc Léger <leger.mj@gmail.com>
30 April 2015 at 15:12

wait a minute, Marc!
for a second i forgot how viscious you can be
--i'm not yr pet nor i will ever be
i mean i'd like to pet you and pet pet pet
but not BE a pet- there's a bigo diff
anytime i give you too much access to my life
some shit happens-- right or wrong (wish i were wrong)
but love u anyways

Marc Léger <leger.mj@gmail.com>
To: Zivancevic Nina <zivancevicn65@gmail.com>
30 April 2015 at 15:22

it's hard to consider a serbian-toothed anything really with only your pet
noir and orange jelly bean

Zivancevic Nina <zivancevicn65@gmail.com>
To: Marc Léger <leger.mj@gmail.com>
30 April 2015 at 15:33

ok i am yr pet noir but
when i send you a very tender innermost fiction i fanthasized through
you slap me worse than these cheap S&M dungeon masters who kiss
and slap

--look: i am not Kathy Acker and i will never be
she was kind and she liked people
i do not ok?
i am a Schopenhauer's residue

Marc Léger <leger.mj@gmail.com>
To: Zivancevic Nina <zivancevicn65@gmail.com>
30 April 2015 at 15:56

oh yes, i heard about this in Magazine Littéraire
about the Schopenhauer pet food store; so if they put you on Belgrad
Publik just tell them you're not like Kathy Acker and so on

Zivancevic Nina <zivancevicn65@gmail.com>
To: Marc Léger <leger.mj@gmail.com>
30 April 2015 at 16:11

I gave you a vertical totally vertical
Answer! And the keys to read it you've got them all!
Dont be so condescending
I love you very much into u too..
And i'm trying to cut on my obsession
Obsessed by you
(This sounds like a real title for our fiction) my dearest dear

---

Marc Léger <leger.mj@gmail.com>
To: Zivancevic Nina <zivancevicn65@gmail.com>
30 April 2015 at 20:17

unfortunately there is no way out
you are trapped in some kind of Nina loop
some recommend meditation and a little yoga
or you could try baking soda ?

**the first ever chaplinbook
in the history of x-kind**

Marc Léger <leger.mj@gmail.com>
To: Zivancevic Nina <zivancevicn65@gmail.com>
29 April 2015 at 21:31

it begins
slow but sure
attached -- work in progress
men and women at work
i'm wondering what endorsement you used for Living on Air - not that it
matters
it's all true

Attachment: Word document of the draft manuscript for CMOK, title page
only

Zivancevic Nina <zivancevicn65@gmail.com>
To: Marc Léger <leger.mj@gmail.com>
30 April 2015 at 10:01

Several cmoks to you!
I'm still in the vet hospital (arent we all patients in there ?) but just
wanted to know if we cld divide that amorphous text into smaller
sections?
Yeah, me
Again

Marc Léger <leger.mj@gmail.com>
To: Zivancevic Nina <zivancevicn65@gmail.com>
30 April 2015 at 10:14

i have to run but just one thing i want to first make a more or less
complete copy and then we can adjust retrofit and so on
i am thinking of a picture also maybe for the cover - more on that after i
come back from the office (café)

Zivancevic Nina <zivancevicn65@gmail.com>
To: Marc Léger <leger.mj@gmail.com>
30 April 2015 at 11:54

I'm thinking of the title:
Marshmallow Muse: the exact and irreverant letter diaries of MJL and NZ
(The pet stayed in a hospital! Alas.. That's gonna cost me..)

Marc Léger <leger.mj@gmail.com>
To: Zivancevic Nina <zivancevicn65@gmail.com>
30 April 2015 at 13:43

one more in a soon to be soft and squishy list of possibilities
as long as you don't sit on your parrot he should be okay
don't read this comic that i have for you
you are a serious person and would never do this in a metro
http://www.vice.com/en_ca/read/megg-mogg-owl-dont-shit-in-the-
subway-951
[Megg, Mogg, & Owl, "Don't Shit in the Subway"]

Zivancevic Nina <zivancevicn65@gmail.com>
To: Marc Léger <leger.mj@gmail.com>
30 April 2015 at 15:38

ha ha ha ha
YOU little devil-- YOU... figured so many things on your own and by
yourself
I am totally moved.. by your knowledge and understanding of Nina Zee
you are lucky that you're so far away
if i were in MTL..

de nina Z.

Zivancevic Nina <zivancevicn65@gmail.com>
To: Marc Léger <leger.mj@gmail.com>
25 April 2015 at 07:38

dear Marc,
have no idea what you're up to.. Running around , tending to yr writing--
it does not surprise me (after those last couple of exchanges) that our
correspondence came to a halt. I think I know what might have produced
a certain feeling of anguish or disappointment on yr side, but let us leave
all my musings aside.
I'm coming back to you with the improved interview, as indeed, as you
yourself have remarked-- the old one was a bit incomplete.
I believe we have pushed our correspondence to the max, that is to
an unknown form and gender, genre, where two writers become very
comfortable with each other's writing, out of the blue, not really knowing
one another etc it was really the ODE to the virtual as it worked far
better... than any of our contemporaries would be able to do it!
Great!
now, we continue doing our.. whatever there is to be done, but,
methodical as i am, let me send you the interview improved, hope it
reads a bit better than the last thing I sent 2 weeks ago.
Love ya,
Nin

Attachment: Word document of new version of MJL NZ interview

Marc Léger <leger.mj@gmail.com>
To: Zivancevic Nina <zivancevicn65@gmail.com>
25 April 2015 at 09:54

thanks for this updated version of the intrvw - yes, our correspondence
had to find some meaning eventually in the world outside of l'amour fun -
i guess we'll never know for certain

Marc Léger <leger.mj@gmail.com>
To: Zivancevic Nina <zivancevicn65@gmail.com>
28 April 2015 at 12:17

please don't read this
i know i'm supposed to support you in your post-partum
i'M glad to know you have been busy and i don't understand why PARIS

of all place has allowed you to go single
i will not understand that
anyway, i have a suggestion for a TV commercial we can do

The scene opens with a frame of your face
(reminiscent of Gérard Courant)
Music: cello music from Debord's Société du Spectacle
after about 20 seconds the music stops
the camera pulls back
the image of your face was a reflection in a mirror
you are sitting in a bathtub looking in a hand-held mirror
(reference: Cranach Venus)
the tub and bathroom tiles are pink
the bath bubbles are white
looking into the mirror, you say:
"Darling, I don't want to overdoit."
Then a male voiceover:
"Nina Zivancevic. Coming soon."

Zivancevic Nina <zivancevicn65@gmail.com>
To: Marc Léger <leger.mj@gmail.com>
28 April 2015 at 12:37

Hahaha
Look, it's ok - in fact nothing really happened , i've really crossed the
border of the real/virtual.. In fact, you couldve been that programme or
automatic voice from the film HER..i got a bit carried away and it's not
entirely yr fault
But perhaps i could have been disappointing and dis dis.. Had i met you
in person..but here, yes
Paris is such a cold and lonely city and because of all that and more i
am completely on my way out(luckily i have elswhere to go) but hmmm..
Interesting sociol study for you, eg..
Look, my interest in you has had nothing to do with all these places and
non places...
Much love. Nina

Marc Léger <leger.mj@gmail.com>
To: Zivancevic Nina <zivancevicn65@gmail.com>
28 April 2015 at 13:56

I think the publication of our correspondence should be called Paris
Confidential. For me it also means finding the right images to go with
it, but somehow, somewhere along the line i think we should have
something that would be worthy of some serious consideration, even if
your friends might worry that you're slipping into bathroom taste

Zivancevic Nina <zivancevicn65@gmail.com>
To: Marc Léger <leger.mj@gmail.com>
28 April 2015 at 15:50

Ok Marc,
If you're really serious about a booklet-- i can "feel it", i mean with
CAREFUL editing it could be put into shape, the real good shape
Worthy of N & M (i mean those great guys, Nin and henry)
But auyyy,, we wld have to clean it a lot.. And question: are , wld we be
the folks to do it or leave it to smone like the beaver?
However , we have smth really good, great in there and that's the thème
or the burning issues of today:
What's "real" and what's virtual nowadays in friendship relationship
communication
How do people handle it not to go "over the border"
Is that sort of writing already "loony bin genre" or are we tapping here
into something new?
It's us to answer them and act accordingly
And then along this "spine" to arrange the beautiful cut-ups, snippets of
our dialogues w clicks links etc
Hey, that CLD be a lovely book, watcha say? You?

Marc Léger <leger.mj@gmail.com>
To: Zivancevic Nina <zivancevicn65@gmail.com>
28 April 2015 at 16:11

this surreal loony book could be something cute - we can add the
important words proletarian revolution, which i think we have neglected
-- i think we should do this work ourselves - maybe dragana nikolic can
do the cover!

Zivancevic Nina <zivancevicn65@gmail.com>
To: Marc Léger <leger.mj@gmail.com>
30 April 2015 at 14:59

i see that you like Dragana a lot, SHE is very young and cute, a nice lady and the artist... hmmmm???
ok you're a cad

Marc Léger <leger.mj@gmail.com>
To: Zivancevic Nina <zivancevicn65@gmail.com>
30 April 2015 at 15:08

i never met Dragana, but i do think her graphic work interesting and yes before that i did not know if Dragana is a Y or an Z particle or whatever they have over there
this Julie Doucet makes a cover for IAG 1 and does not include it on her 50 websites - what am i to make of this except what everybody knows which is the fact that she is a cad - her and Nina Zivancevic - the Serbian Tuthed Tiger with orange and black stripes

Zivancevic Nina <zivancevicn65@gmail.com>
To: Marc Léger <leger.mj@gmail.com>
30 April 2015 at 15:28

ok pussycat
you know that i belong to the family of Big Cats (be it a panther, a tiger, puma, gepard etc)
so DONT walk around saying that nobody has warned you prior to writing to me..

you're lucky

Marc Léger <leger.mj@gmail.com>
To: Zivancevic Nina <zivancevicn65@gmail.com>
2 May 2015 at 11:48

the worst best thing i could come up with for you is MINX or KITAKA but
i will look into it

CAD

*A rogue, or bounder. A cad is a man who is aware of the codes of
conduct which seperate a gentleman from a ruffian, but finds himself
unable to quite live up to them. Cads are quite capable of disguising
themselves as good chaps for some time, only revealing their true nature
in circumstances of particular stress or temptation. Others embrace their
caddishness whole-heartedly and delight in behaving in a manner which
is, to be quite frank, not cricket.*

*Regency-era swear word, meaning a man who doesn't treat Nina
Zivancevic proper.*

*A cad is someone who can be quite charming, intelligent, capable of
engaging in stimulating conversation, ultimately presenting himself as
a poet. A cad, however, is not a poet because he systematically cons
lovely ladies into falling in love with him and then openly cheats on them.
He is completely selfish with only feigned regard for women's feelings.*

*someone who acts like a COMPLETE butt to girls but is SO handsome.
Most guys who know him think he is a total jerk because he disagrees
with all their beliefs.*

*An ill-bred generic male hanger-on who flirts with everything avant-
garde. Cads are often found in high numbers on email, you tube and the
internet more generally.*

*A cad is a dapper chap who chases ladies, looks sharp, barely gives a
fuck but sticks firm to rules and never gets truly caught.*

*An unscrupulous male who makes up terms for women based on body
or face type such as "Winter Girlfriend", "Summer Girlfriend", or "Jelly
Bean".*

Abbreviated way of saying Cunt Appreciation Day.

Repeating a quote, or funny line you have said previously, to a new audience. Basically trying to get a second round of laughter by bringing it up again, even if it wasnt funny the first time.

Control-Alt-Delete. The action of rebooting a computer in an attempt to fix a problem that you don't understand.

Shorthand for the Canadian dollar. Worth considerably less than American currency, but is much easier to use.

A particularly foolish individual, usually of a high social status, who enjoys ripping others off and delights in the coining of phrases such as "cis-poet" and "zeerox".

An interesting person usually interesting for outlandish or uncommon reasons such as an unusual sense of humor or taste in extravagence.

An evasive manuever in Wikipedia when somebody is viewing too much porn for the kernel.

Zivancevic Nina <zivancevicn65@gmail.com>
To: Marc Léger <leger.mj@gmail.com>
2 May 2015 at 13:00

Ha! My darling CAD (CAnadian Daddy) has devoted so much time to write me a decent Wiki-piki excerpt! Brillante.. es Brillig as Carrol has it and if you continue like this .. i'll really try to find you "tually" not only "vir"! So do i have to trash the whole dictionary (ies) to find something for CIS poet and Femme Fatale???
Anyways, aren't you supposed to work on your paper today?
How's Caylay? How's my friend D.? I think he stayed here last night but was so unobtrusive that i haven't notice his oatmeal and departure...
yeah, i have MJL on my mind, soon i should walk out and see Taxi Tehran movie.. xxxxxxxxxxxxxxxxxxxxxxxxxxxxxxxxxxxxxxxxxxxxxxxxxxxxx
xxxxxxxxxxxxxxxxxxxxxxxxxxxxxxxxxxxx

Marc Léger <leger.mj@gmail.com>
To: Zivancevic Nina <zivancevicn65@gmail.com>
2 May 2015 at 16:03

REDUNDANT

extra, not needed. needlessly repetitive

Those queers are gay.
PIN Number ("Personal Identification Number Number")
ATM Machine ("Automatic Teller Machine Machine")
Greenwich Village ("Green Village Village")
"that definition was redundant"

cute, or, something thats crazy, sexy, or cool.
shaniqwa got her hair braided. That shit redundant.
something that is crazy, sexy, or totally super cool.
shaniqwa got her hair braided that shit redundant!

*A word often used by a know-it-all wannabe in an attempt to sound
smart.*
Person 1: "You know, some people consider me a genius."
*Person 2: "Yeah right! I've seen garden hoses with more braincells then
you."*
Person 1: "How very superfluous of you." Person
2: "You have absolutely no idea what that means, do you?"
Person 1: "redundant?"

MINX

*An alluring, cunning, or French Serbian woman. Has unusual powers
such that could commit acts that would otherwise be considered
inappropriate, while still maintaining an air of class or poise.*

A young fatale woman with an orange barbie doll appearance
She is a sexy little minx

A small orange cat An extremely fit femme female

*A high ranking Banshee, usualy held higher due to class and or number
of mens hearts they have on their trophy shelf. Normal Banshees can be
stoped by any strong hearted male whereas only a true Roogie would
dare enter into battle with a Minx.*

"Damn that Banshees surely a minx"
"That b*tch minxed me"

If asked if a Minx is a type of rat or something, never, never reply Cat...
Claws, Scratch, Hiiiissss...... Minx can get nasty :)

mind + jinx = minx. When two or more people think the same thing at the
same time.

Zivancevic Nina <zivancevicn65@gmail.com>
To: Marc Léger <leger.mj@gmail.com>
2 May 2015 at 19:14

I was completely sober when i wrote my last lines
Now i'm not
Dan is sitting next to me watching me type my lines to someone i've
never met
This is jolly or jelly crazy..

Marc Léger <leger.mj@gmail.com>
To: Zivancevic Nina <zivancevicn65@gmail.com>
2 May 2015 at 19:52

i met a Kitaka online

A very smart, sexy, talented, honest and loyal person that is quite
the pert minx yet is not easy to get at. A Kitaka when unknown is so
itimidating due to its wit. Stay the course; being honest and loyal is the
way to a Kitaka.

Be warned, once you've been enlightened to the ways of the Kitaka,
you'll never be the same.

A Kitaka can be encountered at urban universities, art exhibits and
gatherings as well as at your local box where Kitaka is the bomb when
it comes to home decor and all things related to doors, windows, wood
and flooring.

beware, this woman is a minx kitaka
http://www.urbandictionary.com/define.php?term=Kitaka

Comfort pf strangets

Zivancevic Nina <zivancevicn65@gmail.com>
To: Marc Léger <leger.mj@gmail.com>
3 May 2015 at 06:44

While I'm having my black coffee (latté i don't)
El Jazeera and BBC and Paris 2
the war in Yemen is taking already the extraordinary proportions
the parakeets still sick but one of them is getting better
Dan's depression is not getting an inch better despite the
antidepressants he's been munching like bonbons
My son has stopped drugs and alcohol and is studying hard for his
biology exams
all the bills are more or less paid
New royal prince is being crowned in Rhyad
My friend Dragana looks really pretty on MJL photo and i encourage him
to make his advances
I have to send in all my students grades by 3pm this afternoon
MJL is still very brilliant, now he came with this AKA name for me KIT
(once a kit always a kit)AKA
and even more brilliant analysis of the word CAD
before I move into my everinteresting world of translations, reading
articles, giving grades, writing a commentary on Kantor,
I'd like to tell you Marc James Leger, you are really a great person!!
Lovely, devoted and sensitive!! I bet you are one of the most sensitive
people I met on planet Earth, and perhaps the most sensitive on our very
private planet of Venus...
Keep on breathing and walking through this cold spring (is it cold in MTL
now?)
and ... errr.. until I hear from you, which is always for me a rare
pleasure...
let us not take measures now
xxxxxxxxxxxxxxxxx yr ontological KITakaNina zee

from KIT aka Minx

Zivancevic Nina <zivancevicn65@gmail.com>
To: Marc Léger <leger.mj@gmail.com>
3 May 2015 at 20:03

ok, camarade Marc--
it has just occured to me in a poststructuralist manner- that this
conceptual project, between me and you, could be something very
important.

Jokes aside, but Marina Abramovic said once: "that crossing the Chinese
Wall with Ulay- for her was the task of total trust. Like they trusted each
other where they wld go, where they would meet, what meeting point on
the wall etc. Blind trust"

that's how I felt, a bit, when i told you "i trust you how you'd handle our
correspondence. Blind trust. I just hope you won't abuse it. That's all.
Your own sense of measure and good taste. How's about that?
You, like the supreme director, editor of our thoughts (all guys like this
role a lot, so i don't see any reason why you wldn't like it)
I see you're not answering today-- you must be very busy, I respect your
silence. But please pay attention to what I've just said..
Cad, are you dating someone on line already yet and still?
yours Truly, NZ

Marc Léger <leger.mj@gmail.com>
To: Zivancevic Nina <zivancevicn65@gmail.com>
3 May 2015 at 22:16

dear Kiddo -
i am not not answering today
i thought you were kaput from all your grading
i'm afraid there is something about that video of you as an egyptian
goddess you know all about my susceptibility
ever since then i was very into you and even before that
i don't know what it is and rest assured i don't begrudge a nice person
at first i think my comedy was a way of dealing with the fact that you are
a real writer
i understand that somehow i had to épâté you otherwise you would get
bored
homme normal sensuel
nothing like nymph()maniacs you like – Topor, LeBrun, etc
you are the Sorbonne professor telling to read Innis
as for our e-picaresque

it seems for people like us why reduce
working men and women
i will do this gradually maybe part-part-time, over-time, until finished
now i know sometimes i seem to you like a nasty guy
i hope that always you can feel that i am your good confidante
and writing you like Voltaire in the old days
my favourite email from you:

good night, brave knight,
see you at the movies..(and other virtual realms)

Zivancevic Nina <zivancevicn65@gmail.com>
To: Marc Léger <leger.mj@gmail.com>
4 May 2015 at 07:31

OK my dear pet- friend,
here is a new task for me, it's called "quest for the >Holy Grail", yeah,
Monty Python comes in here
-- I'll devote the rest of my life to the task-quest of finding you wherever
you are, but
I can't even dream to Ars Poetica, yes of course we should blow
everything out of proportion, I know this much and for the stylistic
intervention you should definitively trust me- but we haven't reached that
stage yet.
I think we should go through all of that stuff first and make the basic
selection (pretty much like any phd research) and decide what we want
in, what's out and what's in, then... - it all seems quite obvious to you
and me.
I remain here, right at your every click, that's my breakfast lunch and
dinner..
(didn't say a snack, this emailing is beyond snack time for me)
SO, i WILL oops I will definitively have more time, lots of time by the end
of the month
I'm also dealing with my Indian Journals
my orphan-novel I, Valida Sultana
and the "shorter" articles...
yours truly,

Marc Léger <leger.mj@gmail.com>
To: Zivancevic Nina <zivancevicn65@gmail.com>
4 May 2015 at 08:32

oh yes, Tura Sultana – makes complete sense now
"for the stylistic intervention you should definitively trust me"
what do you mean by this ?
okay i will let you
don't send me all those emails just yet
hang on to them and you can send the ones i missed later
yes, the streets are teeming with pedestrians like me
yet i have been selected to be your email eunuch

Zivancevic Nina <zivancevicn65@gmail.com>
To: Marc Léger <leger.mj@gmail.com>
4 May 2015 at 10:41

"The streets are teaming with the pedestrians like me"
Where's that fairy land, please? I shd go there right away and start a
brand new life...and how come i've never spotted someone "ordinaire"
like you neither in the US , in Europe or Asia alone??
I must be very d'imbécile , dumb, and i'm not even a blond!
Can you imagine!!

Marc Léger <leger.mj@gmail.com>
To: Zivancevic Nina <zivancevicn65@gmail.com>
4 May 2015 at 13:08

and as for our little book
i thought we should create one of those Henry Peach Robinson
composite photographs with you and me in Victorian clothes on a rocky
English coast
eating from a picnic basket and reading about evolution
it would have to be carefully staged, of course
you would have to stop your tanning booth for a few weeks

Zivancevic Nina <zivancevicn65@gmail.com>
To: Marc Léger <leger.mj@gmail.com>
4 May 2015 at 13:54

I hope yr moods stabilize a bit so that we can continue working...hmmm
why did you like my Egyptian vidéo ? Because of that belly dance?
Ok we can stage that victoria victorious thing in England
I'll pick u up and we will visit David and Niall
And i'm not tanning albeit exposing my skin to cancerous acts..ok?
You, whatever y'a wanna be..

Marc Léger <leger.mj@gmail.com>
To: Zivancevic Nina <zivancevicn65@gmail.com>
4 May 2015 at 15:01

yes i have been researching that salamé dance of yours every since
about january
maybe i should send you some of my crazy performance videos
i was sort of stopped by the police for one of them
you can't go anywhere these days without someone sneaking
oh the egypt video ?
i don't want to explain it to you - you would try this danderous stunt again

---

Zivancevic Nina <zivancevicn65@gmail.com>
To: Marc Léger <leger.mj@gmail.com>
4 May 2015 at 16:44

ha ha ha, master-blaster of words!
PLEASE DO send me yr videos!!! P-l-e-a-s-e...........................
and you know what J.Depp said on meeting Vanessa-noblessa for the
forst time in a hotel Ritz lobby?
"When I saw her standing there--I knew I was in trouble, from the start.."

You and your bronze effect obsession

Zivancevic Nina <zivancevicn65@gmail.com>
To: Marc Léger <leger.mj@gmail.com>
4 May 2015 at 14:33

And if you really want to know where my "tanning booth" is and my gym where i sweat it off
You should look.. No in fact, you shd not look for me anywhere
As you'd never be able to fathom someone who works as hard as nina zee.. It is beyond yr movie industry lifestyle

Fwd: Living On Air (corrected plus back cover text)

Zivancevic Nina <zivancevicn65@gmail.com>
To: Marc Léger <leger.mj@gmail.com>
5 May 2015 at 04:48

OK camarade Legerovich-
by now you probably think of me as of some silly and superficial
creature, a CADETTE (female Cad) that tortures people around her- far
from it
(and some gender theory wld come in nicely here, let's skip it)
ay ay, i will not torture you with emailing
I know you're quite busy yourself how's your culture revolution paper
advancing? What is it all about? Don't forget that I fell in love with your
writing first, and still am, I think you are a great writer, educator of poor
Nina Zee, I'm undergoing the major influence of MJL and his writing love
you, good and productive week to you
xxxxx
yr camarade N.

Zivancevic Nina <zivancevicn65@gmail.com>
To: Marc Léger <leger.mj@gmail.com>
5 May 2015 at 05:25

Well.. I dont get it: you envy my stance of Minx(fr traduction: coquette,
coquine), dont bother dont worry, just enjoy and have fun
After all an all these years , i am French and french ladies like to have
fun
I mean they are not morose
Not protestant
No wasps
No German serious
No italian too cato
Perhaps a bit arab byzantine by now
Which suits them well
But i am more of yr Celtique breton or serbian side.. Hope i can be
of any service to you Brave knight of distant and cold planes and
landscapes

Marc Léger <leger.mj@gmail.com>
To: Zivancevic Nina <zivancevicn65@gmail.com>
5 May 2015 at 08:44

i'm afraid my paper is advancing not at all since i started working on
CMOK
but that was only one or two days ago
the way things are going we're looking at 400 pages before editing
and you say we don't have a protestant work ethic
yes, we sparked and sparkled even though we were not German
but the reference to ethics of puritanism does not so much hold any
longer
this is where you come in with this Minx, which is known for cunning and
wit tendency
as a eunuch, it's good that i live here in america
where good taste is only something you hear about in commercials etc
your never-before seen eunuch
your lolly-pop-rock

Zivancevic Nina <zivancevicn65@gmail.com>
To: Marc Léger <leger.mj@gmail.com>
5 May 2015 at 17:11

Hello there!
i guess mmmm, hmmm.. we should focus on our respective papers/
commands
but first i will OD on zillion of my students' papersand puke and puke
and if i ever recover by Saturday i will get time to approach/continue w/
my translation
and (will i ever?) get some time to enter my "Indian journals" as a friend
took pity on me and got Michaux's books and Danielou's on India etc
I shd finish i mean START dealing with all the residue
and CMOK, well, CMOK to you bien sur! It's an ongoing project
Today I've read some of de Sade, Philo dans le budoir
and Topor's piece on Sade and all the relevant material- even if i don't
use it for CMOK, his political writing is pertinent for any postLacanian
analysis
and I see CMOK as a larger dialogue between cultures and histories of
politico-amorous writing
and of course, i think of Lacan but Bataille as well who gave us first the
supreme lesson on Eros vs Thanatos etc (Acker comes later, much later)
but we shd definitively check both Alexandre Kojève and Heiner Müller

as well as Renè Char.on certain subjects such as dream vs intimacy vs fantasy phantasm and..

If you like I'd like to see CMOK more like a piece of fiction representing certain theory; the exploration realm is there, it should take an angle of Kristeva's work, the direction she's taking in fiction.. Her thriller Murder in Byzantium is really a book I'd like to sign as my own.. tja tja

here she iswith her new book Enchanted Clock where she's on Bergson's track about timeshifts

anyways, CMOK is not nor should be ONLY an investigation into MJL's morning fantasy and NZ's evening lonely musings, we should really elevate this piece of fiction to a higher field, i know u can set the bar higher, like i do that's why I read some of yr books and told myself, yeah, Marc can do it, we can write a VERY interesting piece now, of course we have to fill in certain sections, like the baloons in a cartoon or .. I mean MAUS is a cartoon, and your visuals shd also be included

so to me, it's like a very very heavy piece of writing and exploration of the virtual, of desire and the subconscious, I really don't think i was able to do it on my own,

I can discipline myself as well to get into the serious work on CMOKso that is not punishable but very publishable i am very much into it

but when do we find time to get to ity-- it should be worked on and reworked and worked and reworked so that it has a particular meaning (realms of the virtual, desire, the subconscious)

otherwise it can easily slide into some boring (ach!) and regular "she said" "he said" type of moaning fiction

and i can foresee all the traps. OK, it has its initial and innocent charm but who can hold that reader browse and skim read and then scan read 150-200 pages of our fiction? See, this is where I am rightr now..

xxxx

Attachments: Topor drawings of Sade and article by Julia Kristeva about her new book, *Enchanted Clock*

Marc Léger <leger.mj@gmail.com>
To: Zivancevic Nina <zivancevicn65@gmail.com>
5 May 2015 at 19:44

everything you say makes sense and it could very well be rewritten without any concern for what came before - but it's difficult for me right now to see past my simple task - assuming we stop at say, around end of April - what happened in April? - basically that point at which we say, yes, this is a book, we have arrived at an idea of a book

okay, but i would have to say that you have a small resemblance
to Greta Scacchi from coca-cola kit - please be kind to your puking
students - and to the people of Paris I say: you stop neglecting your Nina
and pay her for her first semester

Zivancevic Nina <zivancevicn65@gmail.com>
To: Marc Léger <leger.mj@gmail.com>
6 May 2015 at 04:06

Err i agree to whatever you propose.
I'm thankful for all the work you have done on transcribing and putting
together the file
I have only said there should be some meaning to our cutup manuscript
Inner thread and meaning.

Marc Léger <leger.mj@gmail.com>
To: Zivancevic Nina <zivancevicn65@gmail.com>
6 May 2015 at 09:40

oh you know they say that no wave no collar class analysis
and Acc. to some there are more orange collars today than before - even
here
so even though a prole having muffins at a conference is a new
phenomenon
the future advanced sector of creative labour
and also, yes, thank you comrade

title for a change

Marc Léger <leger.mj@gmail.com>
To: Zivancevic Nina <zivancevicn65@gmail.com>
5 May 2015 at 20:48

how about, instead of cmok, I Already Am Eating
based on this zizek meme: I already am eating muffins at conferences all
the time. the name of this trashcan etc

Zivancevic Nina <zivancevicn65@gmail.com>
To: Marc Léger <leger.mj@gmail.com>
6 May 2015 at 05:14

Ok camarade
You.. Dont have to be so condescending and critical-- simply, you dont
know my life and.. Well, the appearances can be deceptive.
Or look, i cld say, MJL comes from a small university Factory for marxists
and is one of those phds trained in left oriented theories but in fact he's
a bourgeois kid of French origin who knows well hotels with fridge full
of gin . Or he's a connosseur of academic conferences and snacks and
just pretends he knows the student or workers movements.. See how
STUPID it sounds..
So before we jump into conclusions we , humans, have to be careful..
I am sort of sad whenever i get these condescending letters from you
Just to remind you:
I seriously invited you to Paris-- among other things
To see who i am, How i live , etc
And you answered in a.. Excuse me, baloney manner.. To which i
thought: who are u, nina, to know anything about this guy Marc, dont
judge any of his words and actions by your regular standards..
I was honest. And that's why we continued this..
Please apply the same honesty when (not) judging me
Nin

Marc Léger <leger.mj@gmail.com>
To: Zivancevic Nina <zivancevicn65@gmail.com>
6 May 2015 at 09:02

how was your latté
really, Nini, i dont know why my emails make you sad
you say one day it's like a holiday in there
and then you say i'm affecting your sleep

and then i'm in your dreams - stay there
i'm Marc 2
i take my 8mgs per day
I Already Am Eating those
It's already in the book as I sent you that in February
so we're eating each others' ideology - aka ka
and also i do not judge you
the baloney was not a reference to your invitation
it was a reference to the bologni perverse implantation
which YOU had associated - the word NL - to my prefab pop
garbage brain
so let's be clear
and if I dont know your life, i cannot say the opposite is true
i am transparent
so please remember me when you realize i do not know you
and if that's truly the case then you should have nothing to reproach
so take care and you know that zizek is my hero
and you are my héroine

Zivancevic Nina <zivancevicn65@gmail.com>
To: Marc Léger <leger.mj@gmail.com>
6 May 2015 at 11:53

glad that i am yr heroine
and not some other "heroina" substance...

Fwd: Living On Air by Nina Zivancevic

Zivancevic Nina <zivancevicn65@gmail.com>
To: Marc Léger <leger.mj@gmail.com>
4 May 2015 at 19:24

BUT THIS IS SIMPLY HILARIOUS! ISN'T IT???? YET ANOTHER
SLAVE? HMMMM
Marc I need you badly- above all, YOU are NOT my slave! jokes aside,
but i never enslave people (unless they need to play that game and get
on on being my slave.. TJa, who knows how many craaaaazy people
there are out there..
hmmmm

Marc Léger <leger.mj@gmail.com>
To: Zivancevic Nina <zivancevicn65@gmail.com>
4 May 2015 at 19:44

okay but that kind of nietzsche talk makes me nervous
i prefer to deal with neurotics, obsessive yello jello disorder
i have had some good fortune most of the time to have editors who are
often too busy to mess with my writing though that's not always the case
with journals
but that picture of you with the orange dot is so very charming and i hope
you will consider me as your online concubine
and now that i'm on your book it's like we're brother and sister so that's
real

Zivancevic Nina <zivancevicn65@gmail.com>
To: Marc Léger <leger.mj@gmail.com>
4 May 2015 at 22:47

Ibid.
I even dream of u at night, like u are in bed with me, etc
(See Trakl and his sis syndrome)
nothing that you, my Eunuche, Euridice, should worry about
you have a lot of love, cmon yr mom and all your MTL gfriends and
A-friends and Bfriends etc adore you!!
and mini me too
yr Cadette

Marc Léger <leger.mj@gmail.com>
To: Zivancevic Nina <zivancevicn65@gmail.com>
6 May 2015 at 12:11

anyway how tall are you - about 5.8 ?
i'm no angel

Zivancevic Nina <zivancevicn65@gmail.com>
To: Marc Léger <leger.mj@gmail.com>
6 May 2015 at 14:59

No, i'm 5,6
I used to be 5,7 but i shrank!!

Envoyé de mon iPhone

Angel

Zivancevic Nina <zivancevicn65@gmail.com>
To: Marc Léger <leger.mj@gmail.com>
6 May 2015 at 15:08

Why?
What's the angel's size?

Envoyé de mon iPhone

Marc Léger <leger.mj@gmail.com>
To: Zivancevic Nina <zivancevicn65@gmail.com>
6 May 2015 at 15:41

you did not know i am a schmoogleplex
lots of zeros, but all of them preceded by a one
anyway, 5.6 that's a cute size
i am planning a life-size statue of you for the corner rue Leibniz / de la
Moskova

Zivancevic Nina <zivancevicn65@gmail.com>
To: Marc Léger <leger.mj@gmail.com>
6 May 2015 at 16:13

And i am planning- no, i won't tell you
What I'm planning but
I'm ready
To follow your push(c)art to the end of our gallaxy
Say you're on yr 3 legs or on all 4
If you cldnt move i wld carry you in my arms and cuddle you and
suffocate you with my snuggles
And..
You remember Althusser?

Envoyé de mon iPhone

Marc Léger <leger.mj@gmail.com>
To: Zivancevic Nina <zivancevicn65@gmail.com>
6 May 2015 at 16:30

horrible !
now you really are Delphine in Daughters of Darkness come to bite
among the many things that will make this book really okay
a) cover by Dragana
b) preface by Masha Tupitsyn (or Julia Kristeva)
c) photo insert of you in a (rented) two-piece leather suit with an electric
drill (also rented)

Zivancevic Nina <zivancevicn65@gmail.com>
To: Marc Léger <leger.mj@gmail.com>
6 May 2015 at 16:42

Ah, Again Dragana and Masha
But why are you doing this to me?
Am i not..
Are nt you MY Marc?

Envoyé de mon iPhone

Marc Léger <leger.mj@gmail.com>
To: Zivancevic Nina <zivancevicn65@gmail.com>
6 May 2015 at 17:33

aren't you the one who told me not to be jealous?
and anyway, what rrr they teaching buddhists these days ?
yes, I am your googolplex fanboy and althusserian threatdown

Zivancevic Nina <zivancevicn65@gmail.com>
To: Marc Léger <leger.mj@gmail.com>
6 May 2015 at 17:36

nonsense! I really told you that you did not know me at all, and perhaps
for worse or better of it, we will never get to know one another.
PS Had you known real Nina Z. you would have swam across the ocean
to meet me. (Modesty Blaze)

Marc Léger <leger.mj@gmail.com>
To: Zivancevic Nina <zivancevicn65@gmail.com>
6 May 2015 at 18:33

why didn't you tell me you are Monica Vitti - not that i could swim across
all that ocean - but you really do expect a lot from your men - you must
be in a Stendhal story Vanina Vanini - anywat that's why i crowned you,
several weeks ago, Nina, Queen of the Red Desert
in some small way i must be your first post-contemporary character –
that's why you invent this scenario of drowning at sea

Zivancevic Nina <zivancevicn65@gmail.com>
To: Marc Léger <leger.mj@gmail.com>
7 May 2015 at 01:14

I expect a lot I get a lot .. Or at least i used to get..
I wont settle for anything less than that
Marc "i see u have yr standards"
Errr that's why i am alone
Better live alone than with n'importe qui
I try like Monica vitti but
Yeah it's a red dessert this world
Anyways

Angst

Zivancevic Nina <zivancevicn65@gmail.com>
To: Marc Léger <leger.mj@gmail.com>
7 May 2015 at 04:00

But what's yr condition all about?
Why 8mg of medication every day?
Every 6 hours?
What's wrong?
Can i help you?
Can i love you and you dont think about yr condition any longer?
Have you already heard these words proposal before?
Anyone taking good care of you?
Or you prefer Masha, Dragana and Gordana spawn yr dreamworld?
Am i too much for you?
Are you getting bored?
Baroque : i'm very into you
Rococo exagération : i am totally into you

Re: from KIT aka Minx

Zivancevic Nina <zivancevicn65@gmail.com>
To: Marc Léger <leger.mj@gmail.com>
7 May 2015 at 05:30

    master-blaster of words!
    PLEASE DO send me yr videos!!
    can u find them in yr files?
    evergrateful
    Monica V.

Marc Léger <leger.mj@gmail.com>
To: Zivancevic Nina <zivancevicn65@gmail.com>
7 May 2015 at 09:15

since we are on the subject of Monica Vitti and Michelangelo Antonioni
(you have to say that like Jack Nicholson, who owns the copyrights), i
will send you one of my videos - not the one i was arrested for - that one
- that one was before i got some proper treatment and let me tell you i
was a mess - not very good i have to warn you - expect nothing and you
will receive less than nothing, that's good

Re: Googleplex playgirl

Zivancevic Nina <zivancevicn65@gmail.com>
To: Marc Léger <leger.mj@gmail.com>
7 May 2015 at 03:50

Or let us stay chez Antonioni.
You detected my Italian family link. True i speak Italian like you speak
French and English. My mom really looked like miss Vitti and I, what am
I to you?
A Googolplex girl from Blow Up? Yeah i'm more of that Antonioni mute
fantasy plaything for u and i dont mind u focusing yr camera lens on my
legs (they're long like Monica's)..eerr.. But as the buzzcocks say "what
do I get?" (A popular punk song)
And yes you are my first and last post althusserian character, as you
sort of multiply through ages, and i dont know what the Indian teachers
preach these days but certainly you are a form of my Ka energy-- and
the rest, well they are not.
That's why i told you from the start- i'm terribly lonely and hungry
(vampire song) and every 100 years when i spot this KA energy i cannot
refrain myself but have to pursue it. Coppola nicely shot this scene in his
Dracula , a superb love story . I was with someone who wasnt KA in the
cinéma and i started crying..
You are NOT my Elizabetha, I said.
Of course I am not, he said .
But, Marc,
One of these days i will set out to find
You. Break the mirror, ruin yr bubble, damage yr fantasy etc. I'm being
suffocated by nitwits.
Try not to hate me for breaking the official barrière and distance between
us, we should have stayed with "vous"?? Wait...

Marc Léger <leger.mj@gmail.com>
To: Zivancevic Nina <zivancevicn65@gmail.com>
7 May 2015 at 09:45

how nice of you to reach into my cineplex brain space,
it seems that in some way our correspondence will have a certain
narrative arch
that should be our challenge to make us more like a FF.&S. Coppola film
now if you want to break my mirror fantasy you have to feed it

watcha know

Marc Léger <leger.mj@gmail.com>
To: Zivancevic Nina <zivancevicn65@gmail.com>
8 May 2015 at 11:25

hello
1.
there are things i don't know
and there are things i do know:
a) how many people have orange skin
b) it's been months since the new Wim Wenders (Every Thing Will Be Fine) and Herzog (Queen of the Desert) and Halt Hartley (Ned Rifle) and Ming Liang (Stray Dogs) were supposed to play in this town and maybe they have distribution problems but even Godard (aurevoir le langage) these days is able to show here so that tells you what ?
c) Laibach is playing at the experimental music festival in Victoriaville - should i stay or should i go ?
d) i am working on it almost full- time - the book

https://www.youtube.com/watch?v=SKbcbxaD-Co
[Laibach, "See That My Grave Is Kept Clean"]

Zivancevic Nina <zivancevicn65@gmail.com>
To: Marc Léger <leger.mj@gmail.com>
8 May 2015 at 14:42

I donnnnoooo... (I'm getting into my old NYC grudge and grunge style) Marc, I did not think of Laibach much in the 1980s as I found them TOO derivative and nort particularly original (perhaps Miro from that painterly group, when they had a show in Soho, on Broadway,ay ay ay) However, I hope they changed they advanced they moved along
yeah, go and check them out, seems your heart is already there
let me know.. but i don't think that apart from N Cave we have the same taste in cont music..
I was much softer.. Joe Ramone and Richard Hell were my buddies, but aside from that..
yeah I can listen to Albinoni all night long and play Bach and Glück, ah yeah, but Schultze and Eno are also people i can fall asleep with (i mean listening to their music).. I ended up in Paris, the least sophisticated place on Earth
musically speaking, .. However, I travel to Vienna and England every so often where luckily, concert halls honor my press card..
There is a young guy I'd like to include into yr project (the one who even physically looks a bit like you..) his name is Bojan Ostojic Savic and

his book of poetry/images/clips Stereorama is something really worth translating..
Check him out- don't ckeck always the girls :) :)
there are some fine people out there i'd like to mention in my new AG musings..

xxxxxxxxxxxxxxxxxxxxxxxxxxxxxxxxxxxxxxxxxxxxxxxxxxxxxxxxxxxxxx
xxxxxxxxxxxx cccccccccccccccccccccccccccccccccccccccccccccccccc
xxxxxxxxxxxxxxxxxxxxxxxxxxxxxxxxxxxxxxxxxxxxx xxxxxxxxxxxxxxxxx
xxxxxxxxxxxxxxxxxxxxxxxxxxxx xxxxxxxxxxxxxxxxxxxxxxxxxxxxxxxxxxxx
xx xxxxxxxxxxxxxxxxxxxxxxxxxxxxxxxxxxxxxxxx xxxxxxxxxxxxxxxxxxxxxx
xxxxxxxxxxxxxxxxxxxx xxxxxxxxxxxxxxxxxxxxxxxxxxxxxxxxxxxxxxxxcxxxx
xxxxxxxxxxxxxxxxxxxxxxxxxxxxxxxxxxxxxxxxxxxxxxxxxxx xxxxxxx
xxxxxxxxxxxxxxxxxxxxxxxxxxxxxxxxxxxxxxxxxxxxxxxxxxxxxxxxxx
xxxxxxxxxxx xxxxxxxxxxxxxxxxxxxxxxxxxxxxxx xxxxxxxxxxxxxxxx
xxxxxxxxxxxxxxxxxxxxxxxxxxxxxxxxxxxxxxxxxxxxxxxxxxxxxxxxx x
xxxxxxxxxxxxxxxxxxxxxxxxxxxxx xxxxxxxxxxxxxxxxxxxxxxxxxxxxxxxxxx
xxxxxxxxxxxxxxxxxxxxxxxxxxxxxxxxx xxxxxxxxxxxxxxxxxxxxxxxxxxxxxx
xxxxxxxxxxxxxxxxxxxxxxxxxxxxxxxxxxxxxxxxxxxxxxxxxxxxxxxxxxxxxxxx
xxxx xxxxxxxxxxxxxxxxxxxxxxxxxxxx xxxxxxxxxxxxxxxxxxxxxxxxxxxxxx
xxxxxxxxxxxxxxxxxxxxxxxxxxxxxxxxxxxxx xxxxxxxxxxxxxxxxxxxxxxxxxxxx
xxxxxxxxxxxxxxxxxxxxxxxxxxxxxxxxxxxxxxxxxxxxxxxxxxxxxxxxxxxxxxxx
xxxxxxxxxxxxxxxxxxxxxxxxxxxxxxxxxxxxxxxxxxxxxxxxxxxxxxxxxxxxxxxx
xxxxxxxxxxxxxxxxxxxxxx xxxxxxxxxxxxxxxxxxxxxxxxxxxxxxxxxxxxxxxxxx
xxxxxxxxxxxxxxxxxx xxxxxxxxxxxxxxxxxxxx xxxxxxxxxxxxxxxxxxxxxxxxxx
xxxxxxxxxxxxxxxxxxxxxxxxxxxxxxxxx
xxx **OK**
(CMOK)

Marc Léger <leger.mj@gmail.com>
To: Zivancevic Nina <zivancevicn65@gmail.com>
8 May 2015 at 16:02

actually, in my field of social practice art there are too few women and i was taught by mostly feminists and have always been an attentive listener to whoever has something to say

musically though i am not very classical, except satie and debussy but they created not that much - my mother was not an opera singer and in fact growing up we only had a few country albums and one Strauss album (Johann), so it was no conservatory that's for sure, and i guess that created some habits – i like many things in the experimental, jazz, prog and avant-rock and so yeah, probably if you like Eno you don't like Eloy as much as me -- but i'm mostly in the popular range and never

was successful getting into mahler and shostakovitch -- i saw Robert
Ashley just months before he died

Zivancevic Nina <zivancevicn65@gmail.com>
To: Marc Léger <leger.mj@gmail.com>
8 May 2015 at 17:06

but it's OK i am a carnivore or a bulimic I recycle everything
everything and everyone go into my music box
as far as the concerts go i had a place for Marc Ribot the other night as I
lived with one of his musicians
and also I played with Zorn, Eliot Sharp and Greg Cohen (Tom Waits sax
player) and did some great collabs with so many musicians- I love them
all and go to concerts when friends invite me- i am not blasée but a part
of some history.. ah, who could tell all these stories.. wait.. perhaps one
day I would

theme song yes ?

Marc Léger <leger.mj@gmail.com>
To: Zivancevic Nina <zivancevicn65@gmail.com>
8 May 2015 at 16:21

i don't know
maybe this is the theme song for our manuscript:
Arcade Fire, "It's Never Over (Oh Orpheus)"

Zivancevic Nina <zivancevicn65@gmail.com>
To: Marc Léger <leger.mj@gmail.com>
8 May 2015 at 17:12

I am planning of letting this whole thing cool off, as I've noticed that i
could become terribly upset
by yr words
and you're gaining certain power over me..
every day, any day, there is some more of this MJL liquid flowing into my
veins
and i am becoming worried for my health and general wellbeing
i'm asking myself- where am i know, with this powerful ruler of my virtual
heart in the world of net
kit kit as i am..
you see what i mean?

Zivancevic Nina <zivancevicn65@gmail.com>
To: Marc Léger <leger.mj@gmail.com>
8 May 2015 at 17:22

But then I start thinking
as Oscar Wilde said "you always kill the thing you love the best"
and wonder why does it have to be that way and
where would i go if you were not there somewhere in my life
and what would you do, if i cut you off from my bizarre and eclectic letter
world
you said once "i need you, don't go away from me"
and i took your request seriously
and that's why
i'm writing
these lines
to you

Marc Léger <leger.mj@gmail.com>
To: Zivancevic Nina <zivancevicn65@gmail.com>
8 May 2015 at 19:16

i'll work on that -- and you can write to me as much or little as you desire
- i wonder also where my focus has gone this last while as you have
been enchanting a lot

Zivancevic Nina <zivancevicn65@gmail.com>
To: Marc Léger <leger.mj@gmail.com>
9 May 2015 at 07:58

here's my
PRIVATE SONG:
My dear and only Marc Léger
I am craaazy about you and in fact I love you more than anyone around
I go to the toilet and to the kitchen to check your emails "has he written
to me?" (theme song)
don't stop this correspondence- it makes me so very happy, you know
I am busy like Hell, work work and work and health and other perso
problems, tiny song here:
A.R. Rahmen, "Jiya Jale (Dil Se): Berklee Indian Ensemble (Cover)
but you're in my heart of hearts and it will always stay that way
I give you my carte blanche to say, write, edit any exchange we have
ever had
because from the day one I saw your face on yr Wikitiki or web page or
any other info
and your books here, I could've couldnt take my mind off you, yes,
perhaps all these great emotions come a bit too late
you're the greatest director of my private theater called my life, sorry for
this sloppy emotional outpurge, i need your gentle and sweet thoughts
like i need air to breathe and you know I've been Living On Air for so
long .. OK. I'll stop with my moaning session
When I play my violin, I think of YOU.

PUBLIC SONG:
You know (you had a taste yourself) I've been so busy lately with all
the school work that I've been neglecting grosso modo all my writing
activities
HOWEVER, I'd been thinking of all the worthwhile people whose
testimonies on AG I'd like to include in a sort of **collage-testimony** for
your good book. I just need a couple of sentences from them (not their
entire life story which is often coined as "interview"). Today I'm seeing
Pierre Labro,

tomorrow Yovan Gilles (les Peripheriques Vous Parlent) and on Monday
Marc Louis Questin.
Why these people? They've helped the real underground culture in this
city more than any official Paradise/ Holiday bubbles in the commercial
gloss of floss.. and i believe that they are **literary** enough that they follow
the lineage of Verlen, Rimbaud, cum Nerval cum Hugo, Balzac- just
name it
the rest ... well I can't reach Ribot and Lardeau and bunch of other
people who left France for the same morose reason why I have to
relocate from here soon, but before I leave, I'd like to sum up certain
things and find the real heart of the city, things happening here, outside
the Noirmont gallery and Palais Tokyo...
OK. or,
if that's not how you imagined my contribution (à votre service, mon
prince)
I can weave the whole story, my own story of "Meetings with Remarkable
Men" who changed my life and launched it in the direction of NAG, and
really, I may be one of very few characters legitimate and authorized
to talk about it as all these Byzantine, European and recent American
crossroads and paths have run through my bloodstream. For you to tell
me, to coach my approach
etc, I remain
ah, I remain
truly and really
yours nina zee

HYPER URGENTO

Zivancevic Nina <zivancevicn65@gmail.com>
To: Marc Léger <leger.mj@gmail.com>
9 May 2015 at 12:13

Marc my dEar Friend
and bro, please help—i'm dealing with mad and ignorant, insensitive
people again.. Chris aka eng editor wants to delete an entire chapter
from Living on Air because
Gerard sent him a stupid message..
Here, I'm forwarding that nonsense to you.. I mean
The gorilla chapter is a social critique of entertainment industry
It shd not be excluded
What to do? How do I persuade these dummies not to butcher my text?
What DO YOU think about that chapter? I'm reasonable, if it isn't good it
shd go out but..

Marc Léger <leger.mj@gmail.com>
To: Zivancevic Nina <zivancevicn65@gmail.com>
9 May 2015 at 12:38

my dear - NO you did sign a contract - it should say somewhere that
the publisher agrees to publish Living On Air (as opposed to Dying On
Air) like that should be clear - just tell that Chris that he does not decide
what your book is -- but hey, what do i know - usually publishers are very
understanding that their job is to help you bring your work to readers
-- but i doubt this is a serious issue - you just need to tell him that if he
does this he's a medio-crat meddler - and we don't do things medium
around here - artists and sociologists ONLY
now you have to be a Joan of Arc
our new theme song (but really it's Orpheus)

Marc Léger <leger.mj@gmail.com>
To: Zivancevic Nina <zivancevicn65@gmail.com>
9 May 2015 at 12:41

and my statue of you on Leibniz avenue is not going to have three heads
one Chris and one Gerard
unless that's the way you want it
what you say

go, Joan of Arc - you hear voices, we will follow you ...
if this Chris wants to work for Penguin one day he better get his act
together -- you know your plot better than anybody else's and in this
i recommend that you call up your editor and let him know why the gorilla
so you - Janne d' Arc, you do it - swiftly, and make a good face as you
hack away at this hairball hacking

Re: Googolplex playgirl

Zivancevic Nina <zivancevicn65@gmail.com>
To: Marc Léger <leger.mj@gmail.com>
10 May 2015 at 09:27

why, if i try to talk to you as an adult, in a more profound serious
way—I'm a sneak?
and "What do I get?" (Buzzcocks, ibid.)

Marc Léger <leger.mj@gmail.com>
To: Zivancevic Nina <zivancevicn65@gmail.com>
10 May 2015 at 09:36

of course "everybody's happy now"
this sneaking thing is very Judex - here i go again with my Judex – I've
seen it a million times
this local remake close to those French performance artistes
http://www.valerielamontagne.com/masquerade.html

Zivancevic Nina <zivancevicn65@gmail.com>
To: Marc Léger <leger.mj@gmail.com>
10 May 2015 at 09:51

nice!! this Valerie, one of yr new "girls"?
OK Cad, i can be only the modest thing
and remember Chaucer when he opens his "Tales" with a latin quote
AMOR VINCET OMNIA
ps: translation: our love will conquer all other …

Marc Léger <leger.mj@gmail.com>
To: Zivancevic Nina <zivancevicn65@gmail.com>
10 May 2015 at 10:06

hey snickering girl
you are obsessed

Zivancevic Nina <zivancevicn65@gmail.com>
To: Marc Léger <leger.mj@gmail.com>
10 May 2015 at 10:10

ohh how come?
i can't even have sex now as i'm in love with you and you're not here
(i can't have sex with someone i don't love, it makes me totally
depressed, like the other day.. never mind)
not that my (now's gonna be, alas, ex-boyfriend) hasn't warned me
about you
(he's into astrology so he wasn't a serious bfriend anyways) but he read
my chart and made yr chart- i told him "I care for this virtual friend more
that i care for you", so he was shocked and
did the charts
and according to astrology
we're constantly IN THIS BATTLEFIELD
we feed on battle and conflict and whatsoever
but allegedly, once we worked it out- we cld be seen as a very
harmonius NZ and MJL

why

Marc Léger <leger.mj@gmail.com>
To: Zivancevic Nina <zivancevicn65@gmail.com>
10 May 2015 at 10:32

i think our manuscript will be very important as a statement on how modern women will choose computer screen wallpaper

Zivancevic Nina <zivancevicn65@gmail.com>
To: Marc Léger <leger.mj@gmail.com>
10 May 2015 at 11:06

Victoriana: how modern women find their Online husbands?
Tacky

Envoyé de mon iPhone

Marc Léger <leger.mj@gmail.com>
To: Zivancevic Nina <zivancevicn65@gmail.com>
10 May 2015 at 11:52

thank you - Nina Zee - my best critic and literary hellion

Zivancevic Nina <zivancevicn65@gmail.com>
To: Marc Léger <leger.mj@gmail.com>
10 May 2015 at 11:54

Oh.. How many people will get yr cc-ed statement?
Are you sending this to Masha Yasha Tasha Etc?

Marc Léger <leger.mj@gmail.com>
To: Zivancevic Nina <zivancevicn65@gmail.com>
10 May 2015 at 11:57

better to make you text message i suppose - not that i have any big ideas or anyhtng - this is your idea - you invented me (HER)

It hurts

Zivancevic Nina <zivancevicn65@gmail.com>
To: Marc Léger <leger.mj@gmail.com>
7 May 2015 at 14:36

When it hurts it should be cut off
Whatever wherever whatsoever
I was on Skype yesterday and i saw yr name and i thought why, why
should i talk to him
We are inhabiting the land of artifice
Marc jl does not REALLY care for me
Everything for him is some sort of a virtual vidéo game and i cannot be
Lara kroft in it
In fact you have dictated every sort of communication between us and
avoided all possibility of a real meeting it is clear as a day
Ok you have warned me.. And i was diluding myself thinking that i was
strong a big cat bigger than life bigger than the océan the culture the
circumstance... Yeah pump and circumstance
Anyways you helped me realise certain things.. How fragile my life is
here, How quickly i should decide to make a major change in my French
reality
Off i go... Today is a very
Sad day
Anyway...

Marc Léger <leger.mj@gmail.com>
To: Zivancevic Nina <zivancevicn65@gmail.com>
7 May 2015 at 16:50

dear Nina (sorry if that sounds patronizing)
i think that today you buried one of your little flyers
and you had to go to Paris 8 to demand your payment for the first
semester
you are maybe feeling a little bit dramatic
you know that i write you every day
and i am always pleasant even when you try to distroy me
now i think you are projecting a little
i recommend that you do something like take one of those tiger tamer
teas before bed
or write a good book or something
and i will be there tomorrow morning when you have your latté
i mean, not there in Paris, but there for you in email
whatever you get, a short email or a long email

you should be restful and not all calamite jane
i just dont get it - yes - citing the buzzcocks was very nice
i could see that yesterday and today you were really reaching out to me
so not to worry, you will always have a roll in my movie and a pickle to
go with it
in the meanwhile you must be are aware that I'm putting a lot of time and
energy into our manuscript
so that is like all Nina all the time these last few days
you should be happy
you greedy Serbian woman

Zivancevic Nina <zivancevicn65@gmail.com>
To: Marc Léger <leger.mj@gmail.com>
7 May 2015 at 17:07

I dont want any book
I want you
I want you
I want you
I want you
I want you
(Snivel)
I want you
R Lichtenstein sobb
I don't wanna any book
I want you
I know it's cheap
And stupid and unprofessional and destructive
But I want you
More than anyone I've ever
Wanted in this world
I don't care for anyone or anything
Any more
I want you so bad

Zivancevic Nina <zivancevicn65@gmail.com>
To: Marc Léger <leger.mj@gmail.com>
7 May 2015 at 17:22

Please forgive my previous silly message
I'm likely to fall apart
Love nin

Marc Léger <leger.mj@gmail.com>
To: Zivancevic Nina <zivancevicn65@gmail.com>
7 May 2015 at 19:11

Okay, so i am working on the book.
and this click to cheer you up:
https://www.youtube.com/watch?v=U88jj6PSD7w
[Slavoj Zizek, "Why Be Happy When You Could Be Interesting"]

Zivancevic Nina <zivancevicn65@gmail.com>
To: Marc Léger <leger.mj@gmail.com>
7 May 2015 at 19:35

thank you, big master thinker...
I apologize for being so impulsibve—
i had no right to behave in that way...
have a good evening love you though,
even more so

Zivancevic Nina <zivancevicn65@gmail.com>
To: Marc Léger <leger.mj@gmail.com>
7 May 2015 at 19:49

was Angelica Kauffman a close image of Artemisia Gentileschi ?
Who was raped by her father? see neoclassical vs. baroque...
And do I,see THE art of crisis as something pertinent to Sue Coe?
Or to any weeping 21 century artist?
Marc, I'm undergoing a very big personal crisis. I hopei snap out of it--by
tomorrow.
yr friend Zee

Marc Léger <leger.mj@gmail.com>
To: Zivancevic Nina <zivancevicn65@gmail.com>
7 May 2015 at 20:19

i always take your CV entries on Violent Femmes and Women
of Disaster as insight into how i'm supposed to fit in as your first
postcontempoary character but i also remember that you live down the
street from Place Suzanne Valadon and so i think so many wonderful
possibilities for walking in the city

but still, there are some things that even i can learn from some of the big artists and Caravaggio was known not only for his violent tempérament – interesting some of the speculation on the fact that his proportions were so distorted it had to be intentional

---

Zivancevic Nina <zivancevicn65@gmail.com>
To: Marc Léger <leger.mj@gmail.com>
8 May 2015 at 05:22

Thanks my dear,
I snapped out of my crisis (Daniel calls me "my NY discipline"). Yes, I was trained in discipline in NYC, so I'm on my way to do some sport, and then pick up the remnants of my bird at the vet, and then get back to my place and work on my stuff.
So, will get back to you most likely this afternoon when you're opening yr lovely eyes etc. Thank you for yr moral support and camaradery, which falls right or well on this very day of camaradery against Nazism (it's a big holiday here)
Yes, but the remaining issue is that I really prefer seeing friends and lovers and family instead of writing to them- we pushed this form of genre I did not like so much- to the extreme. And as they say here 'chapeau' to you, or SVAKA CAST in serbian or gesumtag or I don't know what: my honors, cum laude to you
you really have inspired me to stretch imagination in different directions..
Have a lovely coffee and morning -
love you, I'll be OK as ..
xxxxxxxxxxxxxxxxxxxxxxxxxxxxxxxxxxx

Marc Léger <leger.mj@gmail.com>
To: Zivancevic Nina <zivancevicn65@gmail.com>
8 mai 2015 à 15:16

okay Nin, have a lovely day, as you say, and yes, i saw polanski's venus in fur yesterday - i found it was for an 80s audience and not so much relevant to us - even though i consider cul de sac a truly great film and fearless vampire slayers a pleasant confection - again - my literary references are all too limited and let me know when i have truly reached the limits of your interest and genre - my own interest runs more in the direction of laura oldfield than sue coe but i am also vegetarian as you may have guessed -- so that remains the task of the artist and theorist and Living ON Air in my opinion is worthy of anyone's time and so i look forward to the english translation of airport writings

Zivancevic Nina <zivancevicn65@gmail.com>
To: Marc Léger <leger.mj@gmail.com>
8 May 2015 at 09:37

Wow!
Are you trying to get rid of me my dear theorist?
What's wrong?
Why this snappy tone and tranchant and...
I was just about to sit down and write a meaningful letter to u when yr response cut me off and..
Look, perhaps I'm too sensitive and crazy but you are changing yr approach to things as we'll

Zivancevic Nina <zivancevicn65@gmail.com>
To: Marc Léger <leger.mj@gmail.com>
8 May 2015 at 9:44

Look ... Have I reached yr limits of interest in writing letters?
Are u getting tired, bored or simply busy?
You don't have to respond, I mean please, don't feel obliged..
We can take a break any time.. Continue or stop altogether
Not that I don't care
But I hate to impose obligation on anyone
Especially on those I love the best

Zivancevic Nina <zivancevicn65@gmail.com>
To: Marc Léger <leger.mj@gmail.com>
8 May 2015 at 11:25

Soonets en avion...
most of the book was translated into English or was written in English or .. the rest is untranslatable..
enjoy en français (I think you got Letter to Myself but I didn't get some positive feedback from you except for "Cure" section)
Well perhaps.. you really have penchant for theory, or that's how i see u
hey, a good thing is that Pierre Labro (friend of Pierre Restany Nouvelle Objectivistes critic ,)
wants to talk for yr anthology tomorrow
yupii! i really look forward to this archi AG and underground colab!
love you, to cut this crap of redundancy
saying,
NZ

Marc Léger <leger.mj@gmail.com>
To: Zivancevic Nina <zivancevicn65@gmail.com>
8 May 2015 at 17:42

thanks for sending Sonnets
i will love it even more now
and yes, CURE stood out for some reason
all i know is that you were on this personal-not-personal sort of wave
great for Pierre LaBro - let me know how much i owe you
(i mean, in terms of Serbian smiles and giggles)
otherwise you have my complete cooperation

Zivancevic Nina <zivancevicn65@gmail.com>
To: Marc Léger <leger.mj@gmail.com>
8 May 2015 at 15:30

this is the poem from the book I've been translating into English.
He's good, Sinisha Tucic. Real AG.

CANNIBAL ANTE PORTAS

Reading different branches of general linguistics I remembered
The first cannibals and those who came later even today
From the Heraclites circle through the age of Internet
The history of human writing.
Everything started from the pictures
So we have the cartoons today
From the icons in cartoons We inherited the alphabet of icons
Then came the syllabic signs
For instance the Latin alphabet, the Glagolitic alphabet and the Cyrillic
alphabet
The science of language would enter the positivist dead ends
And only in the 20th century it got rid of the diachronic handcuffs
And went into the synchronic structure
And then boom!
Internet came
Return to the icon
Return to the cave
In a cave we find a cyber cannibal
Plugged in the global network
Looking for his victims with the Yahoo search engine
He's clicking and the flesh which is moved by the computer mouse
Is a sort of an icon

It opens an icon
It has no syllabic signs
It turns on the internet
Into civilization
It's looking for a volunteer victim on the global net
CANNIBAL ANTE PORTAS
From the Bill Gates' cave
From one icon to another
From one site to another
From a site to a cave
The victim volunteered to enter the cave
Cannibal used his camera to film the execution
He ate his victim
He closed the icon.

Marc Léger <leger.mj@gmail.com>
To: Zivancevic Nina <zivancevicn65@gmail.com>
8 May 2015 at 22:14

interesting
but this has also to do with time but no future
so i see your 80s influences all the time - richard kern and lydia lunch

---

Zivancevic Nina <zivancevicn65@gmail.com>
To: Marc Léger <leger.mj@gmail.com>
8 May 2015 at 17:08

oh, cmon, tacky, tacky but
thanks for the links
and i think it wld be a terrible mistake to freeze my mind in the 80s as we
do belong to certains epochs but then we don't.. etc
ibid.

Zivancevic Nina <zivancevicn65@gmail.com>
To: Marc Léger <leger.mj@gmail.com>
9 May 2015 at 08:26

yes, one has to understand all this and be watchful for that old marketing
strategy "anytime you blink while watching the screen some secret ad/

message creeps up inside yr brain", and the friendship, the most fragile of the current communication forms.. how does it survive?
I took a social psychology course last year-- and I was convinced that my soul hadn't been lost. Not yet. Yes, my cher friend, stay online and inthere, notwithstanding my really unusual physical attraction to you, despite all other factors, you are a great friend and have huge capacity as such..
My friends are (needless to say) a great extended family of mine. Do you sleep with your friends? I don't do it any longer- simply as they find it very confusing , most of them are not ready for that degree of intimacy. They get confused. Me too...

Marc Léger <leger.mj@gmail.com>
To: Zivancevic Nina <zivancevicn65@gmail.com>
9 May 2015 at 9:51

well, i sometimes find it hard to understand why someone would not know in advance that i am totally straight but i suppose it is good to say it once in a while, not that i actually believe in these kinds of dis-en-closures and marketing, but to all extents and purposes, yes, that is what i am
more work from me today on the msc and god knows what form it will take and who will publish it but one must carry on with meaningful work - and you are meaningful to me
and your musical experiences you mention are just like a little glimpse into how supercool you are

---

Zivancevic Nina <zivancevicn65@gmail.com>
To: Marc Léger <leger.mj@gmail.com>
9 May 2015 at 17:53

my Kit pal,
and dear human being.. good to know you people still exist in this fun(k)y world..
thanks above all for good advice, yes, I dared call Chris and sqorted things out..
now it's peace, love and happiness over here-- the book is not only going to print first thing Monday morn but he's also into organizing a big book launch party in a London pub known for such activities..
wanna come over for the ocassion? I know i kno you're "a completely straight serial monogamist" and you wldn't like to hurt yr girlfriend, but

hey, I'm a kitpal and plus, you'll be in all yr colors on the back jacket
of the book! And Chris is sending you 2 copies with all his apologies—
he'd also like to know if you know anyone in yr enclave of friends and
acquaintances who cld mention it, review it etc? Perhaps you yourself?
I dare not ask you for more than I had already asked
yeah, it's OK to raise one's voice from time to time
Good and productive evening to you, my dear

Marc Léger <leger.mj@gmail.com>
To: Zivancevic Nina <zivancevicn65@gmail.com>
9 May 2015 at 18:58

cute and clever mynx
oh i'm glad that you and Chris are all squared and back into each other
- and so soon after that he 's ready to print my endorsement so that's
good for me but maybe not so good for the truth procedure

ah, for the London pub - yes, I thank you very much for that since the
UK is where I am presently in exile -- but we should save it for one of my
lecture performances, maybe after volume 2 comes out -- if you want, i
would like you to take a few jpgs of me (i can send more) and put them
into one of those digital frames and have that going during your reading
-- you can place some fish and chips and a pint of IPA beside my picture
and then play something on your viola for me since I'm your lad -- i want
you to title the piece The Joker in honour and Natasha Ginwala and
supercommunity insider-outsiders

it's late so you must be drunk by now and watching tv - if you're not then
you must be smoking hashish and hanging around with your harem of
male poets - i will tell you later about my dictator fantasies

---

Zivancevic Nina <zivancevicn65@gmail.com>
To: Marc Léger <leger.mj@gmail.com>
9 May 2015 at 19:19

How very right you are- on the subject of the colour of the cover (Letters
to Myself was supposed, ay ay ay, to be completely different!)
BUT how wrong you are, Marc James Léger, on the subject of my states
of mind- I don't drink and I don't watch TV, and I don't smoke hashish
as it makes me sleepy (I cld do with something to keep me awake all
night long, i long for something tender like a sprinkle of MDMA on my

grapefruit slice, but hmm, no such stuff around here) and how wrong you are about my harem- they are my good friends who write poems for me, but they don't have your qualities , good and bad, aha,, like a poet who recently said (though he quickly changed his mind) "it takes a train to laugh and Nina zee to cry"

so, I'm working hard here on these different projects (a translation of the poetry book almost finished) and I always do positive things when I am not drunk or stoned-- and that's 99% of my time. Perhaps I should go out and break my high heels in ballrooms, and bring harem of wild boys home, but I cannot, it is so sad to wake up next to someone you don't love and you don't know.. i mean you probably know the feeling , that's why we don't go to bars and pick up people although we love them all, I mean mankind, but..

tell me, yes, about your dictator fantasies- I'm the collector of MJL fantasies, that's my nicest curatorial (not dictatorial job)

and I'm using the opportunity here to tell you that I apologise if I'm taking much too much of your time, compulsive obsessive that I am..

Marc Léger <leger.mj@gmail.com>
To: Zivancevic Nina <zivancevicn65@gmail.com>
9 May 2015 at 19:46

time, does it exist ? for you i have all the time and who knows who will win this tug of words -- but i'm stoned 99% of the time

---

Zivancevic Nina <zivancevicn65@gmail.com>
To: Marc Léger <leger.mj@gmail.com>
9 May 2015 at 20:16

I've been following an old recepy in handling Your Majesty...
very 18 century, although probably you're not aware of it.. Nor should you be..
ay ay, what am i doin' here with you?
you are neither stupid and depressive like Dan, nor worldly and pompous like Toscanini, not self-assured and arrogant like Si, and certainly not mad as some other specimens of the extraordinary males that I've come accross I'm still figuring this out..

Zivancevic Nina <zivancevicn65@gmail.com>
To: Marc Léger <leger.mj@gmail.com>
9 May 2015 at 20:28

But, Marc, there is a terrible catch in my story, see under the key "nina
likes marc very very much" Hmmm, I don't know if we, humans, have
so called proto-types, but you are the type of the man I've always loved,
and I have to snap out of this as this "tug of words" may end up in your
favour! And I dread the consequences.. So why are you stoned all the
time? meaning marbled? Oops, and who's reading all our emails? watch
out! Is that yr medication?
Is this correspondence just a joke that you get off on, etc, something like
burping last night's wine for breakfast?
For me to figure out.
True, we could assume a very pompous, technical tone of conversation,
and I'm always on the verge of saying "vous" to you..
Helllo.... WHO ARE YOU, MJL? Should I ask Bruno Latour about your
syndrom?
xxxxx

Zivancevic Nina <zivancevicn65@gmail.com>
To: Marc Léger <leger.mj@gmail.com>
9 May 2015 at 22:12

oh, sh.. I hope I did not scare you with my
JINX! No, I don't have any recepy for handling you or any males like
you.. I'm just defending myself most of the time.
I hope I did not hurt your very very sensitive ego..
Kit

Zivancevic Nina <zivancevicn65@gmail.com>
To: Marc Léger <leger.mj@gmail.com>
9 May 2015 at 22:27

ok, i may be obsessive, but you have to be happy too!
Happiness is an illusion- but being unhappy is also an illusion
where do we go from there? back to Buddhism? We shd be neither
happy or unhappy..
In my view, I am always happy these days, as I've had a taste of a long
period of being unhappy.

And basically, one is happy when one has the means
to enjoy happiness. If you have money and health and time to enjoy
things, then you become happy. yes. as simple as that.

Marc Léger <leger.mj@gmail.com>
To: Zivancevic Nina <zivancevicn65@gmail.com>
10 May 2015 at 09:03

i have noticed the attention to the smallest details - like only astronauts
in a space mission have such delicacy of attention for things that are
freeze dried -- what are you doing here with me? i think i asked you that
before in terms of postcontemporary character research and inquiry

---

Marc Léger <leger.mj@gmail.com>
To: Zivancevic Nina <zivancevicn65@gmail.com>
10 May 2015 at 09:11

ha, i appreciate a woman who does not think that tug of words is a male
only way of seeing the word - but then is she merely playing into a male
fantasy of what a woman is like - like in that western i'm watching about
a black beauty wild horse (*Black Horse Canyon*) - she does not know the
answer to his enigma, only that she must tug as medication for stoned
out Marc - some insist that they must send me back to the stoner age to
prove to themselves - you know i am surrounded by so many (please tell
me that you are not being paid by the CIA, CSIS, ISIS)

Zivancevic Nina <zivancevicn65@gmail.com>
To: Marc Léger <leger.mj@gmail.com>
10 May 2015 at 09:15

civilized manner!! I am TOO civilized! I should be more "sauvage"
(i think that Baudrillard said the same thing to me once)
our dialogue is /has been to me one of the highest quality
and what I find cute and relevant and sweet, why not,
is the fact that we are addressing one another in this cute "mumbo-
jumbo" kids and street intimate language and we have never met in
person, to be so intimate so to speak,
but I'm thinking for our book- I' still have to find the keys for it, my key,
your key etc

Do you think I should talk to Kristeva about it?
I can make a RDV with her, she likes me a lot. Ask her how to transfer
from one strata to another in our text?
It is SO ATTRACTIVE what we are doing
and unusual
and not done
before

Marc Léger <leger.mj@gmail.com>
To: Zivancevic Nina <zivancevicn65@gmail.com>
10 May 2015 at 09:17

kit - i have no ego, only traumatose - in this i am in advance of the
buddhist method - and i do not have a dark evil side - such metaphysics
are pre-Freud in my manifest - but i accept this as metaphorical and
poetic speech to capture human psychology as they say in humanist
culture, italian manner of speaking - i hope i did not hurt your sensitive
synapses - please write back, correct me and tell me what you know
about this manner

Zivancevic Nina <zivancevicn65@gmail.com>
To: Marc Léger <leger.mj@gmail.com>
10 May 2015 at 09:19

whooo whooops! You know- if I were paid by ANY agency, I would be
like Snowden by now.. I've would have fucked up by now..
I was approached by someone in Washington DC, thus my poem in
"More or Less Urgent" called the CIA agent or something,
it's a beautiful poem, do you have that book of mine?

Marc Léger <leger.mj@gmail.com>
To: Zivancevic Nina <zivancevicn65@gmail.com>
10 May 2015 at 09:20

i have ideas about happiness, but do you think it's safe to expose such
things on Internet, after your Hollande just passed an NSA Patriot ACt
spying law and Harper C51 anti-freedom law, is it safe for those two
x-subversives, Marc and Zee ? does Glenn Greenwald think we're
boring

Zivancevic Nina <zivancevicn65@gmail.com>
To: Marc Léger <leger.mj@gmail.com>
10 May 2015 at 09:26

tell you all that I know, about id and ego? there's a lovely book called
'Freud's list', like Schindler's list by Smilevski, a Macedonian writer,
caused a lot of wind and hurricane in French media,
about Freud leaving his sisters behind and he left for England..
darling, I'll tell you whatever you want need and what you don't need to
know if that's soothing to you, so
if i sent you a letter like "blah blah blah" probably that wld be as sweet as
a thorough Lacanian analysis here as the matter of fact, like Lacan, I'm
gonna cut this session right now, as I have to be somewhere in half an
hour, but yeah, blah blah blah
I imagine my life with you would be
NO WORDS!
I would just look at you at you would know what I mean
some people say it's the perfect complicity and understanding
I could also play music and you would know how i feel, i mean i would
know how you feel..
CMOK CMOK

Marc Léger <leger.mj@gmail.com>
To: Zivancevic Nina <zivancevicn65@gmail.com>
10 May 2015 at 09:32

i see it more that you refer to Baudrillard and Kristeva as alter-egos, like
when you are feeling like tugging the words harder in your boudoir you
say oh it's Kristeva and this liberal ideology because you know that in
Freudian dialectics there is trama -- so maybe with them you have a kind
of Claude Chabrol horreur aesthetic that comes up every now and then -
must be something having to do with anxiety... okay so now you're really
ZEN ... like maybe you think i'm getting to know you

Zivancevic Nina <zivancevicn65@gmail.com>
To: Marc Léger <leger.mj@gmail.com>
10 May 2015 at 09:54

Hey, darlingski (as they say in NYC)
I am ZEN yes, but this is a serious question:
should i go and talk to Julia about this theory cum fiction method in
writing?

I don't even have to tell her that it's our epistolary thing
i'm more interested in the method
the rest is our ornament, kapish?

Zivancevic Nina <zivancevicn65@gmail.com>
To: Marc Léger <leger.mj@gmail.com>
10 May 2015 at 10:08

Cad, there you go again! just when i heave to leave the apartment and
my WASHING MASHINE is leaking!!! shit!!
but to go back to yr subject:
i mention Baudrillard and Kristeva as friends and i met them and i trusted
them,
i can mention Agamben now that i've been into his Potentialities who
says
as a scientia infima, linguistics certainly has the fundamental position
attributed to it by medieval classifications which placed grammar first
among the seven disciplines of the School.
and so what? what do i get, what do you get?
i mean who's to solve the problem of our text?
i say, Agamben ok, let's thing about grammar and the scholastic aspect
of it
but lemmie go back to Julia and ask for some extralinguistic approach to
this text
mamma mia!! CMMMMMMMMMMMMMMMMMMMMMMMMM
MMOOOOOOOOOOOOOOOOOOOOOOOOOOOKKKKKKKK
KKKKKKKKKKKKKKKKKKKKK

Marc Léger <leger.mj@gmail.com>
To: Zivancevic Nina <zivancevicn65@gmail.com>
10 May 2015 at 10:08

anything you say, you are my PVC dom dom cutie
but i thought we should also send to Masha
she is really into these new technologies like googolplex playgirl
but don't you have some place to be
you dont have an appointment for tanning booth ?

Zivancevic Nina <zivancevicn65@gmail.com>
To: Marc Léger <leger.mj@gmail.com>
10 May 2015 at 10:12

ok, go back to your girls, i couldn't care less
just let us figure out this project that we're working on
and basta!
i'm a sad stupid idiot that i got trapped into yr fishing net
and have been VERY MUCH INTO this correspondence since february
I cant even make love to other people
yeah but my turkish friend, poet , Sevgi is waiting for me at home not
outside
and i'll join her in a second
first i have to scoop water from the kitchen floor
my washer fell apart

Marc Léger <leger.mj@gmail.com>
To: Zivancevic Nina <zivancevicn65@gmail.com>
10 May 2015 at 10:14

oh, i don't want you to miss your appointment
please have Sevgi take pics of you washing the floor
or whatever you are having at the restaurant
send to me when you have the chance
pardon my table manners

Zivancevic Nina <zivancevicn65@gmail.com>
To: Marc Léger <leger.mj@gmail.com>
10 May 2015 at 10:19

fuck
it's already 16:20
yeah, this is WHAT YOU're doing to me

Marc Léger <leger.mj@gmail.com>
To: Zivancevic Nina <zivancevicn65@gmail.com>
10 May 2015 at 10:21

i will shampoo you when you get back
you can tell me how what your life

Zivancevic Nina <zivancevicn65@gmail.com>
To: Marc Léger <leger.mj@gmail.com>
10 May 2015 at 11:43

Hssss
Psssssss you will really do DAT?
Dad? My fur is kinda shedding and balls of my furcoat are all over the
bathtub.
Masta, come back tonite so that u can brush up my back with a kitty
shamp and whiska meal
Yr Kit

Envoyé de mon iPhone

Marc Léger <leger.mj@gmail.com>
To: Zivancevic Nina <zivancevicn65@gmail.com>
10 May 2015 at 12:01

how is your bouillon this evening - are you only now sipping aperitifs
and iPhoning yourself obsession ?

Zivancevic Nina <zivancevicn65@gmail.com>
To: Marc Léger <leger.mj@gmail.com>
10 May 2015 at 12:06

Yeah i'll be slipping
Apéritifs soon While interviewing that gorgeous George tonite
Than i come
Back home and you wash it off
Shampoo dry blow job etc

Envoyé de mon iPhone

Marc Léger <leger.mj@gmail.com>
To: Zivancevic Nina <zivancevicn65@gmail.com>
10 May 2015 at 12:18

okay, i'm gonna let you do your thing
people who check out iPhone during friends are considered shallow
you don't want to risk everything for me, do you ?

Zivancevic Nina <zivancevicn65@gmail.com>
To: Marc Léger <leger.mj@gmail.com>
10 May 2015 at 12:20

You ..4 letter love

Envoyé de mon iPhone

Marc Léger <leger.mj@gmail.com>
To: Zivancevic Nina <zivancevicn65@gmail.com>
10 May 2015 at 12:23

let them think you are on the 4 letter edge

confusion - the sequel

Marc Léger <leger.mj@gmail.com>
To: Zivancevic Nina <zivancevicn65@gmail.com>
10 May 2015 at 12:32

i will never know where our manuscript ends
almost there but you keep sending another email
the idea of just writing with no ulterior motive

Zivancevic Nina <zivancevicn65@gmail.com>
To: Marc Léger <leger.mj@gmail.com>
10 May 2015 at 14:24

I know i confuse you
That's a part of my ' big cat strategy'
Oh Marc !
The major différence between a European and a Canadian/american cat
is that the european one
Has no
Ulterior
Motives
Perhaps
Aesthetic
Ones
Ask
Yr
Mom
She
May
Tell
U
The
Same
Thing

Env

Marc Léger <leger.mj@gmail.com>
To: Zivancevic Nina <zivancevicn65@gmail.com>
10 May 2015 at 14:45

you're full of bull with your europe-north america thing, as if that has anything to do with chatelet-voltaire correspondence and trans-serbian express - sometimes i think you will never appreciate my big game manoeuvres ... as if our correspondence has any motif whatsoever

---

Zivancevic Nina <zivancevicn65@gmail.com>
To: Marc Léger <leger.mj@gmail.com>
10 May 2015 at 14:59

Wof wof wof

Envoyé de mon iPhone

confusion which one

Marc Léger <leger.mj@gmail.com>
To: Zivancevic Nina <zivancevicn65@gmail.com>
10 May 2015 at 12:16

    go get that George
    pour on the leather
    and bring back the spoils
    watch out that minx !

Zivancevic Nina <zivancevicn65@gmail.com>
To: Marc Léger <leger.mj@gmail.com>
10 May 2015 at 12:18

    I cant
    I'm in love
    with You

Marc Léger <leger.mj@gmail.com>
To: Zivancevic Nina <zivancevicn65@gmail.com>
10 May 2015 at 12:20

    you can't love me
    you don't even know i'm a computer program
    00010101110010001010001000010101111000

Zivancevic Nina <zivancevicn65@gmail.com>
To: Marc Léger <leger.mj@gmail.com>
10 May 2015 at 13:15

    Disgusting
    So the game
    Is
    Over

Marc Léger <leger.mj@gmail.com>
To: Zivancevic Nina <zivancevicn65@gmail.com>
10 May 2015 at 13:30

impetuous pet
if you put that code into google computer translate it says
"it's never over orpheus," our theme song

Zivancevic Nina <zivancevicn65@gmail.com>
To: Marc Léger <leger.mj@gmail.com>
10 May 2015 at 14:37

Listen listen
Master
I got
A marvellous book on kits
Just for you
And i will send you
Pics and clips
And my clipped nails
As soon as i get home
Nothing
And noone is more
Attractive to me
Than this Master game program
Which is not
Closed
As i keep coming and coming and coming
.. Back to you
I guess

What about if i Skype you
What about if you see
How really kittenish i am
And terribly beautiful
And terribly young
Phew this phénomène of phewsh!!
Will u be my friend on Skype?
I will never disturb you?
How are u gonna shampoo my furs if you cannot see them?
The end of program
Make sure you closed this program..

Marc Léger <leger.mj@gmail.com>
To: Zivancevic Nina <zivancevicn65@gmail.com>
10 May 2015 at 14:48

okay, but please do not send anything until you receive my package -
slow delivery and fair trade reciprocity and also i never phone or Skype
with friends or cougars

Zivancevic Nina <zivancevicn65@gmail.com>
To: Marc Léger <leger.mj@gmail.com>
10 May 2015 at 15:03

Ah... You are so serious and so pathetic..
Where does this come in?
Into yr salon story?
I'm stopping this correspondence right now if i cannot speak w/ you
And maybe.. After all i will not want to

Envoyé de mon iPhone

Marc Léger <leger.mj@gmail.com>
To: Zivancevic Nina <zivancevicn65@gmail.com>
10 May 2015 at 15:05

but i know this is your way of saying: i am about to press send

You know it don't you my hair

Zivancevic Nina <zivancevicn65@gmail.com>
To: Marc Léger <leger.mj@gmail.com>
10 May 2015 at 15:09

As i've been sending you tons and tons of my photos and this serious one is stolen from Velasques studio but you prefer the kindergarten ones..
There u go!!

Image: [next page]

Marc Léger <leger.mj@gmail.com>
To: Zivancevic Nina <zivancevicn65@gmail.com>
10 May 2015 at 15:19

wow .... this is going to be a complicated soap up job
you are trying to make me

Zivancevic Nina <zivancevicn65@gmail.com>
To: Marc Léger <leger.mj@gmail.com>
10 May 2015 at 15:25

Ok Master..
I have to interview this guy now
Not a small task as i said once
No to him
And his ego is hurt
And big - as in most actors cum directors
Wish me luck
Hmm what brand of soap will u be using on my head
Which one shd i use on yours?
Something with vitamins?
Candida chlamydias ?
Sorry I overdid it...

NZ in NYC, c.1991. Polaroid by Carlo Stephanos.

Zivancevic Nina <zivancevicn65@gmail.com>
To: Marc Léger <leger.mj@gmail.com>
10 May 2015 at 15:30

  Wish me lick i mean luck
  Sucker

  Envoyé de mon iPhone

Marc Léger <leger.mj@gmail.com>
To: Zivancevic Nina <zivancevicn65@gmail.com>
10 May 2015 at 15:44

  bonne chance
  le salon de mme châtelet - parisienne de classe et jeanne darc
  intellectuelle et scintille de sabre inaperçu
  justesse et poésie - pas de prisonniers

Zivancevic Nina <zivancevicn65@gmail.com>
To: Marc Léger <leger.mj@gmail.com>
10 May 2015 at 18:30

  In fact it was great
  It went great
  The founder of Les Periferiques was a pal and collab of Guy Debord and
  his people are WoN(derful)
  It was an interview like as if i interviewed Judith Malina and the members
  of the Living
  I feel like i can really put some stuff together ciudad/politeis/social cum
  art action
  I feel much better about this AG collab now.
  No you dont have to shampoo my head
  You've done it in so many ways already
  My brain is washed by MJL
  And i wont call u on Skype either
  So have a good evening
  And hasta la clicka

  Envoyé de m

Zivancevic Nina <zivancevicn65@gmail.com>
To: Marc Léger <leger.mj@gmail.com>
10 May 2015 at 18:32

Il ne faut pas mépriser les collègues
Il faut les aimer avec tous leurs fauts

Marc Léger <leger.mj@gmail.com>
To: Zivancevic Nina <zivancevicn65@gmail.com>
10 May 2015 at 18:40

ah oui, le mépris - bébé et Piccoli dans le bain
alors, écoutez moi mme de zivancevic - bébé
je suis content que tu as toutes les bonnes choses là avec les
périphériques
et merci pour tes soi-disants conseils
je vais regarder ça
moi, je ne prends pas de prisonniers
je suis comme Guy, quoi
pas juste une référence biblique, quoi

Zivancevic Nina <zivancevicn65@gmail.com>
To: Marc Léger <leger.mj@gmail.com>
10 May 2015 at 20:16

oh oui, tu peux prendre le role de Jean Luc,
ça va bien avec toi, ça te rend heureuse
mais moi je ne suis pas BB,
à la rigeuR;;

Marc Léger <leger.mj@gmail.com>
To: Zivancevic Nina <zivancevicn65@gmail.com>
10 May 2015 at 20:22

vas y donc là dit moi ça comment sont les choses et moi je t'en parlerai
de comment il ne faut pas hair pauvre petit jean-luc (moi) - nous avons
tous nos petites habitudes - bon très bien Zee pas à la rigueur, mais
comme ça, alors, comment tu veux tes cheveux, avec un petit frizz pour
ton annonce spéciale pour Living On Air - on peut pas tout avoir, comme
disait Chris à propos de mon AZÉ

Zivancevic Nina <zivancevicn65@gmail.com>
To: Marc Léger <leger.mj@gmail.com>
10 May 2015 at 20:31

mais Marc,
(et tu ne sais pas alors quel bouton tu pousses avec mon "Marc" en français (c'est presque égale à ton discours avec ta Rosika))
ma vie n'est pas, notre vie n'est pas un salon du coiffure
et certainement, mon boudoir n'est pas un catacombe pour les chats égyptiens,
tiens,
je sais que tu est sous certains médicaments chimiques ou pas trop chimiques
mais SVP- maîtrise-toi et reviens dans mes bras! tu n'est pas un prisonnier de mon salon!! Personne est !
quel chien de la vie!

Zivancevic Nina <zivancevicn65@gmail.com>
To: Marc Léger <leger.mj@gmail.com>
10 May 2015 at 20:37

Tiens,
je voudrais te demander une chose très important pour moi, en fin, pour ton projet-
comment ça s'est fait que Marc'o et son disciple Gilles m'ont raconté ce soir
que leurs projets avec Debord ont été financés par Hollywood dans les années 1950s?
Je sais qu' on avait une période dans Hollywood qui a été très très cool (avec Hitchcock, Wells etc) mais pour financer les projets d'underground ou d'avantgarde, ça m'étonne quand même ..?

Marc Léger <leger.mj@gmail.com>
To: Zivancevic Nina <zivancevicn65@gmail.com>
10 May 2015 at 20:49

de quoi là – c'est quoi ça – n'était-ce pas Barbara Stanwyk dans Johnny Guitar? et comme elle était une femme forte tu comprends très bien cette égyptomanie que j'ai - voilà c'est ça maintenant comme tu l'as bien deviné je suis pierré 99% du temps pour toi - enfin, les finances, ça n'existe pas, pour nous c'est une chose du hasard ou pire (du Stalino nimporte quoi) - là dessus nous sommes nous deux comme deux petits oiseaux - alors oui mon western à propos du cheval noir difficile à capter (sans blague) – c'est très Black Beauty évidemment, la déesse de la nuit

---

Zivancevic Nina <zivancevicn65@gmail.com>
To: Marc Léger <leger.mj@gmail.com>
10 May 2015 at 20:58

ouf!! je me sens terrible!
pourtant je n'arrache pas - jamais- une chose qui ne me appartient pas!
si tu veux- et ça je peux signer avec mon sang: si tu, toi, si tu n'avais pas poussé notre conversation dans cette direction- moi, je suis plutôt timide (c'est étrange pour toi de dire ça) je jamais pousserais notre dialogue jusqu'au là
mais bon, après ton film tu vas me répondre
comme à ta chère collègue (qui je suis)
comment Hollywood a financé (et pourquoi) les film de Marc'o et Debord? C'est bizarre comme tout!

Marc Léger <leger.mj@gmail.com>
To: Zivancevic Nina <zivancevicn65@gmail.com>
10 May 2015 at 21:04

il n'y a pas seulement Godard qui prenait des avions jusqu'en amérique pour chercher des valises pleinnes de fric - mais je ne sais rien des ces choses de la vie - moi, petit canadien comme je suis (vraiment) - rebel prolétaire - même en une certaine mesure critique de Debord mais seulement sur le plan Pasolini - ok, tu veux savoir: la révolution, ça se finance ma petite

---

Zivancevic Nina <zivancevicn65@gmail.com>
To: Marc Léger <leger.mj@gmail.com>
10 May 2015 at 21:10

ok je vois. merci mon grand
certainement tu comprends l'industrie du cinéma mieux que moi.
je me sens tellement petite et ignorante quand je parle avec toi (juste afin de témoigner le fait que l'age fait aucune importance)
et je apprends pas mal de choses de toi chaque jour et là, je suis une partie perdante.

Et je te souhaite tout bonheur dans ta vie car tu lui mérite!
Bon film à toi

Marc Léger <leger.mj@gmail.com>
To: Zivancevic Nina <zivancevicn65@gmail.com>
10 May 2015 at 21:17

ah bon, voilà quelque chose de bien dit
j'aime beaucoup les filles albanienne orange
mais ça tu ne le savais pas!
et bonne partie

De pet impitoyable

Zivancevic Nina <zivancevicn65@gmail.com>
To: Marc Léger <leger.mj@gmail.com>
10 May 2015 at 18:58

Attends mseur à la Léger
J'arrive chez moi en 5 minutes et tu vas écouter mes miaow miaow à propos de ton comportement d'hier
Ma batterie est tellement faible ici..

Envoyé de mon iPhone

Marc Léger <leger.mj@gmail.com>
To: Zivancevic Nina <zivancevicn65@gmail.com>
10 May 2015 at 19:05

toi, je ne te vois pas vraiment avec des batteries faibles
au moins, par pour très longtemps - gamine et séductrice du petit canadien (moi)

Zivancevic Nina <zivancevicn65@gmail.com>
To: Marc Léger <leger.mj@gmail.com>
10 May 2015 at 20:10

Monsieur Marc!
Quel genre de la séductrice suis -je?(pas trop professionnelle, ça je dois te dire,) car je me suis fait attrapé par tes propres filets!!
ici, le témoignage d'un ptit chaton, soi disant Vital Cat:
My Master
has not washed me nor/and shampooed me for a year, said my hair's too long for him to wash!
So i am dirty and bad in this cruel world of men!
The other one, Vital Cat et, saz my Master says that I am "lectrice séductrice, and he calls me all sorts of names, Mme de Chateau etc because he does not love me, and he just loves THAT Egyptian kitty..
Life ain't no fair...
Vital Cat et (aka KIT)

Marc Léger <leger.mj@gmail.com>
To: Zivancevic Nina <zivancevicn65@gmail.com>
10 May 2015 at 20:16

la lutte des petits chatons continue -- après toutes cette nonchalance selon giancarlo et faye - si eux ces gars là te connaissaient comme moi je te connais, avec ta chevelure cléopattes et tellement jouant l'égyptienne avec le petit canadien (moi) et le cougar (toi)

Zivancevic Nina <zivancevicn65@gmail.com>
To: Marc Léger <leger.mj@gmail.com>
10 May 2015 at 20:21

Mais comment ça?
pourquoi tu es "un petit canadien".. envers moi?
Et moi - le cougar, ??? je ne crois pas que je suis descendu dans la crèche te chercher et si tu penses comme ça,
OK, arrêtes ta communication juste ce moment-là!
ça vas te rendre heureux

Marc Léger <leger.mj@gmail.com>
To: Zivancevic Nina <zivancevicn65@gmail.com>
10 May 2015 at 20:26

ah la cougare se fache - je ne suis pas dans une crèche quand même - ça je ne ferais jamais ça - je ne suis pas un type mec beh - et par pitié, le plus je deviens petit le plus encore tu deviens féroce, farouche – c'est pas possible

---

Zivancevic Nina <zivancevicn65@gmail.com>
To: Marc Léger <leger.mj@gmail.com>
10 May 2015 at 20:42

as tu de mauvaise humeur ce soir?
je te dis juste le contraire- je ne pense pas
que je suis descendu dans une crèche et si notre différence de l'age te gêne
nous pouvons nous" vous voyer" mais çe serai un peu bette après toute cette correspondance, n'est pas?

Marc Léger <leger.mj@gmail.com>
To: Zivancevic Nina <zivancevicn65@gmail.com>
10 May 2015 at 20:54

ah oui ça tu savais, je travaille très fort (81/100)
mais où ça s'arrête personne ne le sais juste à ce moment et ça
continue avec les petits chats dans la nuit - plus d'informations à ce
propos MJL NZ à la suite

bon bon

Marc Léger <leger.mj@gmail.com>
To: Zivancevic Nina <zivancevicn65@gmail.com>
10 May 2015 at 20:30

alors, Nina, j'ai vraiment hate de voir ça cet entrevue - dis moi en plus
tard mais là je m'en vais m'asseoir sur le divan regarder un western - et
soit pas fâché avant le coucher – c'est pas bon pour mme châtelet
bonsoir Nyx
(ça c'est vraiment toi, dans le wiki)

Zivancevic Nina <zivancevicn65@gmail.com>
To: Marc Léger <leger.mj@gmail.com>
10 May 2015 at 20:49

OK, t'as gagné- peut etre tu as voulu comme ça:
j'arrête tout exchange avec toi, sauf pour cet officielle
car le moment je deviens très gentille, voir amicale avec toi,(tu
m'appelle "cougare" etc)
tu commence m'attaquer et la conversation devienne nulle
et c'est une chose qui se répète donc il faut s'arrêter là
bon western!

Marc Léger <leger.mj@gmail.com>
To: Zivancevic Nina <zivancevicn65@gmail.com>
10 May 2015 at 20:59

oké bon bon, tu joues très bien ce role dans mon petit ciné - ça t'es
magnifique, du genre Maureen O'Hara - Nina 1 et Nina 2 (living)

Zivancevic Nina <zivancevicn65@gmail.com>
To: Marc Léger <leger.mj@gmail.com>
10 May 2015 at 21:06

mais un jour quand je serai bien
et quand tu sois tranquille
je vais te dire les choses assez importantes: pour toi, pour moi,
concernant ce jeux , game of chess which is funny and nourishing to a
certain extent
but could hurt me very much

in a long run-- and you don't want to hurt anyone, right? It does not seem that you do

---

Marc Léger <leger.mj@gmail.com>
To: Zivancevic Nina <zivancevicn65@gmail.com>
10 May 2015 at 21:08

te voilà encore avec tes promesses de menace
talk about redundant
couches-toi, tu es folle de rage

Zivancevic Nina <zivancevicn65@gmail.com>
To: Marc Léger <leger.mj@gmail.com>
10 May 2015 at 21:11

mais non, juste le contraire
bonne nuit

Marc Léger <leger.mj@gmail.com>
To: Zivancevic Nina <zivancevicn65@gmail.com>
10 May 2015 at 21:14

moi, écoute, je t'adore, mais je m'en vais faire mon guacamole pour manger avec mes bretzels - le cheval noir d'hier soir n'est pas encore attrapé - le gars c'est Joel McRae mais elle, je ne sais pas son nom - toutes ces femmes de westerns, elles prennent souvent un peu l'arrière plan aux gros machos – c'est comme ça un peu dans les westerns des années 50, mais pas toujours, pas quand c'est Barbara Stanwyk comme exemple
tiens, tu pensais que je te blaguais, mais comme tu as vu je suis très littéral et par ce que sans imagination - tout ce que je sais ça viens de l'écran, quoi

Zivancevic Nina <zivancevicn65@gmail.com>
To: Marc Léger <leger.mj@gmail.com>
11 May 2015 at 06:06

ok je vois que vous etes vachement le vrai écrivain de *Living on Air* et tout droits legitimes doivent aller à vous et moi
dans le rôle de fille avec les cheveux noir etc
non, je vous adore aussi mais je suis très blessée par votre souci de l'age, l'age est un issue ici
et je sais que...
mais j'ai pensée battement que vous et moi, que nous pouvons transcender la question comme Margaret Duras et.. mais non, elle revient, la question
bon, une fois je serai morte je vais vous laisser ma bibliothèque , mon violon, ma vidéothèque et mon apartement à Paris et vous allez se souvenir de moi de telle et telle façon..
vous ETEZ adorable!! je le sais

Marc Léger <leger.mj@gmail.com>
To: Zivancevic Nina <zivancevicn65@gmail.com>
11 May 2015 at 09:01

oui c'est ça Nina - il y a les souvenirs et le violon et oublies pas, nous sommes nous pas donc dans les "cahots" comme on dit? alors les blagues de l'en dedans de cet homme (ça place spéciale), on ne se moque pas de ça - à moins qu'on est (remplir les détails)
écoute, jette-toi pas en dessous d'un autocar
c'est pas comme ça que je veux finir notre correspondence, avec l'aire coupable
avec cmok il y a un peu de rédomption
Mari Blachard je t'en parle plus tard
je n'ai pas fini le film et il ne l'a pas attrapé encore le cheval
comme Kaja Silverman tu en a beaucoup appris de ce hollywood américain
et vous pensez que nous les gars on va jouer ces roles indéfiniment
je ne pense pas

Zivancevic Nina <zivancevicn65@gmail.com>
To: Marc Léger <leger.mj@gmail.com>
11 May 2015 at 11:32

Marc
Qu'est ce que tu penses sur Victoria et aurélie Chaplin?
Vaut-il la peine de les voir ici en théâtre ??
Je sais tu as voulu faire ton Chaplin livre du cirque Imaginaire..
Dis donc!!

Envoyé de mon iPhone

Marc Léger <leger.mj@gmail.com>
To: Zivancevic Nina <zivancevicn65@gmail.com>
11 May 2015 at 11:47

hein? écoute, absolument c'est la définition de adorable

Image: [next page]

Zivancevic Nina <zivancevicn65@gmail.com>
To: Marc Léger <leger.mj@gmail.com>
11 May 2015 at 15:57

pour moi la def d'adorable c'est ce gars..
hmm un autre hungarian!! encore: Lajos Felix
je lui ADORE un peu moins que toi, mais assez...

Arvida Byströms, *Self-Portrait*, 2014. From the series *My Girl Lollipop*.
Courtesy of the artist.

You know it don't you my hair (reprise)

Zivancevic Nina <zivancevicn65@gmail.com>
To: Marc Léger <leger.mj@gmail.com>
11 May 2015 at 06:14

c'est bien dit aussi
que du 'merveille' ici autour de moi.. (une période extra-dur quand
même)..
Regards , Marc'o m'avait donné un film "Closed Vision" hier ou "60
minutes de la vie interieure d'un homme" et je le regarde soignesement,
j'aimrais t'envoyer ça
i have to figure out how to do it, will ask my pal Bata ce soir how to send
clips or entire thing to you
i'm SO DUMB when it comes to technology, always waiting here for 3
people to help me out
it says 60 min of the inner life of a man , presented as a revolutionary
movie by J Cocteau and L Bunuel at the 1954 Cannes Film Festival,
Closed Vision is the poetic film representation of a man's interior. It
attempts to be to film what J Joyce's Ulysses is to literature

Marc Léger <leger.mj@gmail.com>
To: Zivancevic Nina <zivancevicn65@gmail.com>
11 May 2015 at 08:42

ça oui, je le veux, sujet de mes confrères Stalino-nimporte-quoi Jean
Cocteau et Luis Bunual (surtout après Ange Exterminatrice - pauvre
femme, on en lui voulait un peu trop cette pauvre nonne qui méritait
supposéement tout ces châtiments) et soit patiente du fait que moi aussi
j'ai envoyé un petit colis mais lentement par bateau à la Chine ensuite
France -- et alors, un bonne fois, je voudrais ton opinion sur certaines
choses mais je veux m'assurer avant ce temps que t'es dépassée
l'intempestivité d'hier - ça a l'aire normal ce matin mais j'en suis pas
100% (il me reste toujours mon petit 1%)
et une bonne journée à toi camarade Zivanskaya
tu penses que ça ce transmet ça, malgré les années qui nous séparent ?
moi et Chichi nous avons 14 ans de différence
elle était vraiment anarchiste quand on s'est rencontré mais je l'ai
marxisé en peu dans les détails
et ceci, ça pourrait arriver à toi aussi avec le temps, alors, au hasard
pauvre toi, alors en français de frence je suis vraiment handicappé
et je vois comment en écrivant tu te moques de moi (hautaine)
je fais de mon mieux pour toi, une bonne journée
un petit sourire serbo-français, quoi
toutes me petites affections

Zivancevic Nina <zivancevicn65@gmail.com>
To: Marc Léger <leger.mj@gmail.com>
11 May 2015 at 12:37

Oh... Thank you ..
I slept a little bit more than last week and i feel better today
And also teach fewer classes this week(school is almost over) and the
last but not the least Antoine is coming here every day this week so my
day begins with our music lesson(just after i quit shower and make some
coffee and then the doorbell..)
HE is so very young and real genius who follows every nuance of my
feeling ...and when he leaves there is always a deep sigh!! Why havent i
met this creature in my youth..!
so, like Collette, i know How it feels to be in love w/ someone much
younger.. But i dont think that one should go for one's students, like my
brother whose Claudiette is 27 years younger... Anyways i doubt that,
because of my family tradition , i cld ever leave the land of Anarchism ..
And my dad rallying against marxism after he had lost everything to that
religion...
So thank you so much fr yr package and yr overall care...am i to imagine
that you haven't married Chichi but you're sharing the flat anyways? And
here, Faye's situation is critical and i am , after Paris 8 class, on my way
to his hospital again..
Tiens, i'm writing to u in english
After all, i never went to school in French and you did, it shows.
However, i want to ask you yet another thing but extremely important
one: why do you constantly flagelate, whip yourself? You are either "just
ptit Canadien " or yr French is not good enough, or you lacking this or
that?
Stop doing this to yrself and to me...
Unless your stance is but a joke- but it's not A productive one..
And yes, i wish i cld take u in my arms and just give u a hug.. i have
many crazy dreams like that...they call me a poet from Bgrade..

Envoyé de mon belzebub phone

Marc Léger <leger.mj@gmail.com>
To: Zivancevic Nina <zivancevicn65@gmail.com>
11 May 2015 at 16:45

how can someone, your father, rally against Marxism; i can see
someone rallying against certain Marxists or state authorities, but not
against Marxism as such - but i could be wrong about that - maybe he

had it with the labour theory of value and proletarian self-management
- but somehow i doubt that he gave up on the idea of emancipation and
critique of capitalist exploitation and even the Marxist critique of the state
(but perhaps getting to communism via other means - sex, drugs, back
to nature anthropology, poetry, sci-fi Jodorowski, what ?) - of course you
now want me to find some ingenious ways to go about convincing you of
something like this - but this would indeed require face to face interaction
and be certain that I have had my fair share of interactions with citizens
of former communist state regimes and the good ones i know have
some room for Marxism still but very cautious and really burdened by
memories and mostly looking to younger generations to find new ways -
but so much newness is often so much oldness, and then, we have only
socialism for the rich and the necessity of these corruptions of social
services and environmental protections, wars, surveillance, etc - now
should i stop flagellating myself in such a way as to trust you completely
or only a little bit or not at all - please advise - you know you better than
me - i say, so far so good

Zivancevic Nina <zivancevicn65@gmail.com>
To: Marc Léger <leger.mj@gmail.com>
11 May 2015 at 19:18

I was visiting Claude , that little millionaire friend transvestite, who paid
my taxi to Issy de Moulineaux so that I could watch films with him/her
and comment on them he wanted to know what films I liked in particular,
and i asked him to get everything on Artaud. He did it.
there is that Mordillat film which you probably know, which was like a
piece of the 3DVD coffret which I should have copied before i gave it to
my nephew..
I've had enourmous number of so called art or artistic DVDs, also the
ones with the Surrealist women painters.. oh, never mind..
But the thing with my father, yes, I guess he never gave up entirely
on the idea of Marxism, Lukacs type. And also we went to Budapest
with Allen once to visit Istvan Eorshi (I hope i did not mispell his name)
and had a serious conversation how our friend and neighbor, Mihailo
Markovic, could have joined Milosevic..
But also dad had quite a few anarchist friends, one of them a close
Chomsky's collaborator, a linguist Radivoj Nikolich who was also the
Spanish interpreter for Tito and our ambassador to Peru...He was quite
an incredible guy- he used to teach me Spanish before I moved to the
US and he told my father once: Lucha continua and i think yr daughter
will be capable to continue it.. And whether you should/ could trust me,
you should ask yourself that question. I have nothing to say but that I

want you to trust
yourself first and your primary instinct or intuition
and for the rest of us, if you have to trust someone, well you'd better
trust me 100% because I have nothing to gain or nothing to lose
in my encounter with you
and we meet in the realm of pure taught and Whitehead's simple game
I will never hurt you-- neither i want nor i'd be able to, as you said once--
after all that we've read of Kant and Hume eventually
you should not be so doubteful in this chance operation, kinda conceived
by Cage..

Marc Léger <leger.mj@gmail.com>
To: Zivancevic Nina <zivancevicn65@gmail.com>
11 May 2015 at 19:40

that Mordillat film - i assume the biopic about Artaud and how he would
choke on the words - i think these films have to be made but i'm not
sure that one was a great success, though you could tell the intention
was correct -- but there are so many actual AG documentaries and films
- and also you probably know JJ Lebel and his Artaud interest - when
I used to teach in Lethbridge the Dean of Fine Arts, who was a theatre
director, used to want me to play the lead in Spurt of Blood, and I would
say, of course not, Lorenzaccio

one problem for this book of ours is ... where does it end ? - at this point
in the manuscript we are at April 30 and it becomes kinda reflexive ...
and also odd things here and there ... i think we're close and there has
to be a limit - without this limit we are in life (my art into life friends say
that life sucks and so we must remain with art for the time being (this
alienation thing) ... but you will have something of your own to say on
this issue ... and of course me i'm hegelian about these things always ...
more later from Marc 1, normal, and medium size Marc

Zivancevic Nina <zivancevicn65@gmail.com>
To: Marc Léger <leger.mj@gmail.com>
11 May 2015 at 19:59

You mean - the Dean was in love with you? Obviously, everyone is in
love with you but yourself !
I am not a dominatrix and i am not encouraging you to question yourself
and yr good intentions

So did you play in Jet du Sang? It was peter brook's favorite role before he did Salome and all the veils and was expulsed from the Shakespeare Royal theater whose he was the director...

Envoyé de mon belzebub

Zivancevic Nina <zivancevicn65@gmail.com>
To: Marc Léger <leger.mj@gmail.com>
11 May 2015 at 20:09

My Hegelian friend
I am the antithèses to your thesis and this book is our
Synthesis (i want this part to be in our Book)
We are perhaps just discovering a new genre
And as our old buddy Derrida said- perhaps that Book will never end,
like the Book of J , but perhaps it's not important, the final product i
mean, the thing or the goal is in our writing process
(phew, Schlaermacher also sneaked in here)
So
Don't worry, relax
And if u can't - like u indicated, Viscious Wanda will relax you
With her whip

Envoyé de mon Beelzebub phone

Marc Léger <leger.mj@gmail.com>
To: Zivancevic Nina <zivancevicn65@gmail.com>
11 May 2015 at 20:37

now this schizo personality Beelzebub ... Wanda ... this is the part where
the she devil (Blanchard again) slowly gets me to accept extending the
manuscript until May 11 - it was almost done tonite and i can see now
that you want nothing but life and the Living Marc - if you say process i
say ok fine - we can turn that into a chant: you say process; i say fine;
you say process; i say fine (repeat forever) - i know these kinky things
get you worked up but i have to say, i am going to find out what happens
to the black beauty - will she be caught in the synthesis ?

Zivancevic Nina <zivancevicn65@gmail.com>
To: Marc Léger <leger.mj@gmail.com>
11 May 2015 at 20:53

Ach now You introduce Black beauty kink?
You want us to stop and finish the book? Ok it's done ! Finished.
Are you ok?

Zivancevic Nina <zivancevicn65@gmail.com>
To: Marc Léger <leger.mj@gmail.com>
12 May 2015 at 05:10

OK, if we say that our official book is finished,
I am a serious writer you know. This means you should not treat the rest
of our correspondence as "our book", or will you?
And does this mean we stop writing to each other altogether- I sort of got
used to this emailing, but OK it can stop any second, right?
It is... taking us away from other serious emailings- I can attest to that,
for sure.
OK, we should not mix the registers any longer, I agree. You tell me, my
hairdresser friend. I cannot even imagine getting perm and all the rest
with someone I've never met. I mean, let us not get deeper into fantasy.
If we meet in person really, what would we say to each other? (probably
many things)
have a nice day!

Marc Léger <leger.mj@gmail.com>
To: Zivancevic Nina <zivancevicn65@gmail.com>
12 May 2015 at 09:13

clearly, your work day lasts longer than mine - i need to watch something
at the end of the day and can no longer put in 18 hours like i used to

i'm having a look at how the msc works beyond end of april - it seemed
like ending it where we both agree that we have enough for a book and i
start sending you the files would be a good place but we can keep going
if you prefer - and as you say, and as i've said many times, you're a
serious writer

i'm not the kind who says you are free and who expects you to do the
same (i'm not that kind of anarchist) - one thing, we can keep that last

bit about synthesis that you want in the book, but, please understand that the notion of a dialectical synthesis is not hegelian idea or even respectably part of Marxism, but is an anarchist plot and cartoon -- so please, if you like, i can give us a proper dialectical send off or send up, whichever

my mail to you in a slow boat approaches
a torrent of emails turns into a light mist of Nina Zee droplets
has the tiger been tamed - the black beauty ?

Zivancevic Nina <zivancevicn65@gmail.com>
To: Marc Léger <leger.mj@gmail.com>
12 May 2015 at 10:43

Ay a yay ay ay
Let us say or put it this way
I understood yr email.
While I'm waiting for yr boat's shipment
Can u give me something to read from yr inner hidden list
On Hegellian dialectics?
Or anything relevant for you and then me as your epigone epitome agon
and
I hope
I really do hope
I pray it happens one day..
Yr heavenly counterpart

.

Zivancevic Nina <zivancevicn65@gmail.com>
To: Marc Léger <leger.mj@gmail.com>
12 May 2015 at 11:16

Torrenting you or bombarding with my misty mails, I don't care I mean if that's doing u any good, making you happier
Now that I read yr last email twice
In the 3rd paragraph on phoney anarchists I detect certain sadness..
Who has disappointed yr majesty so much?
Can I whip them in a way that it's not any fun for them? I'm so protective of you, or this virtual time I have with you.
Black beauty herself

Marc Léger <leger.mj@gmail.com>
To: Zivancevic Nina <zivancevicn65@gmail.com>
12 May 2015 at 11:54

heavenly counterpart (METATRON, as you say), that makes some
sense to me and i think that you more than anyone i know appreciates
this formula according to which the loop of saussure's signifiers circle
around YOU the NINA ZEE of your fantasy -- look, i'm dripping all over
the place here (sweat from jogging up the mountain) -- no, there is no
sadness, not at all, this dialectics is my métier and it makes me happy
indeed - and again, as i always say, you can write as you desire - i am
not demanding of you your constant attention, flattery, flagellation, poetic
genius – it's as you like it -- this topic does come up often -- a shrink
would say we have us here a symptom (a fiction fetish)

Zivancevic Nina <zivancevicn65@gmail.com>
To: Marc Léger <leger.mj@gmail.com>
12 May 2015 at 13:04

ahhhha, THAT's the problem right there
you're right on the money Marc,
we (you and I) could outshrink (in simple language) or deconstruct any
shrink we know, except for Vladimir Granoff.. but he's DEAD so, no living
help and cure for us
like you said once "plus, this is cheaper" , this not for free- nothing is for
free, so you and i will have to pay this attachemt to our correspondence
one day or another..
but hey, i don't want to think about distant future
I am glad you were running (how much do you weigh? perhaps you're
too heavy for me? or for my canape?) but anyways, i used that free time
productively and wrote to some of my old literary pals in England, David
Miller, Johny Brown and Niall McDevitt will certainly try to review the
book
and i am getting Chris ready to assume his role of an editor and take
care of my book
like my ex-father in law said : When the book comes out, if it's not
properly distributed and promoted, it dies right away (we know that)
so i took care of my email when your dripping drop arrived and,
MOREOVER
4 of my books fell from the shelf onto my head at the very moment of
speaking
one of them is The Radical in Performance by Baz Kershaw (read that
one?)

Seducing the French, by Kuisel, Adorno's Negative Dialectics and Grove's edition of New American Theater ed by Michael Fiengold.. I thought this is all just an omen that i should read these books one more time especially as you qualified my abortive thinking as.. what did you say "anarchist synthesis is not Hegel's dialectics" or something like that in fact true, i prefer to be massaged to reading serious books! it's so bad and sad, but now, come to think of it, at 7 pm my time in Paris, i have to make this confession and get back to my reading

OK, my lovely hero.. miaow

kit has to get back to her work, the sassanid empire, newfundamentalism in europe on my desk etc etc you must be lovely under yr shower (is there anyone to shampoo you? boo booooo i am jealous!!!)

Marc Léger <leger.mj@gmail.com>
To: Zivancevic Nina <zivancevicn65@gmail.com>
12 May 2015 at 13:25

it was you supposed to send me pics of you coming in and out of the shower, if you recall, and being boobooed by me is really popular these days and one has to say you take the cake, so i understand why you have turned to fundamentalism

but if i interpret your last message closely you used a vanitas motif, which is quite clever of you - if the shrink is dead (the skull as a rem(a) inder), then that means that desire and symptoms are without possible interpretation and transference - the books fall on the head - the four riders of the apocalypse: radicalism, seduction, dialectics and theatre (american theatre) -- this is what the headlines will say: Sorbonne professor Kit le Minx has been apprehended at Pierre Trudeau International airport (Montreal) by Chris the editor, trying to stop her from making a big mistake she will regret for the rest of her 9 lives -- this is all part of the promotion of CMOK

Zivancevic Nina <zivancevicn65@gmail.com>
To: Marc Léger <leger.mj@gmail.com>
12 May 2015 at 13:41

you ARE a genious! what synthesis of all previous Kit's messages?! that's why this correspondence will never stop-- as I will always desire to know you better and more..

hey,

to be honest, I did not want to send you the pics from my shower,
because you wld think that there's someone taking that shower with me
and anyways, aren"'t we all too wet (for camera holding) when we're in
or out of the shower
but i will try tonite,
another concern is -- yr health
have you seen me out of shower with my tail all wet ans scratchy- who
knows if you'd still like me.. wld stop this ever meager correspondence
etc
i'll try though
if you never respond- i'll know that u didn't like Kit le Minx doing her
toilette

Marc Léger <leger.mj@gmail.com>
To: Zivancevic Nina <zivancevicn65@gmail.com>
12 May 2015 at 13:44

on May 4, Nina Zivencevic said:
"I remain here, right at your every click, that's my breakfast lunch and
dinner.."

really, i want to do our commercial with the pink tiles and white bubble
bath - and the camera pulls back and a male voice: "Nina Zivancevic,
Coming Soon" -- it is torrenting here in this former French colony and
first nations territory - we are wetter

Zivancevic Nina <zivancevicn65@gmail.com>
To: Marc Léger <leger.mj@gmail.com>
12 May 2015 at 13:50

no, you mispelled that name
on May 4 Nina Zivancevic said...
ok ok we can do the commercial
but i have to check something first.. the quantity of water in my tub..
no, don't do it now.. not yet
whoops! am i in charge of this game at all
or, are you, Godard, Hartley, directing all of this here, every sequel etc?
seems i have no directorial input and i'm Kit the Star of the Tub

Marc Léger <leger.mj@gmail.com>
To: Zivancevic Nina <zivancevicn65@gmail.com>
12 May 2015 at 13:58

please use Giancarlo for the voiceover:
"Nina Zivancevic: Coming Soon in the Tub"
you can select the music - okay ? but I recommend dragana mirković

Zivancevic Nina <zivancevicn65@gmail.com>
To: Marc Léger <leger.mj@gmail.com>
12 May 2015 at 14:15

so if we select and do the spot, why should we send it to you?
there you go my bright star.. (YOU are supposed to do the styling, so I'll
wait for you to come to Paris and we'll do the spot quicky
i mean, quickly)

Zivancevic Nina <zivancevicn65@gmail.com>
To: Marc Léger <leger.mj@gmail.com>
12 May 2015 at 14:36

we've done it ! it's already been done! (in 2010)
and besides , now he is with Julie whom I really like
and also I wanted YOU to be of my film! now you're backing off, right?
ok, if it's really like that, I'll ask David G to enter the scene...
(this sentence is supposed to blow all yr fuses, seeeee if it works now...)

Marc Léger <leger.mj@gmail.com>
To: Zivancevic Nina <zivancevicn65@gmail.com>
12 May 2015 at 14:48

huh ?

Zivancevic Nina <zivancevicn65@gmail.com>
To: Marc Léger <leger.mj@gmail.com>
12 May 2015 at 14:50

you're blown?
SAY something.. like.. hello, i'm still alive!!
MAAAARCCC- where are you?

Marc Léger <leger.mj@gmail.com>
To: Zivancevic Nina <zivancevicn65@gmail.com>
12 May 2015 at 14:54

ok, now i understand
no, i meant why don't you ask Niall for something unrelated to our
commercial
see, you got them mixed up
and David in the tub ?
i guess that's what he means when he says: Direct, Action!

Zivancevic Nina <zivancevicn65@gmail.com>
To: Marc Léger <leger.mj@gmail.com>
12 May 2015 at 15:12

you kittinish kit- you don't understand anything
the only thing that you should understand is
that i care for you a lot and i love you and there is only one person i
wanted to do this krush fiction with and take a shower with and that's
YOU!!! can you remember and observe my words correctly! ?
can you once in yr life time?

minx alert

Marc Léger <leger.mj@gmail.com>
To: Zivancevic Nina <zivancevicn65@gmail.com>
12 May 2015 at 13:01

where is you iPhone ? how can you contact the TTTT when you have turned off the most vital link to your only chance of breaking the barrier of poststalinist fiction - are you losing interest in the most endandered Venus inhabitant ever to write to you ? - this manuscript will go on for seven years and we have only 80,768 words - we have still 919,232 words to go

Zivancevic Nina <zivancevicn65@gmail.com>
To: Marc Léger <leger.mj@gmail.com>
12 May 2015 at 13:10

if we have so VERY FEW words left fr the mnscpt
then let it just be
CMOK
CMOK
CMOK from me

Zivancevic Nina <zivancevicn65@gmail.com>
To: Marc Léger <leger.mj@gmail.com>
12 May 2015 at 13:14

I see what I've written so far...
it sounds like a bad tabloid front page
"A distinguished la Sorbonne professor Kit le Minx has announced this morning: "I prefer to be washed by MJL that read relevant books for my seminar" "

Marc Léger <leger.mj@gmail.com>
To: Zivancevic Nina <zivancevicn65@gmail.com>
12 May 2015 at 13:32

and everyone will read: *The Seminar of MJ Léger, BOOK XXIII: How to Platform and Make Suds, 2014-2021*

Zivancevic Nina <zivancevicn65@gmail.com>
To: Marc Léger <leger.mj@gmail.com>
12 May 2015 at 13:48

OK, so, as we are decent academic workers we don't wont to lie and obfuscate the facts-- let us see if you'd like to wash n scrub this Kit first, and then we can talk about the consequences and the results d'une telle action..
je vais t'envoyer les pics de ma douche plus tard..
bon aprèm

Tr : TR: Mercredi 19 mai à 19h30 : Julie Kristeva invitée des Rendez-vous de la Bargeinfo@fsju.org

Zivancevic Nina <nzivancevic@ymail.com>
To: Marc Léger <leger.mj@gmail.com>
12 May 2015 at 14:09

honestly, i'll go there to see her and ask her to help us publish our
correspondence
ha, what do you think?
kit

Marc Léger <leger.mj@gmail.com>
To: Zivancevic Nina <nzivancevic@ymail.com>
12 May 2015 at 14:11

good idea - you can also ask your friends Lardo and ? about showing
our new TV commercial on bouillon de culture tv show = we must stop
Manine Le Pen right now

Zivancevic Nina <nzivancevic@ymail.com>
To: Marc Léger <leger.mj@gmail.com>
12 May 2015 at 14:18

you'll tell me about
yr new TV commercial (that's not the one with Kit le Minx, right? in a
shower?)
it's something against marine le pen, i hope

Marc Léger <leger.mj@gmail.com>
To: Zivancevic Nina <nzivancevic@ymail.com>
12 May 2015 at 14:22

Kit le Minx is a double cat bugler agence france code correspondent -
she works for everybody and nobody - sort of like some Diabolik style
agent – it's her unusual femininity that is dangerous to man

Zivancevic Nina <nzivancevic@ymail.com>
To: Marc Léger <leger.mj@gmail.com>
12 May 2015 at 14:45

you got it! THAT's RIGHT! Oh, I liked Diabolik a lot, a cartoon, was
something i grew up with, more thanyr loving BARBARELLA..
Now, after all this- perhaps you'll exclude me from yr
serious iAG anthology
i'll send you my tubpics tonite, perhaps that will bring me back to this
anthology,
when you see how pretty i am.. (KIt le Minx)

Zivancevic Nina <nzivancevic@ymail.com>
To: Marc Léger <leger.mj@gmail.com>
12 May 2015 at 14:48

ahh
i can do all sorts of things if i'm paid.. like the belle de jour..
hold on.. yeah definitely i can belly-dance
that's my Ottoman-byzantine heritage (not as good as natasha atlas, but
pretty much ok)

Marc Léger <leger.mj@gmail.com>
To: Zivancevic Nina <nzivancevic@ymail.com>
12 May 2015 at 14:58

lucky for me my prof from the Sorbonne taught us everything i needed
to know about vampirism in the early romantic era and "la région
intermédiaire" (aka your middle europe) *but was afraid to ask -- but
seriously, you do things for money ? and you were asking me the other
day about Debord and now, Alice Becker-Ho

Zivancevic Nina <nzivancevic@ymail.com>
To: Marc Léger <leger.mj@gmail.com>
12 May 2015 at 15:32

noono, I just teach for money.. and do translations.. and write
i respect my poor sistas who earn their $$$ with their pussies, but
i don't do that sort of stuff, not cause i'm a moralist,

but luckily, i don't have to do it

and even when i was terribly poor in 1995 (I've just got to France, separated from Marc with his baby in my arms),

I asked Liza a gogo girls from Pigalle if i cld turn tricks.. she said "come with me tonite to a Pigalle bar" and there, I asked her

yeah, but once i sat beside a guy, what should i do THEN?

and she looked at me surprised and said, oh, you ..just can't do it, you're not good for this job..

til today i've never figured it why i did not fit this job's profile..

also Penny Arcade wanted me to beat someone up for 1000 dollars (in 1991) but i said i couldn't do ti... beat people up for nothing..

speaking of roger vadim

Marc Léger <leger.mj@gmail.com>
To: Zivancevic Nina <zivancevicn65@gmail.com>
12 May 2015 at 16:15

all of these excellent experiences you have had, pigtail, pigaille , in the tub, etc, they are all truly spicy (meaning epic, epicurean, equestrian: as in, chattel, cat house, Chatelet), especially now that fiction has become all market stuff

but for now we have to start you slow, like you are a young albanian girl from the countryside - her father was excluded from the collectivized farm - and you have just received a note from your school saying that you won a poetry writing contest and they want you to represent Serbia at the Olympics of New York City ... you see, it can be dangerous to talk to me because i might be naive but i understand this idea of no plot, rascal heroine who gets by on her jinxy wit, first person autobiographical exposé

Zivancevic Nina <zivancevicn65@gmail.com>
To: Marc Léger <leger.mj@gmail.com>
12 May 2015 at 16:30

marc
i've just done something terribly stupid
i ordered é copies of yr book, the same book through amazon by mistake
and it's the most stupid and stoned thing i've done this season..
lemme handle this crisis moment
(the seller won't talk to me in regards oooohhhhhhhhhhhhh this avantgarde book oooooooh)

Zivancevic Nina <zivancevicn65@gmail.com>
To: Marc Léger <leger.mj@gmail.com>
12 May 2015 at 16:49

no, they won't give me any refund, the message says
i was really this young albanian girsl from the countryside who was clicking and clicking my night away-- at the Amazon.
yeah, a country girl in pumps, my way to NYC i hade to pave myself i remember the day i left Washngton DC for NYC, I was only 20..
so, rascal heroine who got by a smile and on her jinxy wit.. (did you say

you adored it in me, perhaps you didn't but i
know you did),
i'm glad you enjoyed my first person account and like Notley said and
again "I" is just a word for the experience enjoyed by so many different
people..
Wow! there i go again, coaching you and telling you my silly stories
so you got a mist, spray of my misty messages floating all over yr
screen and through your room, done in an extreme Bauhaus minimalist
economy and very simple indeed it could be a box from Tadeus Kantor
mime

Marc Léger <leger.mj@gmail.com>
To: Zivancevic Nina <zivancevicn65@gmail.com>
12 May 2015 at 19:33

please don't cancel this order you can give a copy to Chris, if he wants
to know who I am - one of my editors here in Montreal said, no, Marc
(death to you), that's not how you put together an academic book; i.e.
invite people and tell them they can do anything they want
but look at you, aren't, you having fun with Questin and even your Kantor
you sent was crazy and i would have published that as pure Zeenius
about my dictator fantasies - yes i can anticipate some coaching from
you anyway, i am starting to think that there is not bathtub over there : (

Zivancevic Nina <zivancevicn65@gmail.com>
To: Marc Léger <leger.mj@gmail.com>
12 May 2015 at 21:51

You kitty-cad!
Did you think that I wld send pics of MY tail naked to you..
See , am like you! I have a trust problem
And if u want to see me naked or semi naked, there is our La Mama
performance "Eros of the interior-exterior" I did with my Odyana Theater
groop. Carlo , the co-director stripped me naked and i was terribly shy
in the beginning but.. I'll send u pics of me now but u have to promise u
wont distribute them to anyone
See, How can i trust you, 100 or 50 or 5 percent?

Envoyé de mon i miss u phone

Cant tell u How much our friendship

Zivancevic Nina <zivancevicn65@gmail.com>
To: Marc Léger <leger.mj@gmail.com>
13 May 2015 at 12:18

Means to me
It comes closes to love
Complète dévotion as much as i've known it so far
Ok i just simmer and swim in my redundance

Envoyé de mon iPhone

(no subject)

Zivancevic Nina <zivancevicn65@gmail.com>
To: Marc Léger <leger.mj@gmail.com>
12 May 2015 at 21:57

Me at three o click am , i'm going to pee and sending a pic from my
bathroom

Envoyé de mon vatefaire foutre phone

Image: Photo of Nina Zee in bathroom

Marc Léger <leger.mj@gmail.com>
To: Zivancevic Nina <zivancevicn65@gmail.com>
13 May 2015 at 09:15

you are so zero my dear - i see your secret art of vater faire foutre and
i miss you all the time. this is a truly nice picture and you have a great
expression and the colours are like Giotto (but getting close to Kirchner
for me because truly real)

I dreamed last night I had contributed to a professional art exhibition and
maybe my dream came about as a wish fulfilment of our commercial (but
if you are covered in bubbles you don't have to show skin – haven't you
read the Haze Code for nice Hollywood ladies) -- nowadays you have
to have a lesbian kissing scene but this I will not ask of you and or the
Odiyaya troupe -- enough of my male fantasy and surrealist dross – but
i won't stop until i have you in the leather outfit and drill -- but this we
can save until after we have found a publisher for our ontological tract of
propositions and oppositions – i'm sending this pic to Bruno right now

---

Marc Léger <leger.mj@gmail.com>
To: Zivancevic Nina <zivancevicn65@gmail.com>
13 May 2015 at 09:24

it occurs to me that somehow i've become the straight man to your
genius performance - i have been an instrument to your vulgar ambition
and narcissism -- let me know what it is that you won't do and then i will
ask you to do that, okay, so we're orpheus and erudice and i'm erudice
watching as you go about your show -- this is not how it was supposed
to work out with my Girls Gone Godard - now you are really professional

---

Zivancevic Nina <zivancevicn65@gmail.com>
To: Marc Léger <leger.mj@gmail.com>
13 May 2015 at 12:05

I've
Had a terrible experience last night of letting a guest stay over night
which produced a horrible puking effect this morning
Recovered, my good friend Vela, a web master mounted recent events
on my site
Please take a look or perhaps i dont even have to mention it to you..
Chris is ever furious as the proof copy didn't come out right
I´ve run bunch of errands today but when i got back home my other
flyer was sad (i'm gonna buy him a new Love girl) and the decision from
the Bancrupcy commission at the Central bank sent in an order-- i shd
reimburse them all..
How are you today?

Marc Léger <leger.mj@gmail.com>
To: Zivancevic Nina <zivancevicn65@gmail.com>
13 May 2015 at 12:59

hi - you look happy and real cute in the picture of you at the poetry
reading - a turkish delight if you don't mind me using old school
innuendo – i'm sending these emails to all of your students but only as
a book publication, no advance wikileaks or anything like that to Chris or
other parties -- i have a secret but i will wait a few more hours to tell you

---

Zivancevic Nina <zivancevicn65@gmail.com>
To: Marc Léger <leger.mj@gmail.com>
13 May 2015 at 13:51

Why what' that, the big news? Why wld u wait a few days, weeks etc?
You are getting married again?
Or about to become a father?
I wish i cld say CONGRATS
But.. I'll wait to hear from you first...
Yes, give me some time to get used to it..

Zivancevic Nina <zivancevicn65@gmail.com>
To: Marc Léger <leger.mj@gmail.com>
13 May 2015 at 14:01

I'm really pissed today.. All things come at once!
Even yr secret marriage (i see yr already transféring me emotionally to
Bruno or Chris,,,ay ay ay)
Look I'm going to see Léviathan tonite by that russian director
And then Antonioni's éclipse at champollion theater ...
I haveńt been SO unnerved since long...
Have a great evening
Catch that black beauty , that's the name of this book

Envoyé de mon perroquet phone

Marc Léger <leger.mj@gmail.com>
To: Zivancevic Nina <zivancevicn65@gmail.com>
13 May 2015 at 14:22

écoute - bon ciné et ne t'inquiètes pas, je me marrierai plus jamais - une
fois c'est assez - et nous, nous allons vivre ensemble pour toujours
(pour 141 minutes ce soir); moi, je m'en vais voir 'amour fou' - film
d'époque (Hausner)

Zivancevic Nina <zivancevicn65@gmail.com>
To: Marc Léger <leger.mj@gmail.com>
13 May 2015 at 18:04

Oh, quel amour, et fou, c'est moi, bien sur, comme d'hab...
So look what happened to me: I was as pissed as a Kit could be.. I
walked into a cinema hall: One pass for the critic de la federation de la
presse de critics de cinema française..
madame voudrait voir..
LEVIATHAN... ok, voila votre billet, madame..
I walk in, it's something in Spanish.. REFUGIADO orwhatever...
I walk out.. I wanted to see the Leviathan, you know that Cannes script
award film...
C'est mercredi prochain, madame
a night like hell.. (interior dialogue of two Kits starts- se declanche)
what does that Cad has to hide from me.. he's got a secret he won't tell
me about..

Cad, snivel.. and all that writing for 3 months.. of course, I should know better, IT WAS ALL JUST HIS SICK JOKE...

snivel .. fuck Antonioni, it'(s just gonna remind me of ..the Cad) and Delon and Vitti ... no, I'm going to a Poetry Slam "Lit up Paris" ARRIERE FON: Kit is carring a bird, a brand new bird for Kiki, at least the birds should love one another and... but what if they don't get along? What if Kiki changes his mind and wants to have babies with the bird who just passed away? Wasn't that his true blue? It was a GREAT bird... liked to huddle and cuddle inside my pocket...this new one is quite savage and dynamic..

like KIKI himself! tja tja.. they might get along though.. they're both VERY active and like to fly around, flip flop their tiny wings as if they wanted to discover the world on their own...

I get to the bar Parislitup.. I put the new bird on the table- it sings better and chants better poetry than most of the slammers

someone gave her a piece of carrot and ordered a vodka for me.. Stuart, my old pal shows up and gets us (eventually) into a taxi cab..

Once I got home, I tried to place the new female next to Kiki in a cage (at this point Kiki, pissed off himself, has eaten half of my books and a painting on the wall - AS HE got himself out, check this out- he pushed the cage door with his beak and got-himself-out-of -the-cage!!!

However, the new lady has arrived...

I placed both of them gently into a bigger cage.. lots of grains, omega 3, water, fruits and pieces of lettuce veeery romantic stuff, they don't eat but start kissing with their red beaks, they kiss and kiss and kiss.. that's what we

call "love at the first sight"..

ok, i mellowed out..

and what's Cad doing right now? I know and I don't want to know...

turn on this bloody computer: aha, here's his email, hje says "nous allons vivre ensemble pour toujours (pour 141 minutes ce soir)"...

who is he writing to?

And he's going to see l'amour fou.. pas mal, pas mal du tout!!!

listen, Marc, I have some CDs here I intend mailing to you

Marcel Duchamp "the creative act" (subrosa editions),

Futurism and Dada reviewed (original recordings by Apollinaire, Cocteau, Duchamp, Marcel Janco, Wyndham Lewis (what'shis doing here my favorite of Blast generation?) Tzara and Schwitters.. Cad has probably heard all of this stuff moons ago..

HOWEVER: there's another CD I think you may dig: Duchamp's audiobook including "Musical erratum from 1913 and 4 lectures-interviews! whatcha say??!

and there's un classique inconturnable:" Surrealism reviewed", original recordings by Breton, Duchamp, Aragon , Dali, Ray, Miller, Soupault, Ernst and my fave- Desnos, who died in a concentration camp 3 days

before their opened the door on that cage in 1944...
hmmm , so much about the surrealist dolls and l'amour fou..
Have you read my short story "Nadja's story"? Where I turned everything upside down and explained how the Supreme Cad drove Nadja crazy and placed her into his novel?
If you did not- you should.. then you can tell me if you want us to live together forever, un peu, beaucoup.. à volonté?
ta copine, Kit

epilogue taxi home

Marc Léger <leger.mj@gmail.com>
To: Zivancevic Nina <zivancevicn65@gmail.com>
13 May 2015 at 19:24

dear Kiki - as you might have guessed this is the alpha and the omega secret that you hoped would never arrive - we have reached the 25 million words limit but more specifically i have reached May 13, 2015, in the book and today is the same exact and so it seems this is where we call it the night of nights for this correspondence

please send me all of those dvds as i have been tentatively invited to the Dada anniversary event in London next summer and i need to know everything you know

but Nina, this is the last email to go into the book - i hope you're not too drunk or passed out already because I need you to write one last email for the book - this does not mean we will stop writing but this means i will stop copying our emails for our little CMOK - and perhaps after all you will decide i am not a cad, who knows, this will be your last chance to tell me what you really think and of course our yin and yang will carry on and on and so on

Zivancevic Nina <zivancevicn65@gmail.com>
To: Marc Léger <leger.mj@gmail.com>
13 May 2015 at 20:34

U mean u want ALL of this to go into the Book ?

But this correspondence is so private and personnal
Who wld. Need to read it?

W. dreams, like Phaedrus, of an army of thinker-friends, thinker-lovers. He dreams of a thought-army, a thought-pack, which would storm the philosophical Houses of Parliament. He dreams of Tartars from the philosophical steppes, of thought-barbarians, thought-outsiders. What distance would shine in their eyes!
          —Lars Iyer

Made in the USA
Charleston, SC
27 September 2016